SUPER HOROSCOPE
SAGITTARIUS
2011
NOVEMBER 23 – DECEMBER 20

B

BERKLEY BOOKS, NEW YORK

THE BERKLEY PUBLISHING GROUP
Published by the Penguin Group
Penguin Group (USA) Inc.
375 Hudson Street, New York, New York 10014, USA
Penguin Group (Canada), 90 Eglinton Avenue East, Suite 700, Toronto, Ontario M4P 2Y3, Canada
(a division of Pearson Penguin Canada Inc.)
Penguin Books Ltd., 80 Strand, London WC2R 0RL, England
Penguin Group Ireland, 25 St. Stephen's Green, Dublin 2, Ireland (a division of Penguin Books Ltd.)
Penguin Group (Australia), 250 Camberwell Road, Camberwell, Victoria 3124, Australia
(a division of Pearson Australia Group Pty. Ltd.)
Penguin Books India Pvt. Ltd., 11 Community Centre, Panchsheel Park, New Delhi—110 017, India
Penguin Group (NZ), 67 Apollo Drive, Rosedale, North Shore 0632, New Zealand
(a division of Pearson New Zealand Ltd.)
Penguin Books (South Africa) (Pty.) Ltd., 24 Sturdee Avenue, Rosebank, Johannesburg 2196,
South Africa

Penguin Books Ltd., Registered Offices: 80 Strand, London WC2R 0RL, England

The publishers regret that they cannot answer individual letters requesting personal horoscope
information.

2011 SUPER HOROSCOPE SAGITTARIUS

Copyright © 1974, 1978, 1979, 1980, 1981, 1982 by Grosset & Dunlap, Inc.

Copyright © 1983, 1984 by Charter Communications, Inc.

Copyright © 1985, 1986, 1987, 1988, 1989, 1990, 1991, 1992, 1993, 1994, 1995, 1996, 1997, 1998,
1999, 2000, 2001, 2002, 2003, 2004, 2005, 2006, 2007, 2008 by The Berkley Publishing Group.

Copyright © 2009, 2010 by Penguin Group (USA) Inc.
Cover design by Steven Ferlauto.

All rights reserved.
No part of this book may be reproduced, scanned, or distributed in any printed or electronic form without
permission. Please do not participate in or encourage piracy of copyrighted materials in violation of the
author's rights. Purchase only authorized editions.
BERKLEY® is a registered trademark of Penguin Group (USA) Inc.
The "B" design is a trademark of Penguin Group (USA) Inc.

PRINTING HISTORY
Berkley trade paperback edition / July 2010

Berkley trade paperback ISBN: 978-0-425-23293-4

Library of Congress Cataloging-in-Publication Data

ISSN: 1535-8976

PRINTED IN THE UNITED STATES OF AMERICA

10 9 8 7 6 5 4 3 2 1

If you purchased this book without a cover, you should be aware that this book is stolen property. It was
reported as "unsold and destroyed" to the publisher, and neither the author nor the publisher has received
any payment for this "stripped book."

Contents

THE CUSP-BORN
SAGITTARIUS

Are you *really* a Sagittarius? If your birthday falls around the fourth week in November, at the very beginning of Sagittarius, will you still retain the traits of Scorpio, the sign of the Zodiac before Sagittarius? And what if you were born near Christmas—are you more Capricorn than Sagittarius? Many people born at the edge, or cusp, of a sign have great difficulty determining exactly what sign they are. If you are one of these people, here's how you can figure it out once and for all.

Consult the cusp table on the facing page, then locate the year of your birth. The table will tell you the precise days on which the Sun entered and left your sign for the year of your birth. In that way you can determine if you are a true Sagittarius—or whether you are a Scorpio or Capricorn—according to the variations in cusp dates from year to year (see also page 17).

If you were born at the beginning or end of Sagittarius, yours is a lifetime reflecting a process of subtle transformation. Your life on Earth will symbolize a significant change in consciousness, for you are about to enter a whole new way of living or are leaving one behind.

If you were born at the beginning of Sagittarius, you may want to read the horoscope for Scorpio as well as Sagittarius, for Scorpio holds the key to many of your hidden weaknesses, sexual uncertainties, wishes, fantasies, and spiritual potentials. You are the symbol of the human mind awakening to its higher capabilities. You are preparing the way for the liberation of your soul into the realms of wisdom and truth. You leave behind greed, blind desire, and shallow lust, as you learn to create and understand yourself. You travel, see new places, see how people live, figure yourself out, acquire knowledge.

You may hide a stubborn and dangerous extremism and you may rely too much on luck, but at some crisis point in your life a change of consciousness will occur to shift your behavior patterns. New worlds open up, as you become aware of immortality and the infinite possibilities of your own mind.

If you were born at the end of Sagittarius, you may want to read the horoscope book for Capricorn as well as Sagittarius, for Capri-

4

corn is a deep part of your materialistic values. You were born with the need to bring your dreams into reality and put your talents and ambitions to practical use.

You need to conquer worry and depression and inhibition. You will learn to take life seriously, but without losing your sense of humor and hope. You must find a balance between believing nothing and believing too much. You need to find the firm middle ground between cynicism and idealism.

THE CUSPS OF SAGITTARIUS

DATES SUN ENTERS SAGITTARIUS (LEAVES SCORPIO)

November 22 every year from 1900 to 2015, except for:

November 21		November 23		
1976	1993	1902	1915	1931
80	1996	03	19	35
84	2000	07	23	39
88	2004	10	27	43
92	2008	11		
	2012			

DATES SUN LEAVES SAGITTARIUS (ENTERS CAPRICORN)

December 22 every year from 1900 to 2015, except for:

December 21						
1912	1944	1964	1977	1989	2000	2010
16	48	65	80	92	2001	2012
20	52	68	81	93	2002	2013
23	53	69	84	94	2004	2014
28	56	72	85	96	2005	
32	57	73	86	97	2008	
36	60	76	88	98	2009	
40	61					

THE ASCENDANT:
SAGITTARIUS RISING

Could you be a "double" Sagittarius? That is, could you have Sagittarius as your Rising sign as well as your Sun sign? The tables on pages 8–9 will tell you Sagittarius what your Rising sign happens to be. Just find the hour of your birth, then find the day of your birth, and you will see which sign of the Zodiac is your Ascendant, as the Rising sign is called. The Ascendant is called that because it is the sign rising on the eastern horizon at the time of your birth. For a more detailed discussion of the Rising sign and the twelve houses of the Zodiac, see pages 17–20.

The Ascendant, or Rising sign, is placed on the 1st house in a horoscope, of which there are twelve houses. The 1st house represents your response to the environment—your unique response. Call it identity, personality, ego, self-image, facade, come-on, body-mind-spirit—whatever term best conveys to you the meaning of the you that acts and reacts in the world. It is a you that is always changing, discovering a new you. Your identity started with birth and early environment, over which you had little conscious control, and continues to experience, to adjust, to express itself. The 1st house also represents how others see you. Has anyone ever guessed your sign to be your Rising sign? People may respond to that personality, that facade, that body type governed by your Rising sign.

Your Ascendant, or Rising sign, modifies your basic Sun sign personality, and it affects the way you act out the daily predictions for your Sun sign. If your Rising sign indeed is Sagittarius, what follows is a description of its effects on your horoscope. If your Rising sign is not Sagittarius, but some other sign of the Zodiac, you may wish to read the horoscope book for that sign.

With Sagittarius on the Ascendant, the planet rising in the 1st house is Jupiter, ruler of Sagittarius. In this position Jupiter confers good health, a pleasing personality, a generous disposition, and an increased vitality. It also confers honors or wealth at some point in your lifetime. You may reap unexpected good fortune in times of hardship.

At some point, too, you may exile yourself from everyday life to serve a larger dedication. You will sacrifice for your ideals. Because you are zealous in your beliefs, you could make enemies behind your back. Again, the influence of Jupiter works to overcome the opposition.

You are the student, the idealist. Your need for wisdom is boundless. And you think big! You are not satisfied gathering concrete facts or analyzing practical information. You want to infer the grand patterns, to abstract, to generalize, and finally to generate new ideas. You are a visionary, a dreamer, a futurist. Philosophy, law, and religion attract you, for their truths go beyond the limits of everyday experience. Though you firmly hold your beliefs, you are not dogmatic. Rather, you romanticize them, and your method of persuasion is more seductive than shrill. You restless types are very adaptable, changing your ideas with each new discovery. Your mind is completely open.

With Sagittarius Rising you can be attracted to great causes. Your ideas are not generated merely to erect an impressive intellectual framework. Enlightened by your deep compassion, they become ideals in the service of humanity. There may be an inspirational quality to the causes you join or to the ideals you generate for a cause. Justice and mercy are concepts to be translated into action. You work hard to do that, but you are not rebellious or bossy or demanding. You are brave and forthright, without being reckless or combative. Cooperation and communication are important goals. You like working in groups; your friendly good humor is a model for all social relationships.

There is another you, a private you, that people do not necessarily know very well but may glimpse when you have gone out of their lives. That you is restless, opportunistic, seemingly rootless. You live so much in your mind that you don't want to be tied down by mundane obligations. In fact, you will escape from situations that limit your freedom of choice or action, even if you must dishonor a commitment to do so. You could shirk responsibility by flying off to some greener pasture, yet be no richer for the new experience. Carried to extremes, your quest for adventure could be self-indulgent, yet wasteful of yourself and selfish to the people around you.

Like the Archer, the zodiacal symbol of Sagittarius, you like to roam and hunt, though ideas and people may be your terrain and game. But some of you really prefer the outdoor life and sports. You certainly like to travel. Change recharges your happy-go-lucky nature. You like to get around but not get stuck in a rut, so just as swiftly as you appear on a scene, you disappear. Many jobs and places of residence are outcomes of your journeys.

The key words for Sagittarius Rising are buoyancy and expansiveness. Channel these forces into modes of industriousness so you do not waste your noble visions.

RISING SIGNS FOR SAGITTARIUS

Hour of Birth*	Date of Birth		
	November 21–25	November 26–30	December 1–5
Midnight	Virgo	Virgo	Virgo
1 AM	Virgo	Virgo	Virgo
2 AM	Libra	Libra	Libra
3 AM	Libra	Libra	Libra
4 AM	Libra	Libra; Scorpio 11/29	Libra
5 AM	Scorpio	Scorpio	Scorpio
6 AM	Scorpio	Scorpio	Scorpio
7 AM	Sagittarius	Sagittarius	Sagittarius
8 AM	Sagittarius	Sagittarius	Sagittarius
9 AM	Sagittarius	Capricorn	Capricorn
10 AM	Capricorn	Capricorn	Capricorn
11 AM	Capricorn; Aquarius 11/25	Aquarius	Aquarius
Noon	Aquarius	Aquarius; Pisces 12/3	Aquarius;
1 PM	Pisces	Pisces	Pisces
2 PM	Aries	Aries	Aries
3 PM	Aries	Taurus	Taurus
4 PM	Taurus	Taurus; Gemini 12/2	Taurus;
5 PM	Gemini	Gemini	Gemini
6 PM	Gemini	Gemini; Cancer 12/2	Gemini;
7 PM	Cancer	Cancer	Cancer
8 PM	Cancer	Cancer	Cancer
9 PM	Leo	Leo	Leo
10 PM	Leo	Leo	Leo
11 PM	Leo	Leo; Virgo 11/30	Virgo

*Hour of birth given here is for Standard Time in any time zone. If your hour of birth was recorded in Daylight Saving Time, subtract one hour from it and consult that hour in the table above. For example, if you were born at 6 AM D.S.T., see 5 AM above.

Hour of Birth*	Date of Birth		
	December 6–10	December 11–16	December 17–22
Midnight	Virgo	Virgo	Virgo; Libra 12/22
1 AM	Libra	Libra	Libra
2 AM	Libra	Libra	Libra
3 AM	Libra	Libra; Scorpio 12/14	Scorpio
4 AM	Scorpio	Scorpio	Scorpio
5 AM	Scorpio	Scorpio	Scorpio; Sagittarius 12/21
6 AM	Sagittarius	Sagittarius	Sagittarius
7 AM	Sagittarius	Sagittarius	Sagittarius
8 AM	Sagittarius	Capricorn	Capricorn
9 AM	Capricorn	Capricorn	Capricorn
10 AM	Capricorn; Aquarius 12/10	Aquarius	Aquarius
11 AM	Aquarius	Aquarius	Aquarius; Pisces 12/18
Noon	Pisces	Pisces	Pisces; Aries 12/22
1 PM	Aries	Aries	Aries
2 PM	Aries	Taurus	Taurus
3 PM	Taurus	Taurus	Taurus; Gemini 12/19
4 PM	Gemini	Gemini	Gemini
5 PM	Gemini	Gemini	Cancer
6 PM	Cancer	Cancer	Cancer
7 PM	Cancer	Cancer	Cancer; Leo 12/22
8 PM	Leo	Leo	Leo
9 PM	Leo	Leo	Leo
10 PM	Leo	Leo; Virgo 12/15	Virgo
11 PM	Virgo	Virgo	Virgo

* See note on facing page.

THE PLACE OF ASTROLOGY IN TODAY'S WORLD

Does astrology have a place in the fast-moving, ultra-scientific world we live in today? Can it be justified in a sophisticated society whose outriders are already preparing to step off the moon into the deep space of the planets themselves? Or is it just a hangover of ancient superstition, a psychological dummy for neurotics and dreamers of every historical age?

These are the kind of questions that any inquiring person can be expected to ask when they approach a subject like astrology which goes beyond, but never excludes, the materialistic side of life.

The simple, single answer is that astrology works. It works for many millions of people in the western world alone. In the United States there are 10 million followers and in Europe, an estimated 25 million. America has more than 4000 practicing astrologers, Europe nearly three times as many. Even down-under Australia has its hundreds of thousands of adherents. In the eastern countries, astrology has enormous followings, again, because it has been proved to work. In India, for example, brides and grooms for centuries have been chosen on the basis of their astrological compatibility.

Astrology today is more vital than ever before, more practicable because all over the world the media devotes much space and time to it, more valid because science itself is confirming the precepts of astrological knowledge with every new exciting step. The ordinary person who daily applies astrology intelligently does not have to wonder whether it is true nor believe in it blindly. He can see it working for himself. And, if he can use it—and this book is designed to help the reader to do just that—he can make living a far richer experience, and become a more developed personality and a better person.

Astrology and Relationships

Astrology is the science of relationships. It is not just a study of planetary influences on man and his environment. It is the study of man himself.

We are at the center of our personal universe, of all our relationships. And our happiness or sadness depends on how we act, how we relate to the people and things that surround us. The emotions that we generate have a distinct effect—for better or worse—on the world around us. Our friends and our enemies will confirm this. Just look in the mirror the next time you are angry. In other words, each of us is a kind of sun or planet or star radiating our feelings on the environment around us. Our influence on our personal universe, whether loving, helpful, or destructive, varies with our changing moods, expressed through our individual character.

Our personal "radiations" are potent in the way they affect our moods and our ability to control them. But we usually are able to throw off our emotion in some sort of action—we have a good cry, walk it off, or tell someone our troubles—before it can build up too far and make us physically ill. Astrology helps us to understand the universal forces working on us, and through this understanding, we can become more properly adjusted to our surroundings so that we find ourselves coping where others may flounder.

The Challenge of Love

The challenge of love lies in recognizing the difference between infatuation, emotion, sex, and, sometimes, the intentional deceit of the other person. Mankind, with its record of broken marriages, despair, and disillusionment, is obviously not very good at making these distinctions.

Can astrology help?

Yes. In the same way that advance knowledge can usually help in any human situation. And there is probably no situation as human, as poignant, as pathetic and universal, as the failure of man's love.

Love, of course, is not just between man and woman. It involves love of children, parents, home, and friends. But the big problems usually involve the choice of partner.

Astrology has established degrees of compatibility that exist between people born under the various signs of the Zodiac. Because people are individuals, there are numerous variations and modifications. So the astrologer, when approached on mate and marriage matters, makes allowances for them. But the fact remains that some groups of people are suited for each other and some are not, and astrology has expressed this in terms of characteristics we all can study and use as a personal guide.

No matter how much enjoyment and pleasure we find in the different aspects of each other's character, if it is not an overall compatibility, the chances of our finding fulfillment or enduring happiness in each other are pretty hopeless. And astrology can help us to find someone compatible.

Astrology and Science

Closely related to our emotions is the "other side" of our personal universe, our physical welfare. Our body, of course, is largely influenced by things around us over which we have very little control. The phone rings, we hear it. The train runs late. We snag our stocking or cut our face shaving. Our body is under a constant bombardment of events that influence our daily lives to varying degrees.

The question that arises from all this is, what makes each of us act so that we have to involve other people and keep the ball of activity and evolution rolling? This is the question that both science and astrology are involved with. The scientists have attacked it from different angles: anthropology, the study of human evolution as body, mind and response to environment; anatomy, the study of bodily structure; psychology, the science of the human mind; and so on. These studies have produced very impressive classifications and valuable information, but because the approach to the problem is fragmented, so is the result. They remain "branches" of science. Science generally studies effects. It keeps turning up wonderful answers but no lasting solutions. Astrology, on the other hand, approaches the question from the broader viewpoint. Astrology began its inquiry with the totality of human experience and saw it as an effect. It then looked to find the cause, or at least the prime movers, and during thousands of years of observation of man and his *universal* environment came up with the extraordinary principle of planetary influence—or astrology, which, from the Greek, means the science of the stars.

Modern science, as we shall see, has confirmed much of astrology's foundations—most of it unintentionally, some of it reluctantly, but still, indisputably.

It is not difficult to imagine that there must be a connection between outer space and Earth. Even today, scientists are not too sure how our Earth was created, but it is generally agreed that it is only a tiny part of the universe. And as a part of the universe, people on Earth see and feel the influence of heavenly bodies in almost every aspect of our existence. There is no doubt that the Sun has the greatest influence on life on this planet. Without it there would be no life, for without it there would be no warmth, no division into day and night, no cycles of time or season at all. This is clear and easy to see. The influence of the Moon, on the other hand, is more subtle, though no less definite.

There are many ways in which the influence of the Moon manifests itself here on Earth, both on human and animal life. It is a well-known fact, for instance, that the large movements of water on our planet—that is the ebb and flow of the tides—are caused by the Moon's gravitational pull. Since this is so, it follows that these water movements do not occur only in the oceans, but that all bodies of water are affected, even down to the tiniest puddle.

The human body, too, which consists of about 70 percent water, falls within the scope of this lunar influence. For example the menstrual cycle of most women corresponds to the 28-day lunar month; the period of pregnancy in humans is 273 days, or equal to nine lunar months. Similarly, many illnesses reach a crisis at the change of the Moon, and statistics in many countries have shown that the crime rate is highest at the time of the Full Moon. Even human sexual desire has been associated with the phases of the Moon. But it is in the movement of the tides that we get the clearest demonstration of planetary influence, which leads to the irresistible correspondence between the so-called metaphysical and the physical.

Tide tables are prepared years in advance by calculating the future positions of the Moon. Science has known for a long time that the Moon is the main cause of tidal action. But only in the last few years has it begun to realize the possible extent of this influence on mankind. To begin with, the ocean tides do not rise and fall as we might imagine from our personal observations of them. The Moon as it orbits around Earth sets up a circular wave of attraction which pulls the oceans of the world after it, broadly in an east to west direction. This influence is like a phantom wave crest, a loop of power stretching from pole to pole which passes over and around the Earth like an invisible shadow. It travels with equal effect across the land masses and, as scientists were recently amazed to observe, caused oysters placed in the dark in the middle of the United States where there is no sea to open their shells to receive the nonexistent tide. If the land-locked oysters react to this invisible signal, what effect does it have on us who not so long ago in evolutionary time came out of the sea and still have its salt in our blood and sweat?

Less well known is the fact that the Moon is also the primary force behind the circulation of blood in human beings and animals, and the movement of sap in trees and plants. Agriculturists have established that the Moon has a distinct influence on crops, which explains why for centuries people have planted according to Moon cycles. The habits of many animals, too, are directed by the movement of the Moon. Migratory birds, for instance, depart only at or near the time of the Full Moon. And certain sea creatures, eels in particular, move only in accordance with certain phases of the Moon.

Know Thyself—Why?

In today's fast-changing world, everyone still longs to know what the future holds. It is the one thing that everyone has in common: rich and poor, famous and infamous, all are deeply concerned about tomorrow.

But the key to the future, as every historian knows, lies in the past. This is as true of individual people as it is of nations. You cannot understand your future without first understanding your past, which is simply another way of saying that you must first of all know yourself.

The motto "know thyself" seems obvious enough nowadays, but it was originally put forward as the foundation of wisdom by the ancient Greek philosophers. It was then adopted by the "mystery religions" of the ancient Middle East, Greece, Rome, and is still used in all genuine schools of mind training or mystical discipline, both in those of the East, based on yoga, and those of the West. So it is universally accepted now, and has been through the ages.

But how do you go about discovering what sort of person you are? The first step is usually classification into some sort of system of types. Astrology did this long before the birth of Christ. Psychology has also done it. So has modern medicine, in its way.

One system classifies people according to the source of the impulses they respond to most readily: the muscles, leading to direct bodily action; the digestive organs, resulting in emotion; or the brain and nerves, giving rise to thinking. Another such system says that character is determined by the endocrine glands, and gives us such labels as "pituitary," "thyroid," and "hyperthyroid" types. These different systems are neither contradictory nor mutually exclusive. In fact, they are very often different ways of saying the same thing.

Very popular, useful classifications were devised by Carl Jung, the eminent disciple of Freud. Jung observed among the different faculties of the mind, four which have a predominant influence on character. These four faculties exist in all of us without exception, but not in perfect balance. So when we say, for instance, that someone is a "thinking type," it means that in any situation he or she tries to be rational. Emotion, which may be the opposite of thinking, will be his or her weakest function. This thinking type can be sensible and reasonable, or calculating and unsympathetic. The emotional type, on the other hand, can often be recognized by exaggerated language—everything is either marvelous or terrible—and in extreme cases they even invent dramas and quarrels out of nothing just to make life more interesting.

The other two faculties are intuition and physical sensation. The sensation type does not only care for food and drink, nice clothes and furniture; he or she is also interested in all forms of physical experience. Many scientists are sensation types as are athletes and nature-lovers. Like sensation, intuition is a form of perception and we all possess it. But it works through that part of the mind which is not under conscious control—consequently it sees meanings and connections which are not obvious to thought or emotion. Inventors and original thinkers are always intuitive, but so, too, are superstitious people who see meanings where none exist.

Thus, sensation tells us what is going on in the world, feeling (that is, emotion) tells us how important it is to ourselves, thinking enables us to interpret it and work out what we should do about it, and intuition tells us what it means to ourselves and others. All four faculties are essential, and all are present in every one of us. But some people are guided chiefly by one, others by another. In addition, Jung also observed a division of the human personality into the extrovert and the introvert, which cuts across these four types.

A disadvantage of all these systems of classification is that one cannot tell very easily where to place oneself. Some people are reluctant to admit that they act to please their emotions. So they deceive themselves for years by trying to belong to whichever type they think is the "best." Of course, there is no best; each has its faults and each has its good points.

The advantage of the signs of the Zodiac is that they simplify classification. Not only that, but your date of birth is personal—it is unarguably yours. What better way to know yourself than by going back as far as possible to the very moment of your birth? And this is precisely what your horoscope is all about, as we shall see in the next section.

WHAT IS A HOROSCOPE?

If you had been able to take a picture of the skies at the moment of your birth, that photograph would be your horoscope. Lacking such a snapshot, it is still possible to recreate the picture—and this is at the basis of the astrologer's art. In other words, your horoscope is a representation of the skies with the planets in the exact positions they occupied at the time you were born.

The year of birth tells an astrologer the positions of the distant, slow-moving planets Jupiter, Saturn, Uranus, Neptune, and Pluto. The month of birth indicates the Sun sign, or birth sign as it is commonly called, as well as indicating the positions of the rapidly moving planets Venus, Mercury, and Mars. The day and time of birth will locate the position of our Moon. And the moment—the exact hour and minute—of birth determines the houses through what is called the Ascendant, or Rising sign.

With this information the astrologer consults various tables to calculate the specific positions of the Sun, Moon, and other planets relative to your birthplace at the moment you were born. Then he or she locates them by means of the Zodiac.

The Zodiac

The Zodiac is a band of stars (constellations) in the skies, centered on the Sun's apparent path around the Earth, and is divided into twelve equal segments, or signs. What we are actually dividing up is the Earth's path around the Sun. But from our point of view here on Earth, it seems as if the Sun is making a great circle around our planet in the sky, so we say it is the Sun's apparent path. This twelvefold division, the Zodiac, is a reference system for the astrologer. At any given moment the planets—and in astrology both the Sun and Moon are considered to be planets—can all be located at a specific point along this path.

Now where in all this are you, the subject of the horoscope? Your character is largely determined by the sign the Sun is in. So that is where the astrologer looks first in your horoscope, at your Sun sign.

The Sun Sign and the Cusp

There are twelve signs in the Zodiac, and the Sun spends approximately one month in each sign. But because of the motion of the Earth around the Sun—the Sun's apparent motion—the dates when the Sun enters and leaves each sign may change from year to year. Some people born near the cusp, or edge, of a sign have difficulty determining which is their Sun sign. But in this book a Table of Cusps is provided for the years 1900 to 2015 (page 5) so you can find out what your true Sun sign is.

Here are the twelve signs of the Zodiac, their ancient zodiacal symbol, and the dates when the Sun enters and leaves each sign for the year 2011. Remember, these dates may change from year to year.

ARIES	Ram	March 20–April 20
TAURUS	Bull	April 20–May 21
GEMINI	Twins	May 21–June 21
CANCER	Crab	June 21–July 22
LEO	Lion	July 23–August 23
VIRGO	Virgin	August 23–September 23
LIBRA	Scales	September 23–October 23
SCORPIO	Scorpion	October 23–November 22
SAGITTARIUS	Archer	November 22–December 22
CAPRICORN	Sea Goat	December 22–January 20
AQUARIUS	Water Bearer	January 20–February 18
PISCES	Fish	February 18–March 20

It is possible to draw significant conclusions and make meaningful predictions based simply on the Sun sign of a person. There are many people who have been amazed at the accuracy of the description of their own character based only on the Sun sign. But an astrologer needs more information than just your Sun sign to interpret the photograph that is your horoscope.

The Rising Sign and the Zodiacal Houses

An astrologer needs the exact time and place of your birth in order to construct and interpret your horoscope. The illustration on the next page shows the flat chart, or natural wheel, an astrologer uses. Note the inner circle of the wheel labeled 1 through 12. These 12 divisions are known as the houses of the Zodiac.

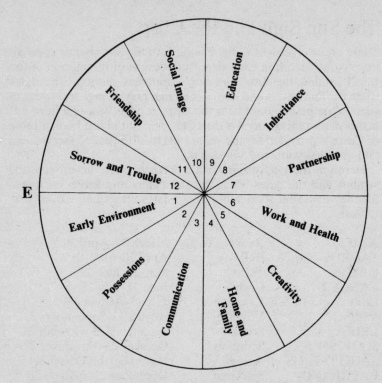

The 1st house always starts from the position marked E, which corresponds to the eastern horizon. The rest of the houses 2 through 12 follow around in a "counterclockwise" direction. The point where each house starts is known as a cusp, or edge.

The cusp, or edge, of the 1st house (point E) is where an astrologer would place your Rising sign, the Ascendant. And, as already noted, the exact time of your birth determines your Rising sign. Let's see how this works.

As the Earth rotates on its axis once every 24 hours, each one of the twelve signs of the Zodiac appears to be "rising" on the horizon, with a new one appearing about every 2 hours. Actually it is the turning of the Earth that exposes each sign to view, but in our astrological work we are discussing apparent motion. This Rising sign marks the Ascendant, and it colors the whole orientation of a horoscope. It indicates the sign governing the 1st house of the chart, and will thus determine which signs will govern all the other houses.

To visualize this idea, imagine two color wheels with twelve divisions superimposed upon each other. For just as the Zodiac is divided into twelve constellations that we identify as the signs, another twelvefold division is used to denote the houses. Now imagine one wheel (the signs) moving slowly while the other wheel (the houses) remains still. This analogy may help you see how the signs keep shifting the "color" of the houses as the Rising sign continues to change every two hours. To simplify things, a Table of Rising Signs has been provided (pages 8–9) for your specific Sun sign.

Once your Rising sign has been placed on the cusp of the 1st house, the signs that govern the rest of the 11 houses can be placed on the chart. In any individual's horoscope the signs do not necessarily correspond with the houses. For example, it could be that a sign covers part of two adjacent houses. It is the interpretation of such variations in an individual's horoscope that marks the professional astrologer.

But to gain a workable understanding of astrology, it is not necessary to go into great detail. In fact, we just need a description of the houses and their meanings, as is shown in the illustration above and in the table below.

THE 12 HOUSES OF THE ZODIAC

1st	Individuality, body appearance, general outlook on life	Personality house
2nd	Finance, possessions, ethical principles, gain or loss	Money house
3rd	Relatives, communication, short journeys, writing, education	Relatives house
4th	Family and home, parental ties, land and property, security	Home house
5th	Pleasure, children, creativity, entertainment, risk	Pleasure house
6th	Health, harvest, hygiene, work and service, employees	Health house
7th	Marriage and divorce, the law, partnerships and alliances	Marriage house
8th	Inheritance, secret deals, sex, death, regeneration	Inheritance house
9th	Travel, sports, study, philosophy, religion	Travel house
10th	Career, social standing, success and honor	Business house
11th	Friendship, social life, hopes and wishes	Friends house
12th	Troubles, illness, secret enemies, hidden agendas	Trouble house

The Planets in the Houses

An astrologer, knowing the exact time and place of your birth, will use tables of planetary motion in order to locate the planets in your horoscope chart. He or she will determine which planet or planets are in which sign and in which house. It is not uncommon, in an individual's horoscope, for there to be two or more planets in the same sign and in the same house.

The characteristics of the planets modify the influence of the Sun according to their natures and strengths.

Sun: Source of life. Basic temperament according to the Sun sign. The conscious will. Human potential.

Moon: Emotions. Moods. Customs. Habits. Changeable. Adaptive. Nurturing.

Mercury: Communication. Intellect. Reasoning power. Curiosity. Short travels.

Venus: Love. Delight. Charm. Harmony. Balance. Art. Beautiful possessions.

Mars: Energy. Initiative. War. Anger. Adventure. Courage. Daring. Impulse.

Jupiter: Luck. Optimism. Generous. Expansive. Opportunities. Protection.

Saturn: Pessimism. Privation. Obstacles. Delay. Hard work. Research. Lasting rewards after long struggle.

Uranus: Fashion. Electricity. Revolution. Independence. Freedom. Sudden changes. Modern science.

Neptune: Sensationalism. Theater. Dreams. Inspiration. Illusion. Deception.

Pluto: Creation and destruction. Total transformation. Lust for power. Strong obsessions.

Superimpose the characteristics of the planets on the functions of the house in which they appear. Express the result through the character of the Sun sign, and you will get the basic idea.

Of course, many other considerations have been taken into account in producing the carefully worked out predictions in this book: the aspects of the planets to each other; their strength according to position and sign; whether they are in a house of exaltation or decline; whether they are natural enemies or not; whether a planet occupies its own sign; the position of a planet in relation to its own house or sign; whether the sign is male or female; whether the sign is a fire, earth, water, or air sign. These are only a few of the colors on the astrologer's pallet which he or she must mix with the inspiration of the artist and the accuracy of the mathematician.

How To Use These Predictions

A person reading the predictions in this book should understand that they are produced from the daily position of the planets for a group of people and are not, of course, individually specialized. To get the full benefit of them our readers should relate the predictions to their own character and circumstances, coordinate them, and draw their own conclusions from them.

If you are a serious observer of your own life, you should find a definite pattern emerging that will be a helpful and reliable guide.

The point is that we always retain our free will. The stars indicate certain directional tendencies but we are not compelled to follow. We can do or not do, and wisdom must make the choice.

We all have our good and bad days. Sometimes they extend into cycles of weeks. It is therefore advisable to study daily predictions in a span ranging from the day before to several days ahead.

Daily predictions should be taken very generally. The word "difficult" does not necessarily indicate a whole day of obstruction or inconvenience. It is a warning to you to be cautious. Your caution will often see you around the difficulty before you are involved. This is the correct use of astrology.

In another section (pages 78–84), detailed information is given about the influence of the Moon as it passes through each of the twelve signs of the Zodiac. There are instructions on how to use the Moon Tables (pages 85–92), which provide Moon Sign Dates throughout the year as well as the Moon's role in health and daily affairs. This information should be used in conjunction with the daily forecasts to give a fuller picture of the astrological trends.

HISTORY OF ASTROLOGY

The origins of astrology have been lost far back in history, but we do know that reference is made to it as far back as the first written records of the human race. It is not hard to see why. Even in primitive times, people must have looked for an explanation for the various happenings in their lives. They must have wanted to know why people were different from one another. And in their search they turned to the regular movements of the Sun, Moon, and stars to see if they could provide an answer.

It is interesting to note that as soon as man learned to use his tools in any type of design, or his mind in any kind of calculation, he turned his attention to the heavens. Ancient cave dwellings reveal dim crescents and circles representative of the Sun and Moon, rulers of day and night. Mesopotamia and the civilization of Chaldea, in itself the foundation of those of Babylonia and Assyria, show a complete picture of astronomical observation and well-developed astrological interpretation.

Humanity has a natural instinct for order. The study of anthropology reveals that primitive people—even as far back as prehistoric times—were striving to achieve a certain order in their lives. They tried to organize the apparent chaos of the universe. They had the desire to attach meaning to things. This demand for order has persisted throughout the history of man. So that observing the regularity of the heavenly bodies made it logical that primitive peoples should turn heavenward in their search for an understanding of the world in which they found themselves so random and alone.

And they did find a significance in the movements of the stars. Shepherds tending their flocks, for instance, observed that when the cluster of stars now known as the constellation Aries was in sight, it was the time of fertility and they associated it with the Ram. And they noticed that the growth of plants and plant life corresponded with different phases of the Moon, so that certain times were favorable for the planting of crops, and other times were not. In this way, there grew up a tradition of seasons and causes connected with the passage of the Sun through the twelve signs of the Zodiac.

Astrology was valued so highly that the king was kept informed of the daily and monthly changes in the heavenly bodies, and the results of astrological studies regarding events of the future. Head astrologers were clearly men of great rank and position, and the office was said to be a hereditary one.

Omens were taken, not only from eclipses and conjunctions of the Moon or Sun with one of the planets, but also from storms and earthquakes. In the eastern civilizations, particularly, the reverence inspired by astrology appears to have remained unbroken since the very earliest days. In ancient China, astrology, astronomy, and religion went hand in hand. The astrologer, who was also an astronomer, was part of the official government service and had his own corner in the Imperial Palace. The duties of the Imperial astrologer, whose office was one of the most important in the land, were clearly defined, as this extract from early records shows:

> This exalted gentleman must concern himself with the stars in the heavens, keeping a record of the changes and movements of the Planets, the Sun and the Moon, in order to examine the movements of the terrestrial world with the object of prognosticating good and bad fortune. He divides the territories of the nine regions of the empire in accordance with their dependence on particular celestial bodies. All the fiefs and principalities are connected with the stars and from this their prosperity or misfortune should be ascertained. He makes prognostications according to the twelve years of the Jupiter cycle of good and evil of the terrestrial world. From the colors of the five kinds of clouds, he determines the coming of floods or droughts, abundance or famine. From the twelve winds, he draws conclusions about the state of harmony of heaven and earth, and takes note of good and bad signs that result from their accord or disaccord. In general, he concerns himself with five kinds of phenomena so as to warn the Emperor to come to the aid of the government and to allow for variations in the ceremonies according to their circumstances.

The Chinese were also keen observers of the fixed stars, giving them such unusual names as Ghost Vehicle, Sun of Imperial Concubine, Imperial Prince, Pivot of Heaven, Twinkling Brilliance, Weaving Girl. But, great astrologers though they may have been, the Chinese lacked one aspect of mathematics that the Greeks applied to astrology—deductive geometry. Deductive geometry was the basis of much classical astrology in and after the time of the Greeks, and this explains the different methods of prognostication used in the East and West.

Down through the ages the astrologer's art has depended, not so much on the uncovering of new facts, though this is important, as on the interpretation of the facts already known. This is the essence of the astrologer's skill.

But why should the signs of the Zodiac have any effect at all on the formation of human character? It is easy to see why people thought they did, and even now we constantly use astrological expressions in our everyday speech. The thoughts of "lucky star," "ill-fated," "star-crossed," "mooning around," are interwoven into the very structure of our language.

Wherever the concept of the Zodiac is understood and used, it could well appear to have an influence on the human character. Does this mean, then, that the human race, in whose civilization the idea of the twelve signs of the Zodiac has long been embedded, is divided into only twelve types? Can we honestly believe that it is really as simple as that? If so, there must be pretty wide ranges of variation within each type. And if, to explain the variation, we call in heredity and environment, experiences in early childhood, the thyroid and other glands, and also the four functions of the mind together with extroversion and introversion, then one begins to wonder if the original classification was worth making at all. No sensible person believes that his favorite system explains everything. But even so, he will not find the system much use at all if it does not even save him the trouble of bothering with the others.

In the same way, if we were to put every person under only one sign of the Zodiac, the system becomes too rigid and unlike life. Besides, it was never intended to be used like that. It may be convenient to have only twelve types, but we know that in practice there is every possible gradation between aggressiveness and timidity, or between conscientiousness and laziness. How, then, do we account for this?

A person born under any given Sun sign can be mainly influenced by one or two of the other signs that appear in their individual horoscope. For instance, famous persons born under the sign of Gemini include Henry VIII, whom nothing and no one could have induced to abdicate, and Edward VIII, who did just that. Obviously, then, the sign Gemini does not fully explain the complete character of either of them.

Again, under the opposite sign, Sagittarius, were both Stalin, who was totally consumed with the notion of power, and Charles V, who freely gave up an empire because he preferred to go into a monastery. And we find under Scorpio many uncompromising characters such as Luther, de Gaulle, Indira Gandhi, and Montgomery, but also Petain, a successful commander whose name later became synonymous with collaboration.

A single sign is therefore obviously inadequate to explain the differences between people; it can only explain resemblances, such as the combativeness of the Scorpio group, or the far-reaching devotion of Charles V and Stalin to their respective ideals—the Christian heaven and the Communist utopia.

But very few people have only one sign in their horoscope chart. In addition to the month of birth, the day and, even more, the hour to the nearest minute if possible, ought to be considered. Without this, it is impossible to have an actual horoscope, for the word horoscope literally means "a consideration of the hour."

The month of birth tells you only which sign of the Zodiac was occupied by the Sun. The day and hour tell you what sign was occupied by the Moon. And the minute tells you which sign was rising on the eastern horizon. This is called the Ascendant, and, as some astrologers believe, it is supposed to be the most important thing in the whole horoscope.

The Sun is said to signify one's heart, that is to say, one's deepest desires and inmost nature. This is quite different from the Moon, which signifies one's superficial way of behaving. When the ancient Romans referred to the Emperor Augustus as a Capricorn, they meant that he had the Moon in Capricorn. Or, to take another example, a modern astrologer would call Disraeli a Scorpion because he had Scorpio Rising, but most people would call him Sagittarius because he had the Sun there. The Romans would have called him Leo because his Moon was in Leo.

So if one does not seem to fit one's birth month, it is always worthwhile reading the other signs, for one may have been born at a time when any of them were rising or occupied by the Moon. It also seems to be the case that the influence of the Sun develops as life goes on, so that the month of birth is easier to guess in people over the age of forty. The young are supposed to be influenced mainly by their Ascendant, the Rising sign, which characterizes the body and physical personality as a whole.

It is nonsense to assume that all people born at a certain time will exhibit the same characteristics, or that they will even behave in the same manner. It is quite obvious that, from the very moment of its birth, a child is subject to the effects of its environment, and that this in turn will influence its character and heritage to a decisive extent. Also to be taken into account are education and economic conditions, which play a very important part in the formation of one's character as well.

People have, in general, certain character traits and qualities which, according to their environment, develop in either a positive or a negative manner. Therefore, selfishness (inherent selfishness, that is) might emerge as unselfishness; kindness and consideration as cruelty and lack of consideration toward others. In the same way, a naturally constructive person may, through frustration, become destructive, and so on. The latent characteristics with which people are born can, therefore, through environment and good or bad training, become something that would appear to be its opposite, and so give the lie to the astrologer's description of their character. But this is not the case. The true character is still there, but it is buried deep beneath these external superficialities.

Careful study of the character traits of various signs of the Zodiac are of immeasurable help, and can render beneficial service to the intelligent person. Undoubtedly, the reader will already have discovered that, while he is able to get on very well with some people, he just "cannot stand" others. The causes sometimes seem inexplicable. At times there is intense dislike, at other times immediate sympathy. And there is, too, the phenomenon of love at first sight, which is also apparently inexplicable. People appear to be either sympathetic or unsympathetic toward each other for no apparent reason.

Now if we look at this in the light of the Zodiac, we find that people born under different signs are either compatible or incompatible with each other. In other words, there are good and bad interrelating factors among the various signs. This does not, of course, mean that humanity can be divided into groups of hostile camps. It would be quite wrong to be hostile or indifferent toward people who happen to be born under an incompatible sign. There is no reason why everybody should not, or cannot, learn to control and adjust their feelings and actions, especially after they are aware of the positive qualities of other people by studying their character analyses, among other things.

Every person born under a certain sign has both positive and negative qualities, which are developed more or less according to our free will. Nobody is entirely good or entirely bad, and it is up to each of us to learn to control ourselves on the one hand and at the same time to endeavor to learn about ourselves and others.

It cannot be emphasized often enough that it is free will that determines whether we will make really good use of our talents and abilities. Using our free will, we can either overcome our failings or allow them to rule us. Our free will enables us to exert sufficient willpower to control our failings so that they do not harm ourselves or others.

Astrology can reveal our inclinations and tendencies. Astrology can tell us about ourselves so that we are able to use our free will to overcome our shortcomings. In this way astrology helps us do our best to become needed and valuable members of society as well as helpmates to our family and our friends. Astrology also can save us a great deal of unhappiness and remorse.

Yet it may seem absurd that an ancient philosophy could be a prop to modern men and women. But below the materialistic surface of modern life, there are hidden streams of feeling and thought. Symbology is reappearing as a study worthy of the scholar; the psychosomatic factor in illness has passed from the writings of the crank to those of the specialist; spiritual healing in all its forms is no longer a pious hope but an accepted phenomenon. And it is into this context that we consider astrology, in the sense that it is an analysis of human types.

Astrology and medicine had a long journey together, and only parted company a couple of centuries ago. There still remain in medical language such astrological terms as "saturnine," "choleric," and "mercurial," used in the diagnosis of physical tendencies. The herbalist, for long the handyman of the medical profession, has been dominated by astrology since the days of the Greeks. Certain herbs traditionally respond to certain planetary influences, and diseases must therefore be treated to ensure harmony between the medicine and the disease.

But the stars are expected to foretell and not only to diagnose.

Astrological forecasting has been remarkably accurate, but often it is wide of the mark. The brave person who cares to predict world events takes dangerous chances. Individual forecasting is less clear cut; it can be a help or a disillusionment. Then we come to the nagging question: if it is possible to foreknow, is it right to foretell? This is a point of ethics on which it is hard to pronounce judgment. The doctor faces the same dilemma if he finds that symptoms of a mortal disease are present in his patient and that he can only prognosticate a steady decline. How much to tell an individual in a crisis is a problem that has perplexed many distinguished scholars. Honest and conscientious astrologers in this modern world, where so many people are seeking guidance, face the same problem.

Five hundred years ago it was customary to call in a learned man who was an astrologer who was probably also a doctor and a philosopher. By his knowledge of astrology, his study of planetary influences, he felt himself qualified to guide those in distress. The world has moved forward at a fantastic rate since then, and yet people are still uncertain of themselves. At first sight it seems fantastic in the light of modern thinking that they turn to the most ancient of all studies, and get someone to calculate a horoscope for them. But is it really so fantastic if you take a second look? For astrology is concerned with tomorrow, with survival. And in a world such as ours, tomorrow and survival are the keywords for the twenty-first century.

SPECIAL OVERVIEW 2011–2020

The second decade of the twenty-first century opens on major planetary shifts that set the stage for challenge, opportunity, and change. The personal planets—notably Jupiter and Saturn—and the generational planets—Uranus, Neptune, and Pluto—have all moved forward into new signs of the zodiac. These fresh planetary influences act to shape unfolding events and illuminate pathways to the future.

Jupiter, the big planet that attracts luck, spends about one year in each zodiacal sign. It takes approximately twelve years for Jupiter to travel through all twelve signs of the zodiac in order to complete a cycle. In 2011 a new Jupiter cycle is initiated with Jupiter transiting Aries, the first sign of the zodiac. As each year progresses over the course of the decade, Jupiter moves forward into the next sign, following the natural progression of the zodiac. Jupiter visits Taurus in 2012, Gemini in 2013, Cancer in 2014, Leo in 2015, Virgo in 2016, Libra in 2017, Scorpio in 2018, Sagittarius in 2019, Capricorn in 2020. Then in late December 2020 Jupiter enters Aquarius just two weeks before the decade closes. Jupiter's vibrations are helpful and fruitful, a source of good luck and a protection against bad luck. Opportunity swells under Jupiter's powerful rays. Learning takes leaps of faith.

Saturn, the beautiful planet of reason and responsibility, spends about two and a half years in each zodiacal sign. A complete Saturn cycle through all twelve signs of the zodiac takes about twenty-nine to thirty years. Saturn is known as the lawgiver: setting boundaries and codes of conduct, urging self-discipline and structure within a creative framework. The rule of law, the role of government, the responsibility of the individual are all sourced from Saturn. Saturn gives as it takes. Once a lesson is learned, Saturn's reward is just and full.

Saturn transits Libra throughout 2011 until early autumn of 2012. Here Saturn seeks to harmonize, to balance, to bring order out of chaos. Saturn in Libra ennobles the artist, the judge, the high-minded, the honest. Saturn next visits Scorpio from autumn 2012 until late December 2014. With Saturn in Scorpio, tactic and strategy combine to get workable solutions and desired results. Saturn's problem-solving tools here can harness dynamic energy for the common good. Saturn in Sagittarius, an idealistic and humanistic transit that stretches from December 2014 into the last day of autumn 2017, promotes activism over mere dogma and debate. Saturn in Sagittarius can be a driving force for good. Saturn tours Capricorn, the sign that Saturn rules, from the first day of winter 2017 into early spring 2020. Saturn in Capricorn is a consolidating transit, bringing things forth and into fruition. Here a plan can be made right, made whole, then launched for success. Saturn starts to visit Aquarius, a sign that Saturn corules and a very good sign for Saturn to visit, in the very last year of the decade. Saturn in Aquarius fosters team spirit, the unity of effort amid diversity. The transit of Saturn in Aquarius until early 2023 represents a period of enlightened activism and unprecedented growth.

Uranus, Neptune, and Pluto spend more than several years in each sign. They produce the differences in attitude, belief, behavior, and taste that distinguish one generation from another—and so are called the generational planets.

Uranus, planet of innovation and surprise, is known as the awakener. Uranus spends seven to eight years in each sign. Uranus started a new cycle when it entered Aries, the first sign of the zodiac, in May 2010. Uranus tours Aries until May 2018. Uranus in Aries accents originality, freedom, independence, unpredictability. There can be a start-stop quality to undertakings given this transit. Despite contradiction and confrontation, significant invention and productivity mark this transit. Uranus next visits Taurus through the end of the decade into 2026. Strategic thinking and timely action characterize the transit of Uranus in Taurus. Here intuition is backed up by common sense, leading to fresh discoveries upon which new industries can be built.

Neptune spends about fourteen years in each sign. Neptune, the visionary planet, enters Pisces, the sign Neptune rules and the final sign of the zodiac, in early April 2011. Neptune journeys through Pisces until 2026 to complete the Neptune cycle of visiting all twelve zodiacal signs. Neptune's tour of Pisces ushers in a long period of great potentiality: universal understanding, universal good, universal love, universal generosity, universal forgiveness—the universal spirit affects all. Neptune in Pisces can oversee the fruition of such noble aims as human rights for all and liberation from all forms of tyranny. Neptune in Pisces is a pervasive influence that changes concepts, consciences, attitudes, actions. The impact of Neptune in Pisces is to illuminate and to inspire.

Pluto, dwarf planet of beginnings and endings, entered the earthy sign of Capricorn in 2008 and journeys there for sixteen years into late 2024. Pluto in Capricorn over the course of this extensive visit has the capacity to change the landscape as well as the humanscape. The transforming energy of Pluto combines with the persevering power of Capricorn to give depth and character to potential change. Pluto in Capricorn brings focus and cohesion to disparate, diverse creativities. As new forms arise and take root, Pluto in Capricorn organizes the rebuilding process. Freedom versus limitation, freedom versus authority is in the framework during this transit. Reasonableness struggles with recklessness to solve divisive issues. Pluto in Capricorn teaches important lessons about adversity, and the lessons will be learned.

THE SIGNS OF THE ZODIAC

Dominant Characteristics

Aries: March 21–April 20

The Positive Side of Aries

The Aries has many positive points to his character. People born under this first sign of the Zodiac are often quite strong and enthusiastic. On the whole, they are forward-looking people who are not easily discouraged by temporary setbacks. They know what they want out of life and they go out after it. Their personalities are strong. Others are usually quite impressed by the Ram's way of doing things. Quite often they are sources of inspiration for others traveling the same route. Aries men and women have a special zest for life that can be contagious; for others, they are a fine example of how life should be lived.

The Aries person usually has a quick and active mind. He is imaginative and inventive. He enjoys keeping busy and active. He generally gets along well with all kinds of people. He is interested in mankind, as a whole. He likes to be challenged. Some would say he thrives on opposition, for it is when he is set against that he often does his best. Getting over or around obstacles is a challenge he generally enjoys. All in all, Aries is quite positive and young-thinking. He likes to keep abreast of new things that are happening in the world. Aries are often fond of speed. They like things to be done quickly, and this sometimes aggravates their slower colleagues and associates.

The Aries man or woman always seems to remain young. Their whole approach to life is youthful and optimistic. They never say

die, no matter what the odds. They may have an occasional setback, but it is not long before they are back on their feet again.

The Negative Side of Aries

Everybody has his less positive qualities—and Aries is no exception. Sometimes the Aries man or woman is not very tactful in communicating with others; in his hurry to get things done he is apt to be a little callous or inconsiderate. Sensitive people are likely to find him somewhat sharp-tongued in some situations. Often in his eagerness to get the show on the road, he misses the mark altogether and cannot achieve his aims.

At times Aries can be too impulsive. He can occasionally be stubborn and refuse to listen to reason. If things do not move quickly enough to suit the Aries man or woman, he or she is apt to become rather nervous or irritable. The uncultivated Aries is not unfamiliar with moments of doubt and fear. He is capable of being destructive if he does not get his way. He can overcome some of his emotional problems by steadily trying to express himself as he really is, but this requires effort.

Taurus: April 21–May 20

The Positive Side of Taurus

The Taurus person is known for his ability to concentrate and for his tenacity. These are perhaps his strongest qualities. The Taurus man or woman generally has very little trouble in getting along with others; it's his nature to be helpful toward people in need. He can always be depended on by his friends, especially those in trouble.

Taurus generally achieves what he wants through his ability to persevere. He never leaves anything unfinished but works on something until it has been completed. People can usually take him at his word; he is honest and forthright in most of his dealings. The Taurus person has a good chance to make a success of his life because of his many positive qualities. The Taurus who aims high seldom falls short of his mark. He learns well by experience. He is thorough and does not believe in shortcuts of any kind. The Bull's thoroughness pays off in the end, for through his deliberateness he learns how to rely on himself and what he has learned. The Taurus person tries to get along with others, as a rule.

He is not overly critical and likes people to be themselves. He is a tolerant person and enjoys peace and harmony—especially in his home life.

Taurus is usually cautious in all that he does. He is not a person who believes in taking unnecessary risks. Before adopting any one line of action, he will weigh all of the pros and cons. The Taurus person is steadfast. Once his mind is made up it seldom changes. The person born under this sign usually is a good family person— reliable and loving.

The Negative Side of Taurus

Sometimes the Taurus man or woman is a bit too stubborn. He won't listen to other points of view if his mind is set on something. To others, this can be quite annoying. Taurus also does not like to be told what to do. He becomes rather angry if others think him not too bright. He does not like to be told he is wrong, even when he is. He dislikes being contradicted.

Some people who are born under this sign are very suspicious of others—even of those persons close to them. They find it difficult to trust people fully. They are often afraid of being deceived or taken advantage of. The Bull often finds it difficult to forget or forgive. His love of material things sometimes makes him rather avaricious and petty.

Gemini: May 21–June 20

The Positive Side of Gemini

The person born under this sign of the Heavenly Twins is usually quite bright and quick-witted. Some of them are capable of doing many different things. The Gemini person very often has many different interests. He keeps an open mind and is always anxious to learn new things.

Gemini is often an analytical person. He is a person who enjoys making use of his intellect. He is governed more by his mind than by his emotions. He is a person who is not confined to one view; he can often understand both sides to a problem or question. He knows how to reason, how to make rapid decisions if need be.

He is an adaptable person and can make himself at home almost anywhere. There are all kinds of situations he can adapt to. He is a person who seldom doubts himself; he is sure of his talents and his ability to think and reason. Gemini is generally most satisfied when he is in a situation where he can make use of his intellect. Never short of imagination, he often has strong talents for invention. He is rather a modern person when it comes to life; Gemini almost always moves along with the times—perhaps that is why he remains so youthful throughout most of his life.

Literature and art appeal to the person born under this sign. Creativity in almost any form will interest and intrigue the Gemini man or woman.

The Gemini is often quite charming. A good talker, he often is the center of attraction at any gathering. People find it easy to like a person born under this sign because he can appear easygoing and usually has a good sense of humor.

The Negative Side of Gemini

Sometimes the Gemini person tries to do too many things at one time—and as a result, winds up finishing nothing. Some Twins are easily distracted and find it rather difficult to concentrate on one thing for too long a time. Sometimes they give in to trifling fancies and find it rather boring to become too serious about any one thing. Some of them are never dependable, no matter what they promise.

Although the Gemini man or woman often appears to be well-versed on many subjects, this is sometimes just a veneer. His knowledge may be only superficial, but because he speaks so well he gives people the impression of erudition. Some Geminis are sharp-tongued and inconsiderate; they think only of themselves and their own pleasure.

Cancer: June 21–July 20

The Positive Side of Cancer

The Moon Child's most positive point is his understanding nature. On the whole, he is a loving and sympathetic person. He would never go out of his way to hurt anyone. The Cancer man or woman is often very kind and tender; they give what they can to others. They hate to see others suffering and will do what they can to help someone in less fortunate circumstances than themselves. They are often very concerned about the world. Their interest in people generally goes beyond that of just their own families and close friends; they have a deep sense of community and respect humanitarian values. The Moon Child means what he says, as a rule; he is honest about his feelings.

The Cancer man or woman is a person who knows the art of patience. When something seems difficult, he is willing to wait until the situation becomes manageable again. He is a person who knows how to bide his time. Cancer knows how to concentrate on one thing at a time. When he has made his mind up he generally sticks with what he does, seeing it through to the end.

Cancer is a person who loves his home. He enjoys being surrounded by familiar things and the people he loves. Of all the signs, Cancer is the most maternal. Even the men born under this sign often have a motherly or protective quality about them. They like to take care of people in their family—to see that they are well loved and well provided for. They are usually loyal and faithful. Family ties mean a lot to the Cancer man or woman. Parents and in-laws are respected and loved. Young Cancer responds very well to adults who show faith in him. The Moon Child has a strong sense of tradition. He is very sensitive to the moods of others.

The Negative Side of Cancer

Sometimes Cancer finds it rather hard to face life. It becomes too much for him. He can be a little timid and retiring, when things don't go too well. When unfortunate things happen, he is apt to just shrug and say, "Whatever will be will be." He can be fatalistic to a fault. The uncultivated Cancer is a bit lazy. He doesn't have very much ambition. Anything that seems a bit difficult he'll gladly leave to others. He may be lacking in initiative. Too sensitive, when he feels he's been injured, he'll crawl back into his shell and nurse his imaginary wounds. The immature Moon Child often is given to crying when the smallest thing goes wrong.

Some Cancers find it difficult to enjoy themselves in environments outside their homes. They make heavy demands on others, and need to be constantly reassured that they are loved. Lacking such reassurance, they may resort to sulking in silence.

Leo: July 21–August 21

The Positive Side of Leo

Often Leos make good leaders. They seem to be good organizers and administrators. Usually they are quite popular with others. Whatever group it is that they belong to, the Leo man or woman is almost sure to be or become the leader. Loyalty, one of the Lion's noblest traits, enables him or her to maintain this leadership position.

Leo is generous most of the time. It is his best characteristic. He or she likes to give gifts and presents. In making others happy, the Leo person becomes happy himself. He likes to splurge when spending money on others. In some instances it may seem that the Lion's generosity knows no boundaries. A hospitable person, the Leo man or woman is very fond of welcoming people to his house and entertaining them. He is never short of company.

Leo has plenty of energy and drive. He enjoys working toward some specific goal. When he applies himself correctly, he gets what he wants most often. The Leo person is almost never unsure of himself. He has plenty of confidence and aplomb. He is a person who is direct in almost everything he does. He has a quick mind and can make a decision in a very short time.

He usually sets a good example for others because of his ambitious manner and positive ways. He knows how to stick to something once he's started. Although Leo may be good at making a joke, he is not superficial or glib. He is a loving person, kind and thoughtful.

There is generally nothing small or petty about the Leo man or woman. He does what he can for those who are deserving. He is a person others can rely upon at all times. He means what he says. An honest person, generally speaking, he is a friend who is valued and sought out.

The Negative Side of Leo

Leo, however, does have his faults. At times, he can be just a bit too arrogant. He thinks that no one deserves a leadership position except him. Only he is capable of doing things well. His opinion of himself is often much too high. Because of his conceit, he is sometimes rather unpopular with a good many people. Some Leos are too materialistic; they can only think in terms of money and profit.

Some Leos enjoy lording it over others—at home or at their place of business. What is more, they feel they have the right to. Egocentric to an impossible degree, this sort of Leo cares little about how others think or feel. He can be rude and cutting.

Virgo: August 22–September 22

The Positive Side of Virgo

The person born under the sign of Virgo is generally a busy person. He knows how to arrange and organize things. He is a good planner. Above all, he is practical and is not afraid of hard work.

Often called the sign of the Harvester, Virgo knows how to attain what he desires. He sticks with something until it is finished. He never shirks his duties, and can always be depended upon. The Virgo person can be thoroughly trusted at all times.

The man or woman born under this sign tries to do everything to perfection. He doesn't believe in doing anything halfway. He always aims for the top. He is the sort of a person who is always learning and constantly striving to better himself—not because he wants more money or glory, but because it gives him a feeling of accomplishment.

The Virgo man or woman is a very observant person. He is sensitive to how others feel, and can see things below the surface of a situation. He usually puts this talent to constructive use.

It is not difficult for the Virgo to be open and earnest. He believes in putting his cards on the table. He is never secretive or underhanded. He's as good as his word. The Virgo person is generally plainspoken and down to earth. He has no trouble in expressing himself.

The Virgo person likes to keep up to date on new developments in his particular field. Well-informed, generally, he sometimes has a keen interest in the arts or literature. What he knows, he knows well. His ability to use his critical faculties is well-developed and sometimes startles others because of its accuracy.

Virgos adhere to a moderate way of life; they avoid excesses. Virgo is a responsible person and enjoys being of service.

The Negative Side of Virgo

Sometimes a Virgo person is too critical. He thinks that only he can do something the way it should be done. Whatever anyone else does is inferior. He can be rather annoying in the way he quibbles over insignificant details. In telling others how things should be done, he can be rather tactless and mean.

Some Virgos seem rather emotionless and cool. They feel emotional involvement is beneath them. They are sometimes too tidy, too neat. With money they can be rather miserly. Some Virgos try to force their opinions and ideas on others.

Libra: September 23–October 22

The Positive Side of Libra

Libras love harmony. It is one of their most outstanding character traits. They are interested in achieving balance; they admire beauty and grace in things as well as in people. Generally speaking, they are kind and considerate people. Libras are usually very sympathetic. They go out of their way not to hurt another person's feelings. They are outgoing and do what they can to help those in need.

People born under the sign of Libra almost always make good friends. They are loyal and amiable. They enjoy the company of others. Many of them are rather moderate in their views; they believe in keeping an open mind, however, and weighing both sides of an issue fairly before making a decision.

Alert and intelligent, Libra, often known as the Lawgiver, is always fair-minded and tries to put himself in the position of the other person. They are against injustice; quite often they take up for the underdog. In most of their social dealings, they try to be tactful and kind. They dislike discord and bickering, and most Libras strive for peace and harmony in all their relationships.

The Libra man or woman has a keen sense of beauty. They appreciate handsome furnishings and clothes. Many of them are artistically inclined. Their taste is usually impeccable. They know how to use color. Their homes are almost always attractively arranged and inviting. They enjoy entertaining people and see to it that their guests always feel at home and welcome.

Libra gets along with almost everyone. He is well-liked and socially much in demand.

The Negative Side of Libra

Some people born under this sign tend to be rather insincere. So eager are they to achieve harmony in all relationships that they will even go so far as to lie. Many of them are escapists. They find facing the truth an ordeal and prefer living in a world of make-believe.

In a serious argument, some Libras give in rather easily even when they know they are right. Arguing, even about something they believe in, is too unsettling for some of them.

Libras sometimes care too much for material things. They enjoy possessions and luxuries. Some are vain and tend to be jealous.

Scorpio: October 23–November 22

The Positive Side of Scorpio

The Scorpio man or woman generally knows what he or she wants out of life. He is a determined person. He sees something through to the end. Scorpio is quite sincere, and seldom says anything he doesn't mean. When he sets a goal for himself he tries to go about achieving it in a very direct way.

The Scorpion is brave and courageous. They are not afraid of hard work. Obstacles do not frighten them. They forge ahead until they achieve what they set out for. The Scorpio man or woman has a strong will.

Although Scorpio may seem rather fixed and determined, inside he is often quite tender and loving. He can care very much for others. He believes in sincerity in all relationships. His feelings about someone tend to last; they are profound and not superficial.

The Scorpio person is someone who adheres to his principles no matter what happens. He will not be deterred from a path he believes to be right.

Because of his many positive strengths, the Scorpion can often achieve happiness for himself and for those that he loves.

He is a constructive person by nature. He often has a deep understanding of people and of life, in general. He is perceptive and unafraid. Obstacles often seem to spur him on. He is a positive person who enjoys winning. He has many strengths and resources; challenge of any sort often brings out the best in him.

The Negative Side of Scorpio

The Scorpio person is sometimes hypersensitive. Often he imagines injury when there is none. He feels that others do not bother to recognize him for his true worth. Sometimes he is given to excessive boasting in order to compensate for what he feels is neglect.

Scorpio can be proud, arrogant, and competitive. They can be sly when they put their minds to it and they enjoy outwitting persons or institutions noted for their cleverness.

Their tactics for getting what they want are sometimes devious and ruthless. They don't care too much about what others may think. If they feel others have done them an injustice, they will do their best to seek revenge. The Scorpion often has a sudden, violent temper; and this person's interest in sex is sometimes quite unbalanced or excessive.

Sagittarius: November 23–December 20

The Positive Side of Sagittarius

People born under this sign are honest and forthright. Their approach to life is earnest and open. Sagittarius is often quite adult in his way of seeing things. They are broad-minded and tolerant people. When dealing with others the person born under the sign of the Archer is almost always open and forthright. He doesn't believe in deceit or pretension. His standards are high. People who associate with Sagittarius generally admire and respect his tolerant viewpoint.

The Archer trusts others easily and expects them to trust him. He is never suspicious or envious and almost always thinks well of others. People always enjoy his company because he is so friendly and easygoing. The Sagittarius man or woman is often good-humored. He can always be depended upon by his friends, family, and co-workers.

The person born under this sign of the Zodiac likes a good joke every now and then. Sagittarius is eager for fun and laughs, which makes him very popular with others.

A lively person, he enjoys sports and outdoor life. The Archer is fond of animals. Intelligent and interesting, he can begin an ani-

mated conversation with ease. He likes exchanging ideas and discussing various views.

He is not selfish or proud. If someone proposes an idea or plan that is better than his, he will immediately adopt it. Imaginative yet practical, he knows how to put ideas into practice.

The Archer enjoys sport and games, and it doesn't matter if he wins or loses. He is a forgiving person, and never sulks over something that has not worked out in his favor.

He is seldom critical, and is almost always generous.

The Negative Side of Sagittarius

Some Sagittarius are restless. They take foolish risks and seldom learn from the mistakes they make. They don't have heads for money and are often mismanaging their finances. Some of them devote much of their time to gambling.

Some are too outspoken and tactless, always putting their feet in their mouths. They hurt others carelessly by being honest at the wrong time. Sometimes they make promises which they don't keep. They don't stick close enough to their plans and go from one failure to another. They are undisciplined and waste a lot of energy.

Capricorn: December 21–January 19

The Positive Side of Capricorn

The person born under the sign of Capricorn, known variously as the Mountain Goat or Sea Goat, is usually very stable and patient. He sticks to whatever tasks he has and sees them through. He can always be relied upon and he is not averse to work.

An honest person, Capricorn is generally serious about whatever he does. He does not take his duties lightly. He is a practical person and believes in keeping his feet on the ground.

Quite often the person born under this sign is ambitious and knows how to get what he wants out of life. The Goat forges ahead and never gives up his goal. When he is determined about something, he almost always wins. He is a good worker—a hard worker. Although things may not come easy to him, he will not complain, but continue working until his chores are finished.

He is usually good at business matters and knows the value of money. He is not a spendthrift and knows how to put something away for a rainy day; he dislikes waste and unnecessary loss.

Capricorn knows how to make use of his self-control. He can apply himself to almost anything once he puts his mind to it. His ability to concentrate sometimes astounds others. He is diligent and does well when involved in detail work.

The Capricorn man or woman is charitable, generally speaking, and will do what is possible to help others less fortunate. As a friend, he is loyal and trustworthy. He never shirks his duties or responsibilities. He is self-reliant and never expects too much of the other fellow. He does what he can on his own. If someone does him a good turn, then he will do his best to return the favor.

The Negative Side of Capricorn

Like everyone, Capricorn, too, has faults. At times, the Goat can be overcritical of others. He expects others to live up to his own high standards. He thinks highly of himself and tends to look down on others.

His interest in material things may be exaggerated. The Capricorn man or woman thinks too much about getting on in the world and having something to show for it. He may even be a little greedy.

He sometimes thinks he knows what's best for everyone. He is too bossy. He is always trying to organize and correct others. He may be a little narrow in his thinking.

Aquarius: January 20–February 18

The Positive Side of Aquarius

The Aquarius man or woman is usually very honest and forthright. These are his two greatest qualities. His standards for himself are generally very high. He can always be relied upon by others. His word is his bond.

Aquarius is perhaps the most tolerant of all the Zodiac personalities. He respects other people's beliefs and feels that everyone is entitled to his own approach to life.

He would never do anything to injure another's feelings. He is never unkind or cruel. Always considerate of others, the Water

Bearer is always willing to help a person in need. He feels a very strong tie between himself and all the other members of mankind.

The person born under this sign, called the Water Bearer, is almost always an individualist. He does not believe in teaming up with the masses, but prefers going his own way. His ideas about life and mankind are often quite advanced. There is a saying to the effect that the average Aquarius is fifty years ahead of his time.

Aquarius is community-minded. The problems of the world concern him greatly. He is interested in helping others no matter what part of the globe they live in. He is truly a humanitarian sort. He likes to be of service to others.

Giving, considerate, and without prejudice, Aquarius have no trouble getting along with others.

The Negative Side of Aquarius

Aquarius may be too much of a dreamer. He makes plans but seldom carries them out. He is rather unrealistic. His imagination has a tendency to run away with him. Because many of his plans are impractical, he is always in some sort of a dither.

Others may not approve of him at all times because of his unconventional behavior. He may be a bit eccentric. Sometimes he is so busy with his own thoughts that he loses touch with the realities of existence.

Some Aquarius feel they are more clever and intelligent than others. They seldom admit to their own faults, even when they are quite apparent. Some become rather fanatic in their views. Their criticism of others is sometimes destructive and negative.

Pisces: February 19–March 20

The Positive Side of Pisces

Known as the sign of the Fishes, Pisces has a sympathetic nature. Kindly, he is often dedicated in the way he goes about helping others. The sick and the troubled often turn to him for advice and assistance. Possessing keen intuition, Pisces can easily understand people's deepest problems.

He is very broad-minded and does not criticize others for their faults. He knows how to accept people for what they are. On the whole, he is a trustworthy and earnest person. He is loyal to his friends and will do what he can to help them in time of need. Generous and good-natured, he is a lover of peace; he is often willing to help others solve their differences. People who have taken a wrong turn in life often interest him and he will do what he can to persuade them to rehabilitate themselves.

He has a strong intuitive sense and most of the time he knows how to make it work for him. Pisces is unusually perceptive and often knows what is bothering someone before that person, himself, is aware of it. The Pisces man or woman is an idealistic person, basically, and is interested in making the world a better place in which to live. Pisces believes that everyone should help each other. He is willing to do more than his share in order to achieve cooperation with others.

The person born under this sign often is talented in music or art. He is a receptive person; he is able to take the ups and downs of life with philosophic calm.

The Negative Side of Pisces

Some Pisces are often depressed; their outlook on life is rather glum. They may feel that they have been given a bad deal in life and that others are always taking unfair advantage of them. Pisces sometimes feel that the world is a cold and cruel place. The Fishes can be easily discouraged. The Pisces man or woman may even withdraw from the harshness of reality into a secret shell of his own where he dreams and idles away a good deal of his time.

Pisces can be lazy. He lets things happen without giving the least bit of resistance. He drifts along, whether on the high road or on the low. He can be lacking in willpower.

Some Pisces people seek escape through drugs or alcohol. When temptation comes along they find it hard to resist. In matters of sex, they can be rather permissive.

Sun Sign Personalities

ARIES: Hans Christian Andersen, Pearl Bailey, Marlon Brando, Wernher Von Braun, Charlie Chaplin, Joan Crawford, Da Vinci, Bette Davis, Doris Day, W.C. Fields, Alec Guinness, Adolf Hitler, William Holden, Thomas Jefferson, Nikita Khrushchev, Elton John, Arturo Toscanini, J.P. Morgan, Paul Robeson, Gloria Steinem, Sarah Vaughn, Vincent van Gogh, Tennessee Williams

TAURUS: Fred Astaire, Charlotte Brontë, Carol Burnett, Irving Berlin, Bing Crosby, Salvador Dali, Tchaikovsky, Queen Elizabeth II, Duke Ellington, Ella Fitzgerald, Henry Fonda, Sigmund Freud, Orson Welles, Joe Louis, Lenin, Karl Marx, Golda Meir, Eva Peron, Bertrand Russell, Shakespeare, Kate Smith, Benjamin Spock, Barbra Streisand, Shirley Temple, Harry Truman

GEMINI: Ruth Benedict, Josephine Baker, Rachel Carson, Carlos Chavez, Walt Whitman, Bob Dylan, Ralph Waldo Emerson, Judy Garland, Paul Gauguin, Allen Ginsberg, Benny Goodman, Bob Hope, Burl Ives, John F. Kennedy, Peggy Lee, Marilyn Monroe, Joe Namath, Cole Porter, Laurence Olivier, Harriet Beecher Stowe, Queen Victoria, John Wayne, Frank Lloyd Wright

CANCER: "Dear Abby," Lizzie Borden, David Brinkley, Yul Brynner, Pearl Buck, Marc Chagall, Princess Diana, Babe Didrikson, Mary Baker Eddy, Henry VIII, John Glenn, Ernest Hemingway, Lena Horne, Oscar Hammerstein, Helen Keller, Ann Landers, George Orwell, Nancy Reagan, Rembrandt, Richard Rodgers, Ginger Rogers, Rubens, Jean-Paul Sartre, O.J. Simpson

LEO: Neil Armstrong, James Baldwin, Lucille Ball, Emily Brontë, Wilt Chamberlain, Julia Child, William J. Clinton, Cecil B. De Mille, Ogden Nash, Amelia Earhart, Edna Ferber, Arthur Goldberg, Alfred Hitchcock, Mick Jagger, George Meany, Annie Oakley, George Bernard Shaw, Napoleon, Jacqueline Onassis, Henry Ford, Francis Scott Key, Andy Warhol, Mae West, Orville Wright

VIRGO: Ingrid Bergman, Warren Burger, Maurice Chevalier, Agatha Christie, Sean Connery, Lafayette, Peter Falk, Greta Garbo, Althea Gibson, Arthur Godfrey, Goethe, Buddy Hackett, Michael Jackson, Lyndon Johnson, D.H. Lawrence, Sophia Loren, Grandma Moses, Arnold Palmer, Queen Elizabeth I, Walter Reuther, Peter Sellers, Lily Tomlin, George Wallace

LIBRA: Brigitte Bardot, Art Buchwald, Truman Capote, Dwight D. Eisenhower, William Faulkner, F. Scott Fitzgerald, Gandhi, George Gershwin, Micky Mantle, Helen Hayes, Vladimir Horowitz, Doris Lessing, Martina Navratalova, Eugene O'Neill, Luciano Pavarotti, Emily Post, Eleanor Roosevelt, Bruce Springsteen, Margaret Thatcher, Gore Vidal, Barbara Walters, Oscar Wilde

SCORPIO: Vivien Leigh, Richard Burton, Art Carney, Johnny Carson, Billy Graham, Grace Kelly, Walter Cronkite, Marie Curie, Charles de Gaulle, Linda Evans, Indira Gandhi, Theodore Roosevelt, Rock Hudson, Katherine Hepburn, Robert F. Kennedy, Billie Jean King, Martin Luther, Georgia O'Keeffe, Pablo Picasso, Jonas Salk, Alan Shepard, Robert Louis Stevenson

SAGITTARIUS: Jane Austen, Louisa May Alcott, Woody Allen, Beethoven, Willy Brandt, Mary Martin, William F. Buckley, Maria Callas, Winston Churchill, Noel Coward, Emily Dickinson, Walt Disney, Benjamin Disraeli, James Doolittle, Kirk Douglas, Chet Huntley, Jane Fonda, Chris Evert Lloyd, Margaret Mead, Charles Schulz, John Milton, Frank Sinatra, Steven Spielberg

CAPRICORN: Muhammad Ali, Isaac Asimov, Pablo Casals, Dizzy Dean, Marlene Dietrich, James Farmer, Ava Gardner, Barry Goldwater, Cary Grant, J. Edgar Hoover, Howard Hughes, Joan of Arc, Gypsy Rose Lee, Martin Luther King, Jr., Rudyard Kipling, Mao Tse-tung, Richard Nixon, Gamal Nasser, Louis Pasteur, Albert Schweitzer, Stalin, Benjamin Franklin, Elvis Presley

AQUARIUS: Marian Anderson, Susan B. Anthony, Jack Benny, John Barrymore, Mikhail Baryshnikov, Charles Darwin, Charles Dickens, Thomas Edison, Clark Gable, Jascha Heifetz, Abraham Lincoln, Yehudi Menuhin, Mozart, Jack Nicklaus, Ronald Reagan, Jackie Robinson, Norman Rockwell, Franklin D. Roosevelt, Gertrude Stein, Charles Lindbergh, Margaret Truman

PISCES: Edward Albee, Harry Belafonte, Alexander Graham Bell, Chopin, Adelle Davis, Albert Einstein, Golda Meir, Jackie Gleason, Winslow Homer, Edward M. Kennedy, Victor Hugo, Mike Mansfield, Michelangelo, Edna St. Vincent Millay, Liza Minelli, John Steinbeck, Linus Pauling, Ravel, Renoir, Diana Ross, William Shirer, Elizabeth Taylor, George Washington

The Signs and Their Key Words

		POSITIVE	NEGATIVE
ARIES	self	courage, initiative, pioneer instinct	brash rudeness, selfish impetuosity
TAURUS	money	endurance, loyalty, wealth	obstinacy, gluttony
GEMINI	mind	versatility	capriciousness, unreliability
CANCER	family	sympathy, homing instinct	clannishness, childishness
LEO	children	love, authority, integrity	egotism, force
VIRGO	work	purity, industry, analysis	faultfinding, cynicism
LIBRA	marriage	harmony, justice	vacillation, superficiality
SCORPIO	sex	survival, regeneration	vengeance, discord
SAGITTARIUS	travel	optimism, higher learning	lawlessness
CAPRICORN	career	depth	narrowness, gloom
AQUARIUS	friends	human fellowship, genius	perverse unpredictability
PISCES	confine- ment	spiritual love, universality	diffusion, escapism

The Elements and Qualities of The Signs

Every sign has both an *element* and a *quality* associated with it. The element indicates the basic makeup of the sign, and the quality describes the kind of activity associated with each.

Element	Sign	Quality	Sign
FIRE............	ARIES LEO SAGITTARIUS	CARDINAL	ARIES LIBRA CANCER CAPRICORN
EARTH	TAURUS VIRGO CAPRICORN	FIXED	TAURUS LEO SCORPIO AQUARIUS
AIR..............	GEMINI LIBRA AQUARIUS		
WATER	CANCER SCORPIO PISCES	MUTABLE	GEMINI VIRGO SAGITTARIUS PISCES

Signs can be grouped together according to their element and quality. Signs of the same element share many basic traits in common. They tend to form stable configurations and ultimately harmonious relationships. Signs of the same quality are often less harmonious, but they share many dynamic potentials for growth as well as profound fulfillment.

Further discussion of each of these sign groupings is provided on the following pages.

The Fire Signs

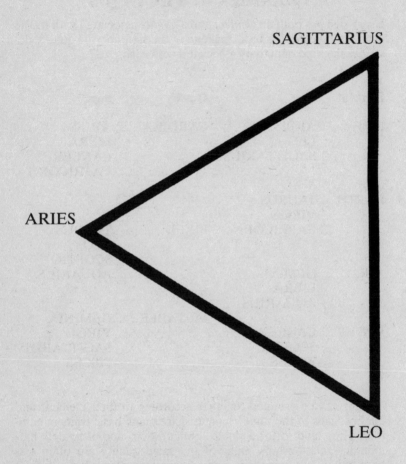

This is the fire group. On the whole these are emotional, volatile types, quick to anger, quick to forgive. They are adventurous, powerful people and act as a source of inspiration for everyone. They spark into action with immediate exuberant impulses. They are intelligent, self-involved, creative, and idealistic. They all share a certain vibrancy and glow that outwardly reflects an inner flame and passion for living.

The Earth Signs

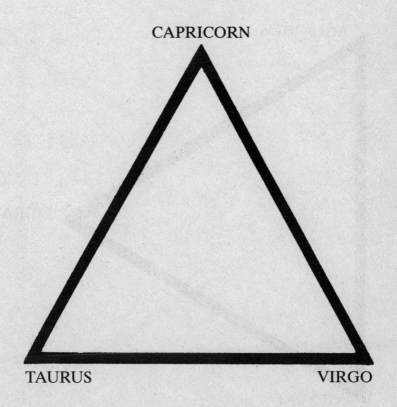

CAPRICORN

TAURUS

VIRGO

This is the earth group. They are in constant touch with the material world and tend to be conservative. Although they are all capable of spartan self-discipline, they are earthy, sensual people who are stimulated by the tangible, elegant, and luxurious. The thread of their lives is always practical, but they do fantasize and are often attracted to dark, mysterious, emotional people. They are like great cliffs overhanging the sea, forever married to the ocean but always resisting erosion from the dark, emotional forces that thunder at their feet.

The Air Signs

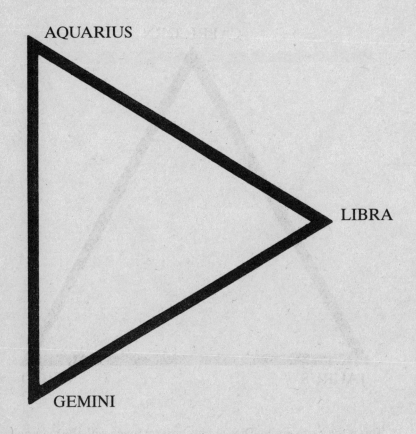

This is the air group. They are light, mental creatures desirous of contact, communication, and relationship. They are involved with people and the forming of ties on many levels. Original thinkers, they are the bearers of human news. Their language is their sense of word, color, style, and beauty. They provide an atmosphere suitable and pleasant for living. They add change and versatility to the scene, and it is through them that we can explore new territory of human intelligence and experience.

The Water Signs

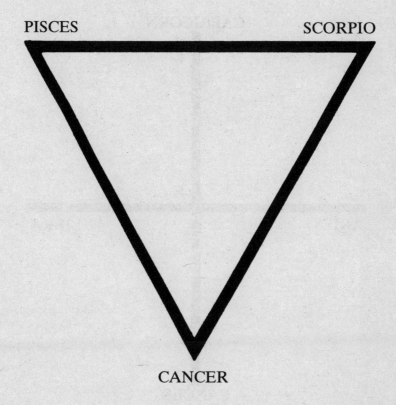

PISCES

SCORPIO

CANCER

This is the water group. Through the water people, we are all joined together on emotional, nonverbal levels. They are silent, mysterious types whose magic hypnotizes even the most determined realist. They have uncanny perceptions about people and are as rich as the oceans when it comes to feeling, emotion, or imagination. They are sensitive, mystical creatures with memories that go back beyond time. Through water, life is sustained. These people have the potential for the depths of darkness or the heights of mysticism and art.

The Cardinal Signs

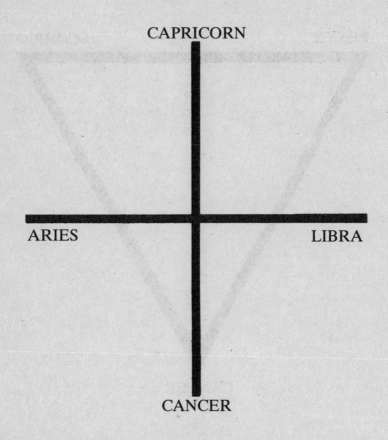

Put together, this is a clear-cut picture of dynamism, activity, tremendous stress, and remarkable achievement. These people know the meaning of great change since their lives are often characterized by significant crises and major successes. This combination is like a simultaneous storm of summer, fall, winter, and spring. The danger is chaotic diffusion of energy; the potential is irrepressible growth and victory.

The Fixed Signs

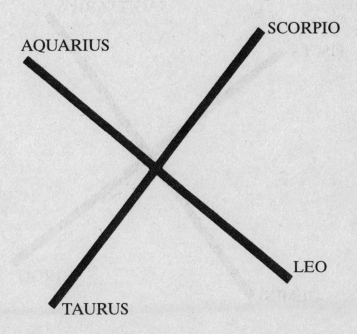

Fixed signs are always establishing themselves in a given place or area of experience. Like explorers who arrive and plant a flag, these people claim a position from which they do not enjoy being deposed. They are staunch, stalwart, upright, trusty, honorable people, although their obstinacy is well-known. Their contribution is fixity, and they are the angels who support our visible world.

The Mutable Signs

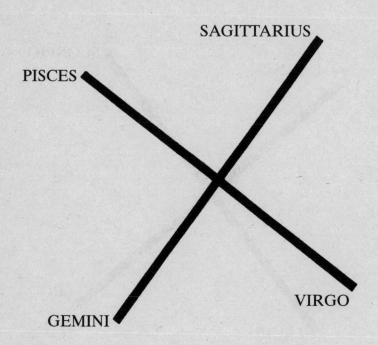

Mutable people are versatile, sensitive, intelligent, ner vous, and deeply curious about life. They are the translators of all energy. They often carry out or complete tasks initiated by others. Combinations of these signs have highly developed minds; they are imaginative and jumpy and think and talk a lot. At worst their lives are a Tower of Babel. At best they are adaptable and ready creatures who can assimilate one kind of experience and enjoy it while anticipating coming changes.

THE PLANETS
OF THE SOLAR SYSTEM

This section describes the planets of the solar system. In astrology, both the Sun and the Moon are considered to be planets. Because of the Moon's influence in our day-to-day lives, the Moon is described in a separate section following this one.

The Planets and the Signs They Rule

The signs of the Zodiac are linked to the planets in the following way. Each sign is governed or ruled by one or more planets. No matter where the planets are located in the sky at any given moment, they still rule their respective signs, and when they travel through the signs they rule, they have special dignity and their effects are stronger.

Following is a list of the planets and the signs they rule. After looking at the list, read the definitions of the planets and see if you can determine how the planet ruling *your* Sun sign has affected your life.

SIGNS	RULING PLANETS
Aries	Mars, Pluto
Taurus	Venus
Gemini	Mercury
Cancer	Moon
Leo	Sun
Virgo	Mercury
Libra	Venus
Scorpio	Mars, Pluto
Sagittarius	Jupiter
Capricorn	Saturn
Aquarius	Saturn, Uranus
Pisces	Jupiter, Neptune

Characteristics of the Planets

The following pages give the meaning and characteristics of the planets of the solar system. They all travel around the Sun at different speeds and different distances. Taken with the Sun, they all distribute individual intelligence and ability throughout the entire chart.

The planets modify the influence of the Sun in a chart according to their own particular natures, strengths, and positions. Their positions must be calculated for each year and day, and their function and expression in a horoscope will change as they move from one area of the Zodiac to another.

We start with a description of the sun.

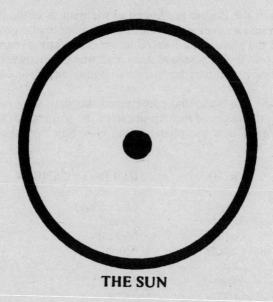

THE SUN

SUN

This is the center of existence. Around this flaming sphere all the planets revolve in endless orbits. Our star is constantly sending out its beams of light and energy without which no life on Earth would be possible. In astrology it symbolizes everything we are trying to become, the center around which all of our activity in life will always revolve. It is the symbol of our basic nature and describes the natural and constant thread that runs through everything that we do from birth to death on this planet.

To early astrologers, the Sun seemed to be another planet because it crossed the heavens every day, just like the rest of the bodies in the sky.

It is the only star near enough to be seen well—it is, in fact, a dwarf star. Approximately 860,000 miles in diameter, it is about ten times as wide as the giant planet Jupiter. The next nearest star is nearly 300,000 times as far away, and if the Sun were located as far away as most of the bright stars, it would be too faint to be seen without a telescope.

Everything in the horoscope ultimately revolves around this singular body. Although other forces may be prominent in the charts of some individuals, still the Sun is the total nucleus of being and symbolizes the complete potential of every human being alive. It is vitality and the life force. Your whole essence comes from the position of the Sun.

You are always trying to express the Sun according to its position by house and sign. Possibility for all development is found in the Sun, and it marks the fundamental character of your personal radiations all around you.

It is the symbol of strength, vigor, wisdom, dignity, ardor, and generosity, and the ability for a person to function as a mature individual. It is also a creative force in society. It is consciousness of the gift of life.

The underdeveloped solar nature is arrogant, pushy, undependable, and proud, and is constantly using force.

MERCURY

Mercury is the planet closest to the Sun. It races around our star, gathering information and translating it to the rest of the system. Mercury represents your capacity to understand the desires of your own will and to translate those desires into action.

In other words it is the planet of mind and the power of communication. Through Mercury we develop an ability to think, write, speak, and observe—to become aware of the world around us. It colors our attitudes and vision of the world, as well as our capacity to communicate our inner responses to the outside world. Some people who have serious disabilities in their power of verbal communication have often wrongly been described as people lacking intelligence.

Although this planet (and its position in the horoscope) indicates your power to communicate your thoughts and perceptions to the world, intelligence is something deeper. Intelligence is distributed throughout all the planets. It is the relationship of the planets to each other that truly describes what we call intelligence. Mercury rules speaking, language, mathematics, draft and design, students, messengers, young people, offices, teachers, and any pursuits where the mind of man has wings.

VENUS

Venus is beauty. It symbolizes the harmony and radiance of a rare and elusive quality: beauty itself. It is refinement and delicacy, softness and charm. In astrology it indicates grace, balance, and the aesthetic sense. Where Venus is we see beauty, a gentle drawing in of energy and the need for satisfaction and completion. It is a special touch that finishes off rough edges. It is sensitivity, and affection, and it is always the place for that other elusive phenomenon: love. Venus describes our sense of what is beautiful and loving. Poorly developed, it is vulgar, tasteless, and self-indulgent. But its ideal is the flame of spiritual love—Aphrodite, goddess of love, and the sweetness and power of personal beauty.

MARS

Mars is raw, crude energy. The planet next to Earth but outward from the Sun is a fiery red sphere that charges through the horoscope with force and fury. It represents the way you reach out for new adventure and new experience. It is energy and drive, initiative, courage, and daring. It is the power to start something and see it through. It can be thoughtless, cruel and wild, angry and hostile, causing cuts, burns, scalds, and wounds. It can stab its way through a chart, or it can be the symbol of healthy spirited adventure, well-channeled constructive power to begin and keep up the drive. If you have trouble starting things, if you lack the get-up-and-go to start the ball rolling, if you lack aggressiveness and self-confidence, chances are there's another planet influencing your Mars. Mars rules soldiers, butchers, surgeons, salesmen—any field that requires daring, bold skill, operational technique, or self-promotion.

JUPITER

This is the largest planet of the solar system. Scientists have recently learned that Jupiter reflects more light than it receives from the Sun. In a sense it is like a star itself. In astrology it rules good luck and good cheer, health, wealth, optimism, happiness, success, and joy. It is the symbol of opportunity and always opens the way for new possibilities in your life. It rules exuberance, enthusiasm, wisdom, knowledge, generosity, and all forms of expansion in general. It rules actors, statesmen, clerics, professional people, religion, publishing, and the distribution of many people over large areas.

Sometimes Jupiter makes you think you deserve everything, and you become sloppy, wasteful, careless and rude, prodigal and lawless, in the illusion that nothing can ever go wrong. Then there is the danger of overconfidence, exaggeration, undependability, and overindulgence.

Jupiter is the minimization of limitation and the emphasis on spirituality and potential. It is the thirst for knowledge and higher learning.

SATURN

Saturn circles our system in dark splendor with its mysterious rings, forcing us to be awakened to what ever we have neglected in the past. It will present real puzzles and problems to be solved, causing delays, obstacles, and hindrances. By doing so, Saturn stirs our own sensitivity to those areas where we are laziest.

Here we must patiently develop *method*, and only through painstaking effort can our ends be achieved. It brings order to a horoscope and imposes reason just where we are feeling least reasonable. By creating limitations and boundary, Saturn shows the consequences of being human and demands that we accept the changing cycles inevitable in human life. Saturn rules time, old age, and sobriety. It can bring depression, gloom, jealousy, and greed, or serious ac cep tance of responsibilities out of which success will develop. With Saturn there is nothing to do but face facts. It rules laborers, stones, granite, rocks, and crystals of all kinds.

THE OUTER PLANETS:
URANUS, NEPTUNE, PLUTO

Uranus, Neptune, Pluto are the outer planets. They liberate human beings from cultural conditioning, and in that sense are the lawbreakers. In early times it was thought that Saturn was the last planet of the system—the outer limit beyond which we could never go. The discovery of the next three planets ushered in new phases of human history, revolution, and technology.

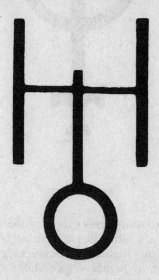

URANUS

Uranus rules unexpected change, upheaval, revolution. It is the symbol of total independence and asserts the freedom of an individual from all restriction and restraint. It is a breakthrough planet and indicates talent, originality, and genius in a horoscope. It usually causes last-minute reversals and changes of plan, unwanted separations, accidents, catastrophes, and eccentric behavior. It can add irrational rebelliousness and perverse bohemianism to a personality or a streak of unaffected brilliance in science and art. It rules technology, aviation, and all forms of electrical and electronic advancement. It governs great leaps forward and topsy-turvy situations, and *always* turns things around at the last minute. Its effects are difficult to predict, since it rules sudden last-minute decisions and events that come like lightning out of the blue.

NEPTUNE

Neptune dissolves existing reality the way the sea erodes the cliffs beside it. Its effects are subtle like the ringing of a buoy's bell in the fog. It suggests a reality higher than definition can usually describe. It awakens a sense of higher responsibility often causing guilt, worry, anxieties, or delusions. Neptune is associated with all forms of escape and can make things seem a certain way so convincingly that you are absolutely sure of something that eventually turns out to be quite different.

It is the planet of illusion and therefore governs the invisible realms that lie beyond our ordinary minds, beyond our simple factual ability to prove what is "real." Treachery, deceit, disillusionment, and disappointment are linked to Neptune. It describes a vague reality that promises eternity and the divine, yet in a manner so complex that we cannot really fathom it at all. At its worst Neptune is a cheap intoxicant; at its best it is the poetry, music, and inspiration of the higher planes of spiritual love. It has dominion over movies, photographs, and much of the arts.

PLUTO

Pluto lies at the outpost of our system and therefore rules finality in a horoscope—the final closing of chapters in your life, the passing of major milestones and points of development from which there is no return. It is a final wipeout, a closeout, an evacuation. It is a distant, subtle but powerful catalyst in all transformations that occur. It creates, destroys, then re creates. Sometimes Pluto starts its influence with a minor event or insignificant incident that might even go unnoticed. Slowly but surely, little by little, everything changes, until at last there has been a total transformation in the area of your life where Pluto has been operating. It rules mass thinking and the trends that society first rejects, then adopts, and finally outgrows.

Pluto rules the dead and the underworld—all the powerful forces of creation and destruction that go on all the time beneath, around, and above us. It can bring a lust for power with strong obsessions.

It is the planet that rules the metamorphosis of the caterpillar into a butterfly, for it symbolizes the capacity to change totally and forever a person's lifestyle, way of thought, and behavior.

THE MOON IN EACH SIGN

The Moon is the nearest planet to the Earth. It exerts more observable influence on us from day to day than any other planet. The effect is very personal, very intimate, and if we are not aware of how it works it can make us quite unstable in our ideas. And the annoying thing is that at these times we often see our own instability but can do nothing about it. A knowledge of what can be expected may help considerably. We can then be prepared to stand strong against the Moon's negative influences and use its positive ones to help us to get ahead. Who has not heard of going with the tide?

The Moon reflects, has no light of its own. It reflects the Sun—the life giver—in the form of vital movement. The Moon controls the tides, the blood rhythm, the movement of sap in trees and plants. Its nature is inconstancy and change so it signifies our moods, our superficial behavior—walking, talking, and especially thinking. Being a true reflector of other forces, the Moon is cold, watery like the surface of a still lake, brilliant and scintillating at times, but easily ruffled and disturbed by the winds of change.

The Moon takes about 27⅓ days to make a complete transit of the Zodiac. It spends just over 2¼ days in each sign. During that time it reflects the qualities, energies, and characteristics of the sign and, to a degree, the planet which rules the sign. When the Moon in its transit occupies a sign incompatible with our own birth sign, we can expect to feel a vague uneasiness, perhaps a touch of irritableness. We should not be discouraged nor let the feeling get us down, or, worse still, allow ourselves to take the discomfort out on others. Try to remember that the Moon has to change signs within 55 hours and, provided you are not physically ill, your mood will probably change with it. It is amazing how frequently depression lifts with the shift in the Moon's position. And, of course, when the Moon is transiting a sign compatible or sympathetic to yours, you will probably feel some sort of stimulation or just be plain happy to be alive.

In the horoscope, the Moon is such a powerful indicator that competent astrologers often use the sign it occupied at birth as the birth sign of the person. This is done particularly when the Sun is on the cusp, or edge, of two signs. Most experienced astrologers, however, coordinate both Sun and Moon signs by reading and confirming from one to the other and secure a far more accurate and personalized analysis.

For these reasons, the Moon tables which follow this section (see pages 86–92) are of great importance to the individual. They show the days and the exact times the Moon will enter each sign of the Zodiac for the year. Remember, you have to adjust the indicated times to local time. The corrections, already calculated for most of the main cities, are at the beginning of the tables. What follows now is a guide to the influences that will be reflected to the Earth by the Moon while it transits each of the twelve signs. The influence is at its peak about 26 hours after the Moon enters a sign. As you read the daily forecast, check the Moon sign for any given day and glance back at this guide.

MOON IN ARIES
This is a time for action, for reaching out beyond the usual self-imposed limitations and faint-hearted cautions. If you have plans in your head or on your desk, put them into practice. New ventures, applications, new jobs, new starts of any kind—all have a good chance of success. This is the period when original and dynamic impulses are being reflected onto Earth. Such energies are extremely vital and favor the pursuit of pleasure and adventure in practically every form. Sick people should feel an improvement. Those who are well will probably find themselves exuding confidence and optimism. People fond of physical exercise should find their bodies growing with tone and well-being. Boldness, strength, determination should characterize most of your activities with a readiness to face up to old challenges. Yesterday's problems may seem petty and exaggerated—so deal with them. Strike out alone. Self-reliance will attract others to you. This is a good time for making friends. Business and marriage partners are more likely to be impressed with the man and woman of action. Opposition will be overcome or thrown aside with much less effort than usual. CAUTION: Be dominant but not domineering.

MOON IN TAURUS
The spontaneous, action-packed person of yesterday gives way to the cautious, diligent, hardworking "thinker." In this period ideas will probably be concentrated on ways of improving finances. A great deal of time may be spent figuring out and going over schemes and plans. It is the right time to be careful with detail.

People will find themselves working longer than usual at their desks. Or devoting more time to serious thought about the future. A strong desire to put order into business and financial arrangements may cause extra work. Loved ones may complain of being neglected and may fail to appreciate that your efforts are for their ultimate benefit. Your desire for system may extend to criticism of arrangements in the home and lead to minor upsets. Health may be affected through overwork. Try to secure a reasonable amount of rest and relaxation, although the tendency will be to "keep going" despite good advice. Work done conscientiously in this period should result in a solid contribution to your future security. CAUTION: Try not to be as serious with people as the work you are engaged in.

MOON IN GEMINI
The humdrum of routine and too much work should suddenly end. You are likely to find yourself in an expansive, quicksilver world of change and self-expression. Urges to write, to paint, to experience the freedom of some sort of artistic outpouring, may be very strong. Take full advantage of them. You may find yourself finishing something you began and put aside long ago. Or embarking on something new which could easily be prompted by a chance meeting, a new acquaintance, or even an advertisement. There may be a yearning for a change of scenery, the feeling to visit another country (not too far away), or at least to get away for a few days. This may result in short, quick journeys. Or, if you are planning a single visit, there may be some unexpected changes or detours on the way. Familiar activities will seem to give little satisfaction unless they contain a fresh element of excitement or expectation. The inclination will be toward untried pursuits, particularly those that allow you to express your inner nature. The accent is on new faces, new places. CAUTION: Do not be too quick to commit yourself emotionally.

MOON IN CANCER
Feelings of uncertainty and vague insecurity are likely to cause problems while the Moon is in Cancer. Thoughts may turn frequently to the warmth of the home and the comfort of loved ones. Nostalgic impulses could cause you to bring out old photographs and letters and reflect on the days when your life seemed to be much more rewarding and less demanding. The love and understanding of parents and family may be important, and, if it is not forthcoming, you may have to fight against bouts of self-pity. The cordiality of friends and the thought of good times with them that are sure to be repeated will help to restore you to a happier frame

of mind. The desire to be alone may follow minor setbacks or re-buffs at this time, but solitude is unlikely to help. Better to get on the telephone or visit someone. This period often causes peculiar dreams and upsurges of imaginative thinking which can be help-ful to authors of occult and mystical works. Preoccupation with the personal world of simple human needs can overshadow any mate-rial strivings. CAUTION: Do not spend too much time thinking—seek the company of loved ones or close friends.

MOON IN LEO

New horizons of exciting and rather extravagant activity open up. This is the time for exhilarating entertainment, glamorous and lav-ish parties, and expensive shopping sprees. Any merrymaking that relies upon your generosity as a host has every chance of being a spectacular success. You should find yourself right in the center of the fun, either as the life of the party or simply as a person whom happy people like to be with. Romance thrives in this heady atmo-sphere and friendships are likely to explode unexpectedly into seri-ous attachments. Children and younger people should be attracted to you and you may find yourself organizing a picnic or a visit to a fun-fair, the movies, or the beach. The sunny company and vitality of youthful companions should help you to find some unsuspected energy. In career, you could find an opening for promotion or ad-vancement. This should be the time to make a direct approach. The period favors those engaged in original research. CAUTION: Bask in popularity, not in flattery.

MOON IN VIRGO

Off comes the party cap and out steps the busy, practical worker. He wants to get his personal affairs straight, to rearrange them, if necessary, for more efficiency, so he will have more time for more work. He clears up his correspondence, pays outstanding bills, makes numerous phone calls. He is likely to make inquiries, or sign up for some new insurance and put money into gilt-edged investment. Thoughts probably revolve around the need for future security—to tie up loose ends and clear the decks. There may be a tendency to be "finicky," to interfere in the routine of others, particularly friends and family members. The motive may be a genuine desire to help with suggestions for updating or streamlining their affairs, but these will probably not be welcomed. Sympathy may be felt for less fortunate sections of the community and a flurry of some sort of voluntary ser-vice is likely. This may be accompanied by strong feelings of respon-sibility on several fronts and health may suffer from extra efforts made. CAUTION: Everyone may not want your help or advice.

MOON IN LIBRA
These are days of harmony and agreement and you should find yourself at peace with most others. Relationships tend to be smooth and sweet-flowing. Friends may become closer and bonds deepen in mutual understanding. Hopes will be shared. Progress by cooperation could be the secret of success in every sphere. In business, established partnerships may flourish and new ones get off to a good start. Acquaintances could discover similar interests that lead to congenial discussions and rewarding exchanges of some sort. Love, as a unifying force, reaches its optimum. Marriage partners should find accord. Those who wed at this time face the prospect of a happy union. Cooperation and tolerance are felt to be stronger than dissension and impatience. The argumentative are not quite so loud in their bellowings, nor as inflexible in their attitudes. In the home, there should be a greater recognition of the other point of view and a readiness to put the wishes of the group before selfish insistence. This is a favorable time to join an art group. CAUTION: Do not be too independent—let others help you if they want to.

MOON IN SCORPIO
Driving impulses to make money and to economize are likely to cause upsets all around. No area of expenditure is likely to be spared the ax, including the household budget. This is a time when the desire to cut down on extravagance can become near fanatical. Care must be exercised to try to keep the aim in reasonable perspective. Others may not feel the same urgent need to save and may retaliate. There is a danger that possessions of sentimental value will be sold to realize cash for investment. Buying and selling of stock for quick profit is also likely. The attention turns to organizing, reorganizing, tidying up at home and at work. Neglected jobs could suddenly be done with great bursts of energy. The desire for solitude may intervene. Self-searching thoughts could disturb. The sense of invisible and mysterious energies in play could cause some excitability. The reassurance of loves ones may help. CAUTION: Be kind to the people you love.

MOON IN SAGITTARIUS
These are days when you are likely to be stirred and elevated by discussions and reflections of a religious and philosophical nature. Ideas of faraway places may cause unusual response and excitement. A decision may be made to visit someone overseas, perhaps a person whose influence was important to your earlier character development. There could be a strong resolution to get away from

present intellectual patterns, to learn new subjects, and to meet more interesting people. The superficial may be rejected in all its forms. An impatience with old ideas and unimaginative contacts could lead to a change of companions and interests. There may be an upsurge of religious feeling and metaphysical inquiry. Even a new insight into the significance of astrology and other occult studies is likely under the curious stimulus of the Moon in Sagittarius. Physically, you may express this need for fundamental change by spending more time outdoors: sports, gardening, long walks appeal. CAUTION: Try to channel any restlessness into worthwhile study.

MOON IN CAPRICORN

Life in these hours may seem to pivot around the importance of gaining prestige and honor in the career, as well as maintaining a spotless reputation. Ambitious urges may be excessive and could be accompanied by quite acquisitive drives for money. Effort should be directed along strictly ethical lines where there is no possibility of reproach or scandal. All endeavors are likely to be characterized by great earnestness, and an air of authority and purpose which should impress those who are looking for leadership or reliability. The desire to conform to accepted standards may extend to sharp criticism of family members. Frivolity and unconventional actions are unlikely to amuse while the Moon is in Capricorn. Moderation and seriousness are the orders of the day. Achievement and recognition in this period could come through community work or organizing for the benefit of some amateur group. CAUTION: Dignity and esteem are not always self-awarded.

MOON IN AQUARIUS

Moon in Aquarius is in the second last sign of the Zodiac where ideas can become disturbingly fine and subtle. The result is often a mental "no-man's land" where imagination cannot be trusted with the same certitude as other times. The dangers for the individual are the extremes of optimism and pessimism. Unless the imagination is held in check, situations are likely to be misread, and rosy conclusions drawn where they do not exist. Consequences for the unwary can be costly in career and business. Best to think twice and not speak or act until you think again. Pessimism can be a cruel self-inflicted penalty for delusion at this time. Between the two extremes are strange areas of self-deception which, for example, can make the selfish person think he is actually being generous. Eerie dreams which resemble the reality and even seem to continue into the waking state are also possible. CAUTION: Look for the fact and not just for the image in your mind.

MOON IN PISCES

Everything seems to come to the surface now. Memory may be crystal clear, throwing up long-forgotten information which could be valuable in the career or business. Flashes of clairvoyance and intuition are possible along with sudden realizations of one's own nature, which may be used for self-improvement. A talent, never before suspected, may be discovered. Qualities not evident before in friends and marriage partners are likely to be noticed. As this is a period in which the truth seems to emerge, the discovery of false characteristics is likely to lead to disenchantment or a shift in attachments. However, when qualities are accepted, it should lead to happiness and deeper feeling. Surprise solutions could bob up for old problems. There may be a public announcement of the solving of a crime or mystery. People with secrets may find someone has "guessed" correctly. The secrets of the soul or the inner self also tend to reveal themselves. Religious and philosophical groups may make some interesting discoveries. CAUTION: Not a time for activities that depend on secrecy.

NOTE: When you read your daily forecasts, use the Moon Sign Dates that are provided in the following section of Moon Tables. Then you may want to glance back here for the Moon's influence in a given sign.

MOON TABLES

CORRECTION FOR NEW YORK TIME, FIVE HOURS WEST OF GREENWICH

Atlanta, Boston, Detroit, Miami, Washington, Montreal,
  Ottawa, Quebec, Bogota, Havana, Lima, Santiago...... Same time
Chicago, New Orleans, Houston, Winnipeg, Churchill,
  Mexico City .... Deduct 1 hour
Albuquerque, Denver, Phoenix, El Paso, Edmonton,
  Helena .... Deduct 2 hours
Los Angeles, San Francisco, Reno, Portland,
  Seattle, Vancouver .... Deduct 3 hours
Honolulu, Anchorage, Fairbanks, Kodiak .... Deduct 5 hours
Nome, Samoa, Tonga, Midway .... Deduct 6 hours
Halifax, Bermuda, San Juan, Caracas, La Paz,
  Barbados .... Add 1 hour
St. John's, Brasilia, Rio de Janeiro, Sao Paulo,
  Buenos Aires, Montevideo .... Add 2 hours
Azores, Cape Verde Islands .... Add 3 hours
Canary Islands, Madeira, Reykjavik .... Add 4 hours
London, Paris, Amsterdam, Madrid, Lisbon,
  Gibraltar, Belfast, Raba .... Add 5 hours
Frankfurt, Rome, Oslo, Stockholm, Prague,
  Belgrade .... Add 6 hours
Bucharest, Beirut, Tel Aviv, Athens, Istanbul, Cairo,
  Alexandria, Cape Town, Johannesburg .... Add 7 hours
Moscow, Leningrad, Baghdad, Dhahran,
  Addis Ababa, Nairobi, Teheran, Zanzibar .... Add 8 hours
Bombay, Calcutta, Sri Lanka .... Add 10$\frac{1}{2}$
Hong Kong, Shanghai, Manila, Peking, Perth............. Add 13 hours
Tokyo, Okinawa, Darwin, Pusan .... Add 14 hours
Sydney, Melbourne, Port Moresby, Guam .... Add 15 hours
Auckland, Wellington, Suva, Wake .... Add 17 hours

2011 MOON SIGN DATES— NEW YORK TIME

JANUARY Day Moon Enters		FEBRUARY Day Moon Enters		MARCH Day Moon Enters	
1. Sagitt.		1. Aquar.	6:22 pm	1. Aquar.	12:15 am
2. Sagitt.		2. Aquar.		2. Aquar.	
3. Capric.	2:40 am	3. Aquar.		3. Pisces	11:48 am
4. Capric.		4. Pisces	6:25 am	4. Pisces	
5. Aquar.	11:09 am	5. Pisces		5. Pisces	
6. Aquar.		6. Aries	5:47 pm	6. Aries	12:15 am
7. Pisces	9:58 pm	7. Aries		7. Aries	
8. Pisces		8. Aries		8. Taurus	12:53 pm
9. Pisces		9. Taurus	6:24 am	9. Taurus	
10. Aries	10:25 am	10. Taurus		10. Taurus	
11. Aries		11. Gemini	5:22 pm	11. Gemini	12:32 am
12. Taurus	10:38 pm	12. Gemini		12. Gemini	
13. Taurus		13. Gemini		13. Cancer	9:31 am
14. Taurus		14. Cancer	12:50 am	14. Cancer	
15. Gemini	8:24 am	15. Cancer		15. Leo	2:34 pm
16. Gemini		16. Leo	4:15 am	16. Leo	
17. Cancer	2:30 pm	17. Leo		17. Virgo	3:54 pm
18. Cancer		18. Virgo	4:40 am	18. Virgo	
19. Leo	5:17 pm	19. Virgo		19. Libra	3:04 pm
20. Leo		20. Libra	4:02 am	20. Libra	
21. Virgo	6:11 pm	21. Libra		21. Scorp.	2:18 pm
22. Virgo		22. Scorp.	4:30 am	22. Scorp.	
23. Libra	7:00 pm	23. Scorp.		23. Sagitt.	3:48 pm
24. Libra		24. Sagitt.	7:47 am	24. Sagitt.	
25. Scorp.	9:17 pm	25. Sagitt.		25. Capric.	8:58 pm
26. Scorp.		26. Capric.	2:33 pm	26. Capric.	
27. Scorp.		27. Capric.		27. Capric.	
28. Sagitt.	1:56 am	28. Capric.		28. Aquar.	6:01 am
29. Sagitt.				29. Aquar.	
30. Capric.	9:05 am			30. Pisces	5:39 pm
31. Capric.				31. Pisces	

Daylight saving time to be considered where applicable.

2011 MOON SIGN DATES— NEW YORK TIME

APRIL Day Moon Enters		MAY Day Moon Enters		JUNE Day Moon Enters	
1. Pisces		1. Aries		1. Gemini	
2. Aries	6:17 pm	2. Taurus	12:59 am	2. Gemini	
3. Aries		3. Taurus		3. Cancer	3:37 am
4. Taurus	6:47 pm	4. Gemini	12:10 pm	4. Cancer	
5. Taurus		5. Gemini		5. Leo	10:04 am
6. Taurus		6. Cancer	9:33 pm	6. Leo	
7. Gemini	6:23 am	7. Cancer		7. Virgo	2:34 pm
8. Gemini		8. Cancer		8. Virgo	
9. Cancer	4:03 pm	9. Leo	4:36 am	9. Libra	5:32 pm
10. Cancer		10. Leo		10. Libra	
11. Leo	10:38 pm	11. Virgo	9:00 am	11. Scorp.	7:34 pm
12. Leo		12. Virgo		12. Scorp.	
13. Leo		13. Libra	10:58 am	13. Sagitt.	9:39 pm
14. Virgo	1:41 am	14. Libra		14. Sagitt.	
15. Virgo		15. Scorp.	11:33 am	15. Sagitt.	
16. Libra	2:00 am	16. Scorp.		16. Capric.	1:00 am
17. Libra		17. Sagitt.	12:24 pm	17. Capric.	
18. Scorp.	1:20 am	18. Sagitt.		18. Aquar.	5:48 am
19. Scorp.		19. Capric.	3:17 pm	19. Aquar.	
20. Sagitt.	1:51 am	20. Capric.		20. Pisces	3:46 pm
21. Sagitt.		21. Aquar.	9:33 pm	21. Pisces	
22. Capric.	5:25 am	22. Aquar.		22. Pisces	
23. Capric.		23. Aquar.		23. Aries	3:25 am
24. Aquar.	1:00 pm	24. Pisces	7:25 am	24. Aries	
25. Aquar.		25. Pisces		25. Taurus	3:54 pm
26. Pisces	11:59 pm	26. Aries	7:37 pm	26. Taurus	
27. Pisces		27. Aries		27. Taurus	
28. Pisces		28. Aries		28. Gemini	2:57 am
29. Aries	12:34 pm	29. Taurus	8:03 am	29. Gemini	
30. Aries		30. Taurus		30. Cancer	11:14 am
		31. Gemini	6:57 pm		

Daylight saving time to be considered where applicable.

2011 MOON SIGN DATES—
NEW YORK TIME

JULY Day Moon Enters		AUGUST Day Moon Enters		SEPTEMBER Day Moon Enters	
1. Cancer		1. Virgo	3:43 am	1. Scorp.	1:49 pm
2. Leo	4:44 pm	2. Virgo		2. Scorp.	
3. Leo		3. Libra	5:05 am	3. Sagitt.	4:05 am
4. Virgo	8:16 pm	4. Libra		4. Sagitt.	
5. Virgo		5. Scorp.	6:58 am	5. Capric.	9:05 pm
6. Libra	10:55 pm	6. Scorp.		6. Capric.	
7. Libra		7. Sagitt.	10:22 am	7. Capric.	
8. Libra		8. Sagitt.		8. Aquar.	4:43 am
9. Scorp.	1:32 am	9. Capric.	3:39 pm	9. Aquar.	
10. Scorp.		10. Capric.		10. Pisces	2:28 pm
11. Sagitt.	4:48 am	11. Aquar.	10:49 pm	11. Pisces	
12. Sagitt.		12. Aquar.		12. Pisces	
13. Capric.	9:14 am	13. Aquar.		13. Aries	1:50 am
14. Capric.		14. Pisces	7:55 am	14. Aries	
15. Aquar.	3:31 pm	15. Pisces		15. Taurus	2:26 pm
16. Aquar.		16. Aries	7:03 pm	16. Taurus	
17. Aquar.		17. Aries		17. Taurus	
18. Pisces	12:14 am	18. Aries		18. Gemini	3:07 am
19. Pisces		19. Taurus	7:37 am	19. Gemini	
20. Aries	11:26 am	20. Taurus		20. Cancer	1:55 pm
21. Aries		21. Gemini	7:54 am	21. Cancer	
22. Taurus	11:59 pm	22. Gemini		22. Leo	8:56 pm
23. Taurus		23. Gemini		23. Leo	
24. Taurus		24. Cancer	5:32 am	24. Virgo	11:50 pm
25. Gemini	11:35 am	25. Cancer		25. Virgo	
26. Gemini		26. Leo	11:10 am	26. Libra	11:52 pm
27. Cancer	8:13 pm	27. Leo		27. Libra	
28. Cancer		28. Virgo	1:14 pm	28. Scorp.	11:06 pm
29. Cancer		29. Virgo		29. Scorp.	
30. Leo	1:17 am	30. Libra	1:26 pm	30. Sagitt.	11:42 pm
31. Leo		31. Libra			

Daylight saving time to be considered where applicable.

2011 MOON SIGN DATES—
NEW YORK TIME

OCTOBER
Day Moon Enters

1. Sagitt.
2. Sagitt.
3. Capric. 3:17 am
4. Capric.
5. Aquar. 10:19 am
6. Aquar.
7. Pisces 8:14 pm
8. Pisces
9. Pisces
10. Aries 7:58 am
11. Aries
12. Taurus 8:36 pm
13. Taurus
14. Taurus
15. Gemini 9:16 am
16. Gemini
17. Cancer 8:39 pm
18. Cancer
19. Cancer
20. Leo 5:07 am
21. Leo
22. Virgo 9:42 am
23. Virgo
24. Libra 10:50 am
25. Libra
26. Scorp. 10:09 am
27. Scorp.
28. Sagitt. 9:46 am
29. Sagitt.
30. Capric. 11:40 am
31. Capric.

NOVEMBER
Day Moon Enters

1. Aquar. 5:09 pm
2. Aquar.
3. Aquar.
4. Pisces 2:19 am
5. Pisces
6. Aries 2:03 pm
7. Aries
8. Aries
9. Taurus 2:46 am
10. Taurus
11. Gemini 3:11 pm
12. Gemini
13. Gemini
14. Cancer 2:20 am
15. Cancer
16. Leo 11:18 am
17. Leo
18. Virgo 5:20 pm
19. Virgo
20. Libra 8:17 pm
21. Libra
22. Scorp. 8:59 pm
23. Scorp.
24. Sagitt. 8:58 pm
25. Sagitt.
26. Capric. 10:06 pm
27. Capric.
28. Capric.
29. Aquar. 2:03 am
30. Aquar.

DECEMBER
Day Moon Enters

1. Pisces 9:46 pm
2. Pisces
3. Aries 8:52 pm
4. Aries
5. Aries
6. Taurus 9:36 am
7. Taurus
8. Gemini 9:53 pm
9. Gemini
10. Gemini
11. Cancer 8:27 am
12. Cancer
13. Leo 4:49 pm
14. Leo
15. Virgo 11:00 pm
16. Virgo
17. Virgo
18. Libra 3:07 am
19. Libra
20. Scorp. 5:34 am
21. Scorp.
22. Sagitt. 7:04 am
23. Sagitt.
24. Capric. 8:58 am
25. Capric.
26. Aquar. 12:15 pm
27. Aquar.
28. Pisces 6:46 pm
29. Pisces
30. Pisces
31. Aries 4:49 am

Daylight saving time to be considered where applicable.

2011 PHASES OF THE MOON— NEW YORK TIME

New Moon	First Quarter	Full Moon	Last Quarter
Jan. 4	Jan. 12	Jan. 19	Jan. 26
Feb. 2	Feb. 11	Feb. 18	Feb. 24
March 4	March 12	March 19	March 26
April 3	April 11	April 17	April 24
May 3	May 10	May 17	May 24
June 1	June 8	June 15	June 23
July 1	July 8	July 15	July 23
July 30	August 6	August 13	August 21
August 28	Sept. 4	Sept. 12	Sept. 20
Sept. 27	Oct. 3	Oct. 11	Oct. 19
Oct. 26	Nov. 2	Nov. 10	Nov. 18
Nov. 25	Dec. 2	Dec. 10	Dec. 17
Dec. 24	Jan. 1 ('12)	Jan. 9 ('12)	Jan. 16 ('12)

Each phase of the Moon lasts approximately seven to eight days, during which the Moon's shape gradually changes as it comes out of one phase and goes into the next.

There will be a solar eclipse during the New Moon phase on January 4, on June 1, on July 1, and on November 25.

There will be a lunar eclipse during the Full Moon phase on June 15 and on December 10.

2011 FISHING GUIDE

	Good	Best
January	3-4-6-9-14-20-28-31	2-8-18-27
February	2-10-14-19-24-28	5-15-23
March	5-7-12-14-20-25-27	4-13-22-31
April	1-6-10-11-13-21-25-27	2-10-19-28
May	3-5-11-12-18-21-26	8-16-25
June	1-18-12-17-20-22	4-12-21
July	6-11-21-22-26-28-31	1-2-10-19-29
August	2-5-10-18-26-28-30	6-15-25
September	1-6-9-17-23-24-25	2-11-21-29
October	6-16-20-22-24-28	8-18-27
November	5-10-15-19-25	4-14-23
December	3-8-13-17-20-22-23-35	2-12-21-29

2011 PLANTING GUIDE

	Aboveground Crops	Root Crops
January	1-4-8-9-10-18-19	24-25-26-31
February	5-6-15-16	1-21-22-28
March	5-6-14-15-18	1-20-21-27-28-29
April	10-11-12-15-16	18-22-23-24
May	8-9-12-13-16-17	20-21-30-31
June	4-5-8-9-12-13-14	17-18-19-27-38
July	18-19-20-29-30	14-15-23-24-25
August	15-16-25-26-29	20-21
September	12-22-23-26-27	17-18-27-28
October	19-20-23-24	13-14-15-25
November	15-16-19-20-23	10-11-21-22-23
December	12-13-17-18-21-22	19-20

	Pruning	Weeds and Pests
January	11-12	20-21
February	13-14	17-18
March	13-16-17	29-30
April	13-14	25-26-27
May	10-11	24
June	15-16	29-30
July	12-13	13-14-15
August	8-9-10	12-13
September	4-5	9-10
October	11-12	6-7
November	8-9	2-3-4
December	4-5-6	1-10-11

MOON'S INFLUENCE OVER PLANTS

Centuries ago it was established that seeds planted when the Moon is in signs and phases called Fruitful will produce more growth than seeds planted when the Moon is in a Barren sign.

Fruitful Signs: Taurus, Cancer, Libra, Scorpio, Capricorn, Pisces
Barren Signs: Aries, Gemini, Leo, Virgo, Sagittarius, Aquarius
Dry Signs: Aries, Gemini, Sagittarius, Aquarius

Activity	Moon In
Mow lawn, trim plants	**Fruitful sign:** 1st & 2nd quarter
Plant flowers	**Fruitful sign:** 2nd quarter; best in Cancer and Libra
Prune	**Fruitful sign:** 3rd & 4th quarter
Destroy pests; spray	**Barren sign:** 4th quarter
Harvest potatoes, root crops	**Dry sign:** 3rd & 4th quarter; Taurus, Leo, and Aquarius

MOON'S INFLUENCE OVER YOUR HEALTH

ARIES	Head, brain, face, upper jaw
TAURUS	Throat, neck, lower jaw
GEMINI	Hands, arms, lungs, shoulders, ner vous system
CANCER	Esophagus, stomach, breasts, womb, liver
LEO	Heart, spine
VIRGO	Intestines, liver
LIBRA	Kidneys, lower back
SCORPIO	Sex and eliminative organs
SAGITTARIUS	Hips, thighs, liver
CAPRICORN	Skin, bones, teeth, knees
AQUARIUS	Circulatory system, lower legs
PISCES	Feet, tone of being

Try to avoid work being done on that part of the body when the Moon is in the sign governing that part.

MOON'S INFLUENCE OVER DAILY AFFAIRS

The Moon makes a complete transit of the Zodiac every 27 days 7 hours and 43 minutes. In making this transit the Moon forms different aspects with the planets and consequently has favorable or unfavorable bearings on affairs and events for persons according to the sign of the Zodiac under which they were born.

When the Moon is in conjunction with the Sun it is called a New Moon; when the Moon and Sun are in opposition it is called a Full Moon. From New Moon to Full Moon, first and second quarter—which takes about two weeks—the Moon is increasing or waxing. From Full Moon to New Moon, third and fourth quarter, the Moon is decreasing or waning.

Activity	Moon In
Business: buying and selling new, requiring public support	Sagittarius, Aries, Gemini, Virgo 1st and 2nd quarter
meant to be kept quiet	3rd and 4th quarter
Investigation	3rd and 4th quarter
Signing documents	1st & 2nd quarter, Cancer, Scorpio, Pisces
Advertising	2nd quarter, Sagittarius
Journeys and trips	1st & 2nd quarter, Gemini, Virgo
Renting offices, etc.	Taurus, Leo, Scorpio, Aquarius
Painting of house/apartment	3rd & 4th quarter, Taurus, Scorpio, Aquarius
Decorating	Gemini, Libra, Aquarius
Buying clothes and accessories	Taurus, Virgo
Beauty salon or barber shop visit	1st & 2nd quarter, Taurus, Leo, Libra, Scorpio, Aquarius
Weddings	1st & 2nd quarter

Sagittarius

SAGITTARIUS

Character Analysis

People born under this ninth sign of the Zodiac are quite often self-reliant and intelligent. Generally, they are quite philosophical in their outlook on life. They know how to make practical use of their imagination.

There is seldom anything narrow about a Sagittarius man or woman. He or she is generally very tolerant and considerate. They would never consciously do anything that would hurt another's feelings. They are gifted with a good sense of humor and believe in being honest in relationships with others. At times Sagittarius is a little short of tact. They are so intent on telling the truth that sometimes they can be blunt.

Nevertheless, Sagittarius men and women mean well, and people who enjoy a relationship with them are often willing to overlook this flaw. Sagittarius may even tell people true things about themselves that they do not wish to hear. At times this can cause a strain in the relationship. Sagittarius often wishes that others were as forthright and honest as he or she is—no matter what the consequences.

Sagittarius men and women are positive and optimistic and love life. They often help others to snap out of an ill mood. Their joie de vivre is often infectious. People enjoy being around Sagittarius because they are almost always in a good mood.

Quite often people born under the sign of Sagittarius are fond of the outdoors. They enjoy sporting events and often excel in them. Like the Archer, the zodiacal symbol of the sign, Sagittarius men and women are fond of animals, especially horses and dogs.

Generally, the Archer is healthy—in mind and in body. They have pluck. They enjoy the simple things of life. Fresh air and good comradeship are important to them. On the other hand, they are fond of developing their minds. Many Sagittarius cannot read or study enough. They like to keep abreast of things. They are interested in theater and the arts in general. Some of them are quite religious. Some choose a religious life.

Because they are outgoing for the most part, they sometimes come in touch with situations that others are never confronted with. In the long run this tends to make their life experiences quite rich and varied. They are well-balanced. They like to be active. And they enjoy using their intellects.

It is important to the person born under this sign that justice prevails. They dislike seeing anyone treated unfairly. If Sagittarius feels that the old laws are out of date or unrealistic, he or she will fight to have them changed. At times they can be true rebels. It is important to the Archer that law is carried out impartially. In matters of law, they often excel.

Sagittarius are almost always fond of travel. It seems to be imbedded in their natures. At times, they feel impelled to get away from familiar surroundings and people. Faraway places have a magical attraction for someone born under this sign. They enjoy reading about foreign lands and strange customs.

Many people who are Sagittarius are not terribly fond of living in big cities; they prefer the quiet and greenery of the countryside. Of all the signs of the Zodiac the sign of Sagittarius is closest to mother nature. They can usually build a trusting relationship with animals. They respect wildlife in all its forms.

Sagittarius is quite clever in conversation. He or she has a definite way with words. They like a good argument. They know how to phrase things exactly. Their sense of humor often has a cheerful effect on their manner of speech. They are seldom without a joke.

At times, the Sagittarius wit is apt to hurt someone's feelings, but this is never intentional. A slip of the tongue sometimes gets the Archer into social difficulties. As a result, there can be argumentative and angry scenes. But Sagittarius men and women cool down quickly. They are not given to holding grudges. They are willing to forgive and forget.

On the whole, Sagittarius is good-natured and fun-loving. They find it easy to take up with all sorts of people. In most cases, their social circle is large. People enjoy their company and their parties. Many friends share the Sagittarius interest in the outdoor life as well as intellectual pursuits.

Sagittarius sometimes can be impulsive. They are not afraid of risk. On the contrary, they can be foolhardy in the way they court danger. But Sagittarius men and women are very sporting in all they that do. If they should wind up the loser, they will not waste time grieving about it. They are fairly optimistic—they believe in good luck.

Health

Often people born under the sign of Sagittarius are quite athletic. They are healthy-looking—quite striking in a robust way. Often they are rather tall and well-built. They are enthusiastic people and like being active or involved. Exercise and sports may interest them a great deal.

Sagittarius cannot stand not being active. They have to be on the go. As they grow older, they seem to increase in strength and physical ability. At times they may have worries, but they never allow them to affect humor or health.

It is important to Sagittarius men and women to remain physically sound. They are usually very physically fit, but their nervous system may be somewhat sensitive. Too much activity—even while they find action attractive—may put a severe strain on them after a time. The Archer should try to concentrate their energies on as few objects as possible. However, usually they have many projects scattered here and there, and can be easily exhausted.

At times, illnesses fall upon the Archer suddenly or strangely. Some Sagittarius are accident-prone. They are not afraid of taking risks and as a result are sometimes careless in the way they do things. Injuries often come to them by way of sports or other vigorous activities.

Sometimes men and women of this sign try to ignore signs of illness—especially if they are engaged in some activity that has captured their interest. This results in a severe setback at times.

In later life, Sagittarius sometimes suffers from stomach disorders. High blood pressure is another ailment that might affect them. They should also be on guard for signs of arthritis and sciatica. In spite of these possible dangers, the average Sagittarius manages to stay quite youthful and alert through their many interests and pastimes.

Occupation

Sagittarius is someone who can be relied upon in a work situation. They are loyal and dependable. They are energetic workers, anxious to please superiors. They are forward-looking by nature and enjoy working in modern surroundings and toward progressive goals.

Challenges do not frighten Sagittarius. They are flexible and can work in confining situations even though they may not enjoy it. Work that gives them a chance to move around and meet new people is well suited to their character. If they have to stay in one locale, they become sad and ill-humored. They can take orders but they would rather be in a situation where they do not have to. They are difficult to please at times, and may hop from job to job before feeling that it is really time to settle down. Sagittarius do their best work when they are allowed to work on their own.

Sagittarius individuals are interested in expressing themselves in the work they do. If they occupy a position that does not allow them to be creative, they will seek outside activities. Such hobbies or pastimes give them a chance to develop and broaden their talents.

Some Sagittarius do well in the field of journalism. Others make good teachers and public speakers. They are generally quite flexible and would do well in many different positions. Some excel as foreign ministers or in music. Others do well in government work or in publishing.

Men and women born under this ninth sign are often more intelligent than the average person. The cultivated Sagittarius knows how to employ intellectual gifts to their best advantage. In politics and religion, Sagittarius often displays brilliance.

The Sagittarius man or woman is pleasant to work with. They are considerate of colleagues and would do nothing that might upset the working relationship. Because they are so self-reliant, they often inspire teammates. Sagittarius likes to work with detail. Their ideas are both practical and idealistic. Sagittarius is curious by nature and is always looking for ways of expanding their knowledge.

Sagittarius are almost always generous. They rarely refuse someone in need, but are always willing to share what they have. Whether they are up or down, Sagittarius can always be relied upon to help someone in dire straits. Their attitude toward life may be happy-go-lucky in general. They are difficult to depress no matter what the situation. They are optimistic and forward-looking. Money always seems to fall into their hands.

The average Sagittarius is interested in expansion and promotion. Sometimes these concerns weaken their projects rather than strengthen them. Also, the average Sagittarius is more interested in contentment and joy than in material gain. However, they will do their best to make the most of any profit that comes their way.

When Sagittarius does get hooked on a venture, he or she is often willing to take risks to secure a profit. In the long run they are successful. They have a flair for carrying off business deals. It is the cultivated Sagittarius who prepares in advance for any business contingency. In that way he or she can bring knowledge and experience to bear on their professional and financial interests.

Home and Family

Not all Sagittarius are very interested in home life. Many of them set great store in being mobile. Their activities outside the home may attract them more than those inside the home. Not exactly homebodies, Sagittarius, however, can adjust themselves to a stable domestic life if they put their minds to it.

People born under this sign are not keen on luxuries and other displays of wealth. They prefer the simple things. Anyone entering their home should be able to discern this. They are generally neat. They like a place that has plenty of space—not too cluttered with imposing furniture.

Even when they settle down, Sagittarius men and women like to keep a small corner of their life just for themselves. Independence is important to them. If necessary, they will insist upon it, no matter what the situation. They like a certain amount of beauty in the home, but they may not be too interested in keeping things looking nice. Their interests lead them elsewhere. Housekeeping may bore them to distraction. When forced to stick to a domestic routine, they can become somewhat disagreeable.

Children bring Sagittarius men and women a great deal of happiness. They are fond of family life. Friends generally drop in any old time to visit for they know they will always be welcomed and properly entertained. The Archer's love for their fellow man is well known.

The Sagittarius parent may be bewildered at first by a newborn baby. They may worry about holding such a tiny tot for fear of injuring the little one. Although some Sagittarius may be clumsy, they do have a natural touch with small children and should not worry about handling them properly. As soon as the infant begins to grow up and develop a definite personality, Sagittarius can relax and relate. There is always a strong tie between children and the Sagittarius parent.

Children are especially drawn to Sagittarius because they seem to understand them better than other adults.

One is apt to find children born under this sign a little restless and disorganized at times. They are usually quite independent in their ways and may ask for quite a bit of freedom while still young. They don't like being fussed over by adults. They like to feel that their parents believe in them and trust them on their own.

Social Relationships

Sagittarius enjoys having people around. It is not difficult for them to make friends. They are very sociable by nature. Most of the friends they make they keep for life.

Sagittarius men and women are broad-minded, so they have all sorts of pals and casual acquaintances. They appreciate people for their good qualities, however few a person might have. Sagittarius are not quick to judge and are usually very forgiving. They are not impressed by what a friend has in the way of material goods.

Sagittarius men and women are generally quite popular. They are much in demand socially. People like their easy disposition and good humor. Their friendship is valued by others. Quite often in spite of their chumminess, Sagittarius is rather serious. Light conversation may be somewhat difficult for them.

Sagittarius men and women believe in speaking their minds, in saying what they feel. Yet at times, they can appear quiet and retiring. It all depends on their mood. Some people feel that there are two sides to the Sagittarius personality. This characteristic is reflected in the zodiacal symbol for the sign—a double symbol: the hunter and the horse intertwined, denoting two different natures.

It may be difficult for some people to get to know a Sagittarius man or woman. In some instances Sagittarius employ silence as a sort of protection. When people pierce through, however, and will not leave him or her in peace, Sagittarius can become quite angry.

On the whole, Sagittarius is kind and considerate. Their nature is gentle and unassuming. With the wrong person, though, they can become somewhat disagreeable. They do become angry, but they cool down quickly and are willing to let bygones be bygones. Sagittarius individuals never hold a grudge against anyone.

Companionship and harmony in all social relationships is necessary for Sagittarius. They are willing to make some sacrifices for it. Any partner, friend, or mate must be a good listener. There are times when Sagittarius feel it necessary to pour their hearts out. They are willing to listen to someone's problems and want the same considerate treatment in return.

A partner, friend, or lover should also be able to take an interest in any hobbies, pastimes, or sports a Sagittarius wants to pursue. If not, Sagittarius men and women will be tempted to go their own way even more so than their nature dictates.

Sagittarius individuals do not beat around the bush. They do say what they mean. Being direct is one of their strongest qualities. Sometimes it pays off, sometimes it doesn't. They often forget that the one they love may be very sensitive and can take offhand remarks personally.

Sagittarius has a tendency to be too blunt and to reveal secrets, innocently or otherwise, that hurt people's feelings. A friend or partner may not be able to overlook this flaw or may not be able to correct it either in a subtle or direct way. When making jokes or casual comments, Sagittarius sometimes strikes a sensitive chord in a companion, which can result in a serious misunderstanding.

But the cultivated Sagittarius learns the boundaries of social behavior. They know when not to go too far. Understanding a partner's viewpoint is the first step toward assuring a good relationship down the road.

Love and Marriage

Sagittarius individuals are faithful to their loved ones. They are affectionate and not at all possessive. Love is important for them spiritually as well as physically. For some Sagittarius, romance is a chance to escape reality—a chance for adventure.

Quite often a mate or lover finds it difficult to keep up with Sagittarius—they are so active and energetic. When Sagittarius men and women fall in love, however, they are quite easy to handle.

Sagittarius do like having freedom. They will make concessions in a steady relationship. Still there will be a part of themselves that they keep from others. He or she is very intent on preserving their individual rights, no matter what sort of relationship they are engaged in. Sagittarius ideals are generally high, and they are important. Sagittarius is looking for someone with similar standards, not someone too lax or too conventional.

In love, Sagittarius men and women may be a bit childlike at times. As a result of this they are apt to encounter various disappointments before they find the one meant for them. At times he or she says things they really shouldn't, and this causes the end of a romantic relationship.

Men and women born under this sign may have many love affairs before they feel ready to settle down with just one person. If the person they love does not exactly measure up to their standards, they are apt to overlook this—depending on how strong their love is—and accept the person for what that person is.

On the whole, Sagittarius men and women are not envious. They are willing to allow a partner needed freedoms—within reason. Sagittarius does this so they will not have to jeopardize their own liberties. Live and let live could easily be their motto. If their ideals and freedom are threatened, Sagittarius fights hard to protect what they believe is just and fair.

They do not want to make any mistakes in love, so they take their time when choosing someone to settle down with. They are direct and positive when they meet the right one. They do not waste time.

The average Sagittarius may be a bit altar-shy. It may take a bit of convincing before Sagittarius agree that married life is right for them. This is generally because they do not want to lose their freedom. Sagittarius is an active person who enjoys being around a lot of other people. Sitting quietly at home does not interest them at all. At times it may seem that he or she wants to have things their own way, even in marriage. It may take some doing to get Sagittarius to realize that in marriage, as in other things, give-and-take plays a great role.

Romance and the Sagittarius Woman

The Sagittarius woman is kind and gentle. Most of the time she is very considerate of others and enjoys being of help in some way to her friends. She can be quite active and, as a result, be rather difficult to catch. On the whole, she is optimistic and friendly. She believes in looking on the bright side of things. She knows how to make the best of situations that others feel are not worth salvaging. She has plenty of pluck.

Men generally like her because of her easygoing manner. Quite often she becomes friends with a man before venturing on to romance. There is something about her that makes her more of a companion than a lover. The woman Archer can best be described as sporting and broad-minded.

She is almost never possessive. She enjoys her own freedom too much to want to make demands on that of another person.

She is always youthful in her disposition. She may seem naive or guileless at times. Generally it takes her longer really to mature than it does others. She tends to be impulsive and may easily jump from one thing to another. If she has an unfortunate experience in love early in life, she may shy away from fast or intimate contacts for a while. She is usually very popular. Not all the men who are attracted to her see her as a possible lover, but more as a friend or companion.

The woman born under the sign of the Archer generally believes in true love. She may have several romances before she decides to settle down. For her there is no particular rush. She is willing to have a long romantic relationship with the man she loves before making marriage plans.

The Sagittarius woman is often the outdoors type and has a strong liking for animals—especially dogs and horses. Quite often she excels in sports. She is not generally someone who is content to stay at home and cook and take care of the house. She would rather be out attending to her other interests. When she does household work, however, she does it well.

She makes a good companion as well as a wife. She usually enjoys participating with her husband in his various interests and affairs. Her sunny disposition often brightens up the dull moments of a love affair.

At times her temper may flare, but she is herself again after a few moments. She would never butt into her husband's business affairs, but she does enjoy being asked for her opinion from time to time. Generally she is up to date on all that her husband is doing and can offer him some pretty sound advice.

The Sagittarius woman is seldom jealous of her husband's interest in other people—even if some of them are of the opposite sex. If she has no reason to doubt his love, she never questions it.

She makes a loving and sympathetic mother. She knows all the sports news and probably has the latest board game to play with her children. Her cheerful manner makes her an invaluable playmate and encouraging guide.

Romance and the Sagittarius Man

The Sagittarius man is often an adventurer. He likes taking chances in love as well as in life. He may hop around quite a bit—from one romance to another—before really thinking about settling down. Many men born under this sign feel that marriage would mean the end of their freedom, so they avoid it as much as possible. Whenever a romance becomes too serious, they move on.

Many Sagittarius men are impulsive in love. Early marriages for some often end unpleasantly. A male Archer is not a very mature person, even at an age when most others are. He takes a bit more time. He may not always make a wise choice in a love partner.

He is affectionate and loving but not at all possessive. Because he is rather lighthearted in love, he sometimes gets into trouble.

Most Sagittarius men find romance an exciting adventure. They make attentive lovers and are never cool or indifferent. Love should also have a bit of fun in it for him too. He likes to keep things light and gay. Romance without humor can at times be difficult for him to accept. The woman he loves should also be a good sport. She should have as open and fun-loving a disposition as he has if she is to understand him properly.

He wants his mate to share his interest in the outdoor life and animals. If she is good at sports, she is likely to win his heart. The average Sagittarius generally has an interest in athletics of various sorts—from bicycling to baseball.

His mate must also be a good intellectual companion, someone who can easily discuss those matters which interest him. Physical love is important to him—but so is spiritual love. A good romance will contain these in balance.

His sense of humor may sometimes seem a little unkind to someone who is not used to being laughed at. He enjoys playing jokes now and again. It is the child in his nature that remains a part of his character even when he grows old and gray.

He is not a homebody. He is responsible, however, and will do what is necessary to keep a home together. Still and all, the best wife for him is one who can manage household matters single-handedly if need be.

He loves the children, especially as they grow older and begin to take on definite personalities.

Woman—Man

SAGITTARIUS WOMAN
ARIES MAN

In some ways, the Aries man resembles a wandering mountain sheep seeking high land. He has an insatiable thirst for knowledge. He's ambitious and is apt to have his finger in many pies. He can do with a woman like you—someone attractive, quick-witted, and smart.

He is not interested in a clinging vine for a mate. He wants someone who is there when he needs her, someone who listens and understands what he says, someone who can give advice if he should ever need it, which is not likely to be often.

The Aries man wants a woman who will look good on his arm without hanging on it too heavily. He is looking for a woman who has both feet on the ground and yet is mysterious and enticing, a kind of domestic Helen of Troy whose face or fine dinner can launch a thousand business deals if need be. That woman he's in search of sounds a little like you, doesn't she? If the shoe fits, put it on. You won't regret it.

The Aries man makes a good husband. He is faithful and attentive. He is an affectionate man. He'll make you feel needed and loved. Love is a serious matter for the Aries man. He does not believe in flirting or playing the field—especially after he's found the woman of his dreams. He'll expect you to be as constant in your affection as he is in his. He'll expect you to be one hundred percent his. He won't put up with any nonsense while romancing you.

The Aries man may be pretty progressive and modern about many things. However, when it comes to pants wearing, he's downright conventional: it's strictly male attire. The best role you can take in the relationship is a supporting one. He's the boss and that's that. Once you have learned to accept that, you'll find the going easy.

The Aries man, with his endless energy and drive, likes to relax in the comfort of his home at the end of the day. The good homemaker can be sure of holding his love. He'll watch a sports match with you from his favorite armchair. If you see to it that everything in the house is where he expects to find it, you'll have no difficulty keeping the relationship on an even keel.

Life and love with an Aries man may be just the medicine you need. He'll be a good provider. He'll spoil you if he's financially able.

The Aries father is young at heart and will spoil children every chance he gets. So naturally the kids will take to him like ducks to water. His quick mind and energetic behavior appeal to the young. His ability to jump from one thing to another will delight the kids and keep them active. You will have to introduce some rules of the game so that the children learn how to start things properly and finish them before running off elsewhere.

SAGITTARIUS WOMAN
TAURUS MAN

If you've got your heart set on a man born under the sign of Taurus, you'll have to learn the art of being patient. Taurus take their time about everything—even love.

The steady and deliberate Taurus man is a little slow on the draw. It may take him quite a while before he gets around to popping that question. For the woman who doesn't mind twiddling her thumbs, the waiting and anticipating almost always pays off in the end. Taurus men want to make sure that every step they take is a good one, particularly if they feel that the path they're on is one that leads to the altar.

If you are in the mood for a whirlwind romance, you had better cast your net in shallower waters. Moreover, most Taurus prefer to do the angling themselves. They are not keen on a woman taking the lead. Once she does, they might drop her like a dead fish. If you let yourself get caught in his net, you'll find that he's fallen for you—hook, line, and sinker.

The Taurus man is fond of a comfortable home life. It is very important to him. If you keep those home fires burning you will have no trouble keeping that flame in your Taurus mate's heart aglow. You have a talent for homemaking; use it. Your taste in furnishings is excellent. You know how to make a house come to life with colors and decorations.

Taurus, the strong, steady, and protective Bull, may not be your idea of a man on the move. Still he's reliable. Perhaps he could be the anchor for your dreams and plans. He could help you to acquire a more balanced outlook and approach to your life. If you're given to impulsiveness, he could help you to curb it. He's the man who is always there when you need him.

When you tie the knot with a man born under Taurus, you can put away fears about creditors pounding on the front door. Taurus are practical about everything including bill paying. When he carries you over that threshold, you can be certain that the entire house is paid for, not only the doorsill.

As a wife, you won't have to worry about putting aside your many interests for the sake of back-breaking house chores. Your Taurus husband will see to it that you have all the latest time-saving appliances and comforts.

The Taurus father has much love and affection for the children, and he has no trouble demonstrating his warmth. Yet he does not believe in spoiling the kids. The Taurus father believes that children have a place, and they should know their place at all times. He is an excellent disciplinarian and will see to it that the youngsters grow up to be polite, obedient, and respectful. You will provide mirth and fun to balance things out.

SAGITTARIUS WOMAN
GEMINI MAN

If opposites attract, as the notion goes, then Gemini and Sagittarius should be swell together. The fact that you two are astrologically related—being zodiacal partners as well as zodiacal opposites—does not automatically guarantee that you will understand each other, at least at first. Gemini is an air sign, you are a fire sign, so the initial contact between you should be warm and breezy.

The Gemini man is quite a catch. Many a woman has set her cap for him and failed to bag him. Generally, Gemini men are intelligent, witty, and outgoing. Many of them tend to be versatile.

On the other hand, some of them seem to lack that sort of common sense that you set so much store in. Their tendency to start a half-dozen projects, then toss them up in the air out of boredom may do nothing more than exasperate you.

One thing that causes a Twin's mind and affection to wander is a bore. But it is unlikely that the active Sagittarius woman would ever allow herself to be accused of dullness. The Gemini man who has caught your heart will admire you for your ideas and intellect—perhaps even more than for your athletic talents and good looks.

A strong-willed woman could easily fill the role of rudder for her Gemini's ship-without-a-sail. The intelligent Gemini is often aware of his shortcomings and doesn't mind if someone with better bearings gives him a shove in the right direction—when it's needed. The average Gemini doesn't have serious ego hang-ups and will even accept a well-deserved chewing out from his mate or girlfriend gracefully.

A successful and serious-minded Gemini could make you a very happy woman, perhaps, if you gave him half the chance. Although he may give you the impression that he has a hole in his head, the Gemini man generally has a good head on his shoulders and can make efficient use of it when he wants to. Some of them, who have learned the art of being steadfast, have risen to great heights in their professions.

Once you convince yourself that not all people born under the sign of the Twins are witless grasshoppers, you won't mind dating a few—to test your newborn conviction. If you do wind up walking down the aisle with one, accept the fact that married life with him will mean your taking the bitter with the sweet.

Life with a Gemini man can be more fun than a barrel of clowns. You'll never be allowed to experience a dull moment. But don't leave money matters to him, or you'll both wind up behind the eight ball.

Gemini men are always attractive to the opposite sex. You'll perhaps have to allow him an occasional harmless flirt. It will seldom amount to more than that if you're his ideal mate.

Gemini is your zodiacal mate, as well as your zodiacal opposite, so the Gemini-Sagittarius couple will make delightful parents together. Airy Gemini will create a very open, experimental environment for the kids. He loves them so much, he sometimes lets them do what they want. You will keep the kids in line and prevent them from running the household. But you and your Gemini mate's combined sense of humor is infectious, so the youngsters will naturally come to see the fun and funny sides of life.

SAGITTARIUS WOMAN
CANCER MAN

Chances are you won't hit it off too well with the man born under Cancer if your plans concern love. But then, Cupid has been known to do some pretty unlikely things. The Cancer man is very sensitive—thin-skinned and occasionally moody. You've got to keep on your toes—and not step on his—if you're determined to make a go of the relationship.

The Cancer man may be lacking in some of the qualities you seek in a man. But when it comes to being faithful and being a good provider, he's hard to beat.

The perceptive woman will not mistake the Crab's quietness for sullenness or his thriftiness for penny-pinching. In some respects, he is like that wise old owl out on a limb. He may look like he's dozing but actually he hasn't missed a thing.

Cancers possess a well of knowledge about human behavior. They can come across with some pretty helpful advice to those in trouble or in need. He can certainly guide you in making investments both in time and money. He may not say much, but he's always got his wits about him.

The Crab may not be the match or catch for a woman like you. At times, you are likely to find him downright dull. True to his sign, he can be fairly cranky and crabby when handled the wrong way. He is perhaps more sensitive than he should be.

If you're smarter than your Cancer friend, be smart enough not to let him know. Never give him the idea that you think he's a little short on brainpower. It would send him scurrying back into his shell. And all that ground lost in the relationship will perhaps never be recovered.

The Crab is most content at home. Once settled down for the night or the weekend, wild horses couldn't drag him any farther than the gatepost—that is, unless those wild horses were dispatched by his mother.

The Crab is sometimes a Momma's boy. If his mate does not put her foot down, he will see to it that his mother always comes first. No self-respecting wife would ever allow herself to play second fiddle, even if it's to her mother-in-law. With a little bit of tact, however, she'll find that slipping into that number-one position is as easy as pie (that legendary one his mother used to bake).

If you pamper your Cancer man, you'll find that mother turns up less and less, at the front door and in conversations.

Cancers make proud, patient, and protective fathers. But they can be a little too protective. Their sheltering instincts can interfere with a youngster's natural inclination to test the waters outside the home. Still, the Cancer father doesn't want to see his kids learning about life the hard way from the streets. Your qualities of optimism and encouragement and your knowledge of right and wrong will guide the youngsters along the way.

SAGITTARIUS WOMAN
LEO MAN

For the woman who enjoys being swept off her feet in a romantic whirlwind fashion, Leo is the sign of such love. When the Lion puts his mind to romancing, he doesn't stint. It's all wining and dining and dancing till the wee hours of the morning.

Leo is all heart and knows how to make his woman feel like a woman. The woman in constant search of a man she can look up to need go no farther: Leo is ten-feet tall—in spirit if not in stature. He's a man not only in full control of his faculties but in full control of just about any situation he finds himself in. Leo is a winner.

The Leo man may not look like Tarzan, but he knows how to roar and beat his chest if he has to. The woman who has had her fill of weak-kneed men finds in a Leo someone she can at last lean upon. He can support you not only physically but spiritually as well. He's good at giving advice that pays off.

Leos are direct people. They don't believe in wasting time or effort. They almost never make unwise investments.

Many Leos rise to the top of their professions. Through example, they often prove to be a source of great inspiration to others.

Although he's a ladies' man, Leo is very particular about his ladies. His standards are high when it comes to love interests. The idealistic and cultivated woman should have no trouble keeping her balance on the pedestal the Lion sets her on.

Leo believes that romance should be played on a fair give-and-take basis. He won't stand for any monkey business in a love relationship. It's all or nothing.

You'll find him a frank, off-the-shoulder person. He generally says what is on his mind.

If you decide upon a Leo man for a mate, you must be prepared to stand behind him full force. He expects it—and usually deserves it. He's the head of the house and can handle that position without a hitch. He knows how to go about breadwinning and, if he has his way (and most Leos do have their own way), he'll see to it that you'll have all the luxuries you crave and the comforts you need.

It's unlikely that the romance in your marriage will ever die out. Lions need love like flowers need sunshine. They're ever amorous and generally expect similar attention and affection from their mates. Leos are fond of going out on the town. They love to give parties, as well as to go to them. Because you, too, love to throw a party, you and your Leo mate will be the most popular host and hostess in town.

Leo fathers have a tendency to spoil the children—up to a point. That point is reached when the children become the center of attention, and Leo feels neglected. Then the Leo father becomes strict and insists that his rules be followed. You will have your hands full pampering both your Leo mate and the children. As long as he comes first in your affections, the family will be creative and joyful.

SAGITTARIUS WOMAN
VIRGO MAN

Although the Virgo man may be a bit of a fussbudget at times, his seriousness and dedication to common sense may help you to overlook his tendency to be too critical about minor things.

Virgo men are often quiet, respectable types who set great store in conservative behavior and levelheadedness. He'll admire you for your practicality and tenacity, perhaps even more than for your good looks. He's seldom bowled over by a glamour-puss. When he gets his courage up, he turns to a serious and reliable girl for romance.

The Virgo man will be far from a Valentino while dating. In fact, you may wind up making all the passes. Once he does get his motor running, however, he can be a warm and wonderful fellow—to the right lover.

He's gradual about love. Chances are your romance with him will start out looking like an ordinary friendship. Once he's sure you're no fly-by-night flirt and have no plans of taking him for a ride, he'll open up and rain sunshine all over your heart.

Virgo men tend to marry late in life. Virgo believes in holding out until he's met the right woman. He may not have many names in his little black book; in fact, he may not even have a black book. He's not interested in playing the field; leave that to men of the more flamboyant signs. The Virgo man is so particular that he may remain romantically inactive for a long period. His woman has to be perfect or it's no go.

If you find yourself feeling weak-kneed for a Virgo, do your best to convince him that perfect is not so important when it comes to love. Help him to realize that he's missing out on a great deal by not considering the near perfect or whatever it is you consider yourself to be. With your surefire perseverance, you will most likely be able to make him listen to reason and he'll wind up reciprocating your romantic interests.

The Virgo man is no block of ice. He'll respond to what he feels to be the right feminine flame. Once your love life with a Virgo man starts to bubble, don't give it a chance to fall flat. You may never have a second chance at winning his heart.

If you should ever break up with him, forget about patching it up. He'd prefer to let the pieces lie scattered. Once married, though, he'll stay that way—even if it hurts. He's too conscientious to try to back out of a legal deal of any sort.

The Virgo man is as neat as a pin. He's thumbs down on sloppy housekeeping. Keep everything bright, neat, and shiny. That goes for the children, too, at least by the time he gets home.

The Virgo father appreciates good manners, courtesy, and cleanliness from the children. He will instill a sense of order in the household, and he expects youngsters to respect his wishes. He can become very worried about scrapes, bruises, and all sorts of minor mishaps when the kids go out to play. Your easygoing faith in the children's safety will counteract Virgo's tendency to fuss and fret over them.

SAGITTARIUS WOMAN
LIBRA MAN

If there's a Libra in your life, you are most likely a very happy woman. Men born under this sign have a way with women. You'll always feel at ease in a Libra's company. You can be yourself when you're with him.

The Libra man can be moody at times. His moodiness is often puzzling. One moment he comes on hard and strong with declarations of his love, the next moment you find that he's left you like yesterday's mashed potatoes. He'll come back, though, don't worry. Libras are like that. Deep down inside he really knows what he wants even though he may not appear to.

You'll appreciate his admiration of beauty and harmony. If you're dressed to the teeth and never looked lovelier, you'll get a ready compliment—and one that's really deserved. Libras don't indulge in idle flattery. If they don't like something, they are tactful enough to remain silent.

Libras will go to great lengths to preserve peace and harmony—they will even tell a fat lie if necessary. They don't like showdowns or disagreeable confrontations. The frank woman is all for getting whatever is bothering her off her chest and out into the open, even if it comes out all wrong. To the Libra, making a clean breast of everything seems like sheer folly sometimes.

You may lose your patience while waiting for your Libra friend to make up his mind. It takes him ages sometimes to make a decision. He weighs both sides carefully before committing himself to anything. You seldom dillydally, at least about small things. So it's likely that you will find it difficult to see eye-to-eye with a hesitating Libra when it comes to decision-making methods.

All in all, though, he is kind, considerate, and fair. He is interested in the real truth. He'll try to balance everything out until he has all the correct answers. It's not difficult for him to see both sides of a story.

He's a peace-loving man. Even a rough-and-tumble sports event, and certainly a violent one, will make Libra shudder.

Libras are not show-offs. Generally, they are well-balanced, modest people. Honest, wholesome, and affectionate, they are serious about every love encounter they have. If Libra should find that the woman he's dating is not really suited to him, he will end the relationship in such a tactful manner that no hard feelings will come about.

The Libra father is patient and fair. He can be firm without exercising undue strictness or discipline. Although he can be a harsh judge at times, with the youngsters he will radiate sweetness and light in the hope that they will grow up to imitate his gentle manner. To balance the essential refinement the children will acquire from their Libra father, you will teach them a few rough-and-ready ways to enjoy recreation.

SAGITTARIUS WOMAN
SCORPIO MAN

Scorpio shares at least one trait in common with Sagittarius. You both are blunt. But Scorpio, who can be vengeful and vindictive, intends an insult as an insult, not just a thoughtless comment. Many find Scorpio's sting a fate worse than death. When his anger breaks loose, you better clear out of the vicinity.

The average Scorpio may strike you as a brute. He'll stick pins into the balloons of your plans and dreams if they don't line up with what he thinks is right. If you do anything to irritate him—just anything—you'll wish you hadn't. He'll give you a sounding out that would make you pack your bags and go back to Mother—if you were that kind of woman.

The Scorpio man hates being tied down to home life. He would rather be out on the battlefield of life, belting away at whatever he feels is a just and worthy cause, instead of staying home nestled in a comfortable armchair with the evening paper. If you have a strong homemaking streak, don't keep those home fires burning too brightly too long; you may just run out of firewood.

As passionate as he is in business affairs and politics, the Scorpio man still has plenty of fire and light stored away for the pursuit of romance and lovemaking.

Most women are easily attracted to him—perhaps you are no exception. Those who allow a man born under this sign to sweep them off their feet quickly find that they're dealing with a pepper pot of seething excitement. The Scorpio man is passionate with a capital P, you can be sure of that. When you two meet on the playing field of love, Scorpio will be much more intense and competitive than you.

If you can match his intensity and adapt to his mood swings, you are fair game. If you're the kind of woman who can keep a stiff upper lip, take it on the chin, turn a deaf ear, and all of that, because you feel you are still under his love spell in spite of everything—lots of luck.

If you have decided to take the bitter with the sweet, prepare yourself for a lot of ups and downs. Chances are you won't have as much time for your own affairs and interests as you'd like. The Scorpio's love of power may cause you to be at his constant beck and call.

Scorpios like fathering large families. He is proud of his children, but often he fails to live up to his responsibilities as a parent. In spite of the extremes in his personality, the Scorpio man is able to transform the conflicting characteristics within himself when he becomes a father. When he takes his fatherly duties seriously, he is a powerful teacher. He believes in preparing his children for the hard knocks life sometimes delivers. He is adept with difficult youngsters because he knows how to tap the best in each child.

SAGITTARIUS WOMAN
SAGITTARIUS MAN

The woman who has set her cap for a man born under the sign of Sagittarius may have to apply an awful amount of strategy before she can get him to drop down on bended knee. Although some Sagittarius may be marriage-shy, they're not ones to skitter away from romance. A high-spirited woman may find a relationship with a Sagittarius—whether a fling or the real thing—a very enjoyable experience.

As you know, Sagittarius are bright, happy, and healthy people. You all have a strong sense of fair play. You all are a source of inspiration to others. You're full of ideas and drive.

You'll be taken by the Sagittarius man's infectious grin and his lighthearted friendly nature. If you do wind up being the woman in his life, you'll find that he's apt to treat you more like a buddy than the love of his life. It's just his way. Sagittarius are often chummy instead of romantic.

You'll admire his broad-mindedness in most matters—including those of the heart. If, while dating you, he claims that he still wants to play the field, he'll expect you to enjoy the same liberty. Once he's promised to love, honor, and obey, however, he does just that. Marriage for him, once he's taken that big step, is very serious business.

A woman who has a keen imagination and a great love of freedom will not be disappointed if she does tie up with the Archer. The Sagittarius man is often quick-witted. Men of this sign have a genuine interest in equality. They hate prejudice and injustice.

If he does insist on a night out with the boys once a week, he won't scowl if you decide to let him shift for himself in the kitchen once a week while you pursue some of your own interests. He believes in fairness.

He's not much of a homebody. Quite often he's occupied with

faraway places either in his dreams or in reality. He enjoys—just as you do—being on the go or on the move. He's got ants in his pants and refuses to sit still for long stretches at a time. Humdrum routine, especially at home, bores him. So the two of you will probably go out a lot or throw lots of parties at home.

He likes surprising people. He'll take great pride in showing you off to his friends. He'll always be a considerate mate; he will never embarrass or disappoint you intentionally.

He's very tolerant when it comes to friends, and you'll most likely spend a lot of time entertaining people—which suits you party animals royally.

The Sagittarius father, unlike you, may be bewildered and made utterly nervous by a newborn. He will dote on any infant son or daughter from a safe distance because he can be clumsy and frightened handling the tiny tot. The Sagittarius dad usually becomes comfortable with youngsters once they have passed through the baby stage. As soon as they are old enough to walk and talk, he will encourage each and every visible sign of talent and skill.

SAGITTARIUS WOMAN
CAPRICORN MAN

A with-it woman like you is likely to find the average Capricorn man a bit of a drag. The man born under this sign is often a closed up person and difficult to get to know. Even if you do get to know him, you may not find him very interesting.

In romance, Capricorn men are a little on the rusty side. You'll probably have to make all the passes.

You may find his plodding manner irritating and his conservative, traditional ways downright maddening. He's not one to take a chance on anything. If it was good enough for his father, it's good enough for him. Capricorn can be habit-bound. He follows a way that is tried and true.

Whenever adventure rears its tantalizing head, the Goat will turn the other way. Unlike you, he is not prone to taking risks.

He may be just as ambitious as you are, perhaps even more so. But his ways of accomplishing his aims are more subterranean than yours. He operates from the background a good deal of the time. At a gathering you may never even notice him. But he's there, taking everything in, sizing everyone up, planning his next careful move.

Although Capricorns may be intellectual to a degree, it is not generally the kind of intelligence you appreciate. He may not be as quick or as bright as you. It may take him ages to understand a joke, and you love jokes.

If you do decide to take up with a man born under the sign of the Goat, you ought to be pretty good in the cheering up department.

The Capricorn man often acts as though he's constantly being followed by a cloud of gloom.

The Capricorn man is most himself when in the comfort and privacy of his own home. The security possible within four walls can make him a happy man. He'll spend as much time as he can at home. If he is loaded down with extra work, he'll bring it home instead of finishing it up at the office.

You'll most likely find yourself frequently confronted by his relatives. Family is very important to the Capricorn—his family that is. They had better take an important place in your life, too, if you want to keep your home a happy one.

Although his caution in most matters may all but drive you up the wall, you'll find that his concerned way with money is justified most of the time. He'll plan everything right down to the last penny.

The Capricorn father is a dutiful parent and takes a lifelong interest in seeing that his children make something of themselves. He may not understand their hopes and dreams because he often tries to put his head on their shoulders. The Capricorn father believes that there are certain goals to be achieved, and there is a traditional path to achieving them. He can be quite a scold if the youngsters break the rules. Your easygoing, joyful manner will moderate Capricorn's rigid approach and will make things fun again for the children.

SAGITTARIUS WOMAN
AQUARIUS MAN

Aquarius individuals love everybody—even their worst enemies sometimes. Through your love relationship with an Aquarius you'll find yourself running into all sorts of people, ranging from near genius to downright insane—and they're all friends of his.

As a rule, Aquarius are extremely friendly and open. Of all the signs, they are perhaps the most tolerant. In the thinking department, they are often miles ahead of others.

You'll most likely find your relationship with this man a challenging one. Your high respect for intelligence and imagination may be reason enough for you to set your heart on a Water Bearer. You'll find that you can learn a lot from him.

In the holding-hands phase of your romance, you may find that your Water Bearer friend has cold feet. Aquarius take quite a bit of warming up before they are ready to come across with that first goodnight kiss. More than likely, he'll just want to be your pal in the beginning. For him, that's an important first step in any relationship—love included.

The poetry and flowers stage—if it ever comes—will come later. Aquarius is all heart. Still, when it comes to tying himself down to one person and for keeps, he is almost always sure to hesitate.

He may even try to get out of it if you breathe down his neck too heavily.

The Aquarius man is no Romeo, and he wouldn't want to be. The kind of love life he's looking for is one that's made up mainly of companionship. He may not be very romantic, but still the memory of his first romance will always hold an important position in his heart. So in a way he is like Romeo after all. Some Aquarius wind up marrying their childhood sweethearts.

You won't find it difficult to look up to a man born under the sign of the Water Bearer, but you may find the challenge of trying to keep up with him dizzying. He can pierce through the most complicated problem as if it were simple math. You may find him a little too lofty and high-minded. But don't judge him too harshly if that's the case. He's way ahead of his time.

If you marry this man, he'll stay true to you. Don't think that once the honeymoon is over, you'll be chained to the kitchen sink forever. Your Aquarius husband will encourage you to keep active in your own interests and affairs. You'll most likely have a minor tiff now and again but never anything serious.

The Aquarius father has an almost intuitive understanding of children. He sees them as individuals in their own right, not as extensions of himself or as beings who are supposed to take a certain place in the world. He can talk to the kids on a variety of subjects, and his knowledge can be awe-inspiring. Your dedication to learning and your desire to educate the children will be bolstered by your Aquarius mate. And your love of sports and games, the fun physical activities in life, will balance the airy Aquarius intellectualism.

SAGITTARIUS WOMAN
PISCES MAN

The man born under Pisces is quite a dreamer. Sometimes he's so wrapped up in his dreams that he's difficult to reach. To the average, active woman, he may seem a little passive.

He's easygoing most of the time. He seems to take things in his stride. He'll entertain all kinds of views and opinions from just about everyone, nodding or smiling vaguely, giving the impression that he's with them one hundred percent while that may not be the case at all. His attitude may be why bother when he's confronted with someone wrong who thinks he's right. The Pisces man will seldom speak his mind if he thinks he'll be rigidly opposed.

The Pisces man is oversensitive at times. He's afraid of getting his feelings hurt. He'll sometimes imagine a personal affront when none's been made. Chances are you'll find this complex of his maddening. At times you may feel like giving him a swift kick where it hurts the most. It wouldn't do any good, though. It would just add fuel to the fire of his complex.

One thing you'll admire about this man is his concern for people who are sickly or troubled. He'll make his shoulder available to anyone in the mood for a good cry. He can listen to one hard-luck story after another without seeming to tire. When his advice is asked, he is capable of coming across with some words of wisdom. He often knows what is bothering someone before that person is aware of it. It's almost intuitive with Pisces.

Still, at the end of the day, this man will want some peace and quiet. If you've got a problem when he comes home, don't unload it in his lap. If you do, you are apt to find him short-tempered. He's a good listener but he can only take so much.

Pisces are not aimless although they may seem so at times. The positive sort of Pisces man is quite often successful in his profession and is likely to wind up rich and influential. Material gain, however, is never a direct goal for a man born under this sign.

The weaker Pisces are usually content to stay on the level where they find themselves. They won't complain too much if the roof leaks or if the fence is in need of repair.

Because of their seemingly laissez-faire manner, people under the sign of the Fishes—needless to say—are immensely popular with children. For tots the Pisces father plays the double role of confidant and playmate. It will never enter the mind of a Pisces to discipline a child, no matter how spoiled or incorrigible that child becomes.

Man—Woman

SAGITTARIUS MAN
ARIES WOMAN

The Aries woman is quite a charmer. When she tugs at the strings of your heart, you'll know it. She's a woman who's in search of a knight in shining armor. She is a very particular person with very high ideals. She won't accept anyone but the man of her dreams.

The Aries woman never plays around with passion. She means business when it comes to love.

Don't get the idea that she's a dewy-eyed damsel. She isn't. In fact, she can be practical and to the point when she wants to be. She's a dame with plenty of drive and ambition.

With an Aries woman behind you, you can go far in life. She knows how to help her man get ahead. She's full of wise advice; you only have to ask. The Aries woman has a keen business sense. Many of them become successful career women. There is nothing passive or retiring about her. She is equipped with a good brain and she knows how to use it.

Your union with her could be something strong, secure, and romantic. If both of you have your sights fixed in the same direction, there is almost nothing that you could not accomplish.

The Aries woman is proud and capable of being quite jealous. While you're with her, never cast your eye in another woman's direction. It could spell disaster for your relationship. The Aries woman won't put up with romantic nonsense when her heart is at stake.

If the Aries woman backs you up in your business affairs, you can be sure of succeeding. However, if she only is interested in advancing her own career and puts her interests before yours, she can be sure to rock the boat. It will put a strain on the relationship. The overambitious Aries woman can be a pain in the neck and make you forget you were in love with her once.

The cultivated Aries woman makes a wonderful wife and mother. She has a natural talent for homemaking. With a pot of paint and some wallpaper, she can transform the dreariest domicile into an abode of beauty and snug comfort. The perfect hostess—even when friends just happen by—she knows how to make guests feel at home.

You'll also admire your Aries because she knows how to stand on her own two feet. Hers is an independent nature. She won't break down and cry when things go wrong, but will pick herself up and try to patch up matters.

The Aries woman makes a fine, affectionate mother. Although she is not keen on burdensome responsibilities, like you she relishes the joy that children bring. The Aries woman is skilled at juggling both career and motherhood, so her kids will never feel that she is an absentee parent. In fact, as the youngsters grow older, they might want some of the liberation that is so important to her. One of your roles is to encourage the children's quest for independence.

SAGITTARIUS MAN
TAURUS WOMAN

The woman born under the sign of Taurus may lack a little of the sparkle and bubble you often like to find in a woman. The Taurus woman is generally down to earth and never flighty. It's important to her that she keep both feet flat on the ground. She is not fond of bounding all over the place, especially if she's under the impression that there's no profit in it.

On the other hand, if you hit it off with a Taurus woman, you won't be disappointed in the romance area. The Taurus woman is all woman and proud of it, too. She can be very devoted and loving once she decides that her relationship with you is no fly-by-night romance. Basically, she's a passionate person. In sex, she's direct and to the point. If she really loves you, she'll let you know she's yours—and without reservations.

Better not flirt with other women once you've committed yourself to her. She's capable of being very jealous and possessive.

She'll stick by you through thick and thin. It's almost certain that if the going ever gets rough, she won't go running home to her mother. She can adjust to the hard times just as graciously as she can to the good times.

Taurus are, on the whole, pretty even-tempered. They like to be treated with kindness. Beautiful things and aesthetic objects make them feel loved and treasured.

You may find her a little slow and deliberate. She likes to be safe and sure about everything. Let her plod along if she likes. Don't coax her, but just let her take her own sweet time. Everything she does is done thoroughly and, generally, without mistakes.

Don't deride her for being a slowpoke. It could lead to a tirade of insults that could put even your blunt manner to shame. The Taurus woman doesn't anger readily but when prodded often enough, she's capable of letting loose with a cyclone of ill will. If you treat her with kindness and consideration, you'll have no cause for complaint.

The Taurus woman loves doing things for her man. She's a whiz in the kitchen and can whip up feasts fit for a king if she thinks they'll be royally appreciated. She may not fully understand you, but she'll adore you and be faithful to you if she feels you're worthy of it.

The Taurus woman makes a wonderful mother. She knows how to keep her children loved, cuddled, and warm. She may have some difficult times with them when they reach adolescence, and start to rebel against her strictness. You can inject a sense of adventure even in the most mundane of household responsibilities, so you will moderate your Taurus mate's insistence on discipline.

SAGITTARIUS MAN
GEMINI WOMAN

You may find a romance with a woman born under the sign of the Twins a many-splendored thing. In her you can find the intellectual companionship you often look for in a friend or mate.

Gemini, your astrological mate, can appreciate your aims and desires because she travels pretty much the same road as you do intellectually. At least she will travel part of the way. She may share your interests, but she will lack your tenacity.

She suffers from itchy feet. She can be here, there, all over the place and at the same time, or so it would seem. Her eagerness to move around may make you dizzy. Still, you'll enjoy and appreciate her liveliness and mental agility.

Geminis have sparkling personalities. You'll be attracted by her warmth and grace. While she's on your arm, you'll probably notice that many male eyes are drawn to her. She may even return a gaze or two, but don't let that worry you. All women born under this sign have nothing against a harmless flirt once in a while. They enjoy this sort of attention. If Gemini feels she is already spoken for, however, she will never let such attention get out of hand.

Although she may not be as handy as you'd like in the kitchen, you'll never go hungry for a filling and tasty meal. The Gemini woman is always in a rush. She won't feel like she's cheating by breaking out the instant mashed potatoes or the frozen peas. She may not be much of a good cook but she is clever. With a dash of this and a suggestion of that, she can make an uninteresting TV dinner taste like a gourmet meal.

Then, again, maybe you've struck it rich and have a Gemini lover or mate who finds complicated recipes a challenge to her intellect. If so, you'll find every meal an experiment—a tantalizing and mouth-watering surprise.

When you're beating your brains out over the Sunday crossword puzzle and find yourself stuck, just ask your Gemini partner. She'll give you all the right answers without batting an eyelash.

Like you, she loves all kinds of people. You may even find that you're a bit more particular than she. Often all that a Gemini requires is that her friends be interesting—and stay interesting. One thing she's not able to abide is a dullard.

Leave the party organizing to your Gemini sweetheart or mate, and you'll never have a chance to know a dull moment. She'll bring out the swinger in you if you give her half the chance.

The Gemini mother has a youthful streak that guides her in bringing up children through the various stages. She enjoys her kids, which can be the most sincere form of love. Like you—and like them—the Gemini mother is often restless, adventurous, and easily bored. She will never complain about the children's fleeting interests because she understands how they will change as they mature. Gemini-Sagittarius parents, being true zodiacal mates as well as zodiacal opposites, can encourage variety and experience in life so the kids really get to know what the world is like.

SAGITTARIUS MAN
CANCER WOMAN

If you fall in love with a Cancer woman, be prepared for anything. Cancer is sometimes difficult to understand when it comes to love. In one hour, she can unravel a whole gamut of emotions that will leave you in a tizzy. She'll undoubtedly keep you guessing.

You may find her a little too uncertain and sensitive for your liking. You'll most likely spend a good deal of time encouraging her, helping her to erase her foolish fears. Tell her she's a living doll a dozen times a day, and you'll be well loved in return.

Be careful of the jokes you make when in her company. Don't let any of them revolve around her, her personal interests, or her family. If you do, you'll most likely reduce her to tears. She can't stand being made fun of. It will take bushels of roses and tons of chocolates—not to mention the apologies—to get her to come back out of her shell.

In matters of money managing, she may not easily come around to your way of thinking. Money will never burn a hole in her pocket. You may get the notion that your Cancer sweetheart or mate is a direct descendent of Scrooge. If she has her way, she'll hang onto that first dollar you earned. She's not only that way with money, but with everything right on up from bakery string to jelly jars. She's a saver. She never throws anything away, no matter how trivial.

Once she returns your love, you'll find you have an affectionate, self-sacrificing, and devoted woman for life. Her love for you will never alter unless you want it to. She'll put you high upon a pedestal and will do everything—even if it's against your will—to keep you up there.

Cancer women love home life. For them, marriage is an easy step. They're domestic with a capital D. The Cancer woman will do her best to make your home comfortable and cozy. She, herself, is more at ease at home than anywhere else. She makes an excellent hostess. The best in her comes out when she is in her own environment, one she has created to meet her own and her family's needs.

Cancer women make the best mothers. Each will consider every complaint of her child a major catastrophe. With her, children always come first. If you're lucky, you'll run a close second. You'll perhaps see her as too devoted to the children. You may have a hard time convincing her that her apron strings are a little too tight.

SAGITTARIUS MAN
LEO WOMAN

If you can manage a woman who likes to kick up her heels every now and again, then the Lioness was made for you. You'll have to learn to put away jealous fears when you take up with a woman born under the sign of Leo. She's often the kind that makes heads turn and tongues wag. You don't have to believe any of what you hear. It's most likely jealous gossip or wishful thinking.

The Leo woman has more than a fair share of grace and glamour. She knows it, and she knows how to put it to good use. Needless to say, other women in her vicinity turn green with envy and will try anything to put her out of the running.

If she's captured your heart and fancy, woo her full force—if your intention is eventually to win her. Shower her with expensive gifts and promise her the moon, if you're in a position to go that far. Then you'll

find her resistance beginning to weaken. It's not that she's such a difficult cookie. She'll probably pamper you once she's decided you're the
man for her. But she does enjoy a lot of attention. What's more, she
feels she's entitled to it. Her mild arrogance, however, is becoming.

The Leo woman knows how to transform the crime of excessive
pride into a very charming misdemeanor. It sweeps most men—or
rather, all men—right off their feet. Those who do not succumb to
her leonine charm are few and far between.

If you've got an important business deal to clinch and you have
doubts as to whether you can bring it off as you should, take your
Leo mate along to the business luncheon. It will be a cinch that you'll
have that contract—lock, stock, and barrel—in your pocket before
the meeting is over. She won't have to say or do anything, just be there
at your side. The grouchiest oil magnate can be transformed into a
gushing, obedient schoolboy if there's a Leo woman in the room.

If you're rich and want to see to it that you stay that way, don't
give your Leo spouse a free hand with the charge accounts and credit
cards. When it comes to spending, Leo tends to overdo. If you're poor,
you have no worries because the luxury-loving Leo will most likely
never recognize your existence—let alone consent to marry you.

A Leo mother can be so proud of her children that she is sometimes blind to their faults. Yet when she wants them to learn and take
their rightful place in the social scheme of things, the Leo mother
can be strict. She is a patient teacher, lovingly explaining the rules
the youngsters are expected to follow. Easygoing and friendly, like
you are, she loves to pal around with the kids and show them off on
every occasion. Your family will be a bundle of joy.

SAGITTARIUS MAN
VIRGO WOMAN

The Virgo woman may be a little too difficult for you to understand
at first. Her waters run deep. Even when you think you know her,
don't take any bets on it. She's capable of keeping things hidden in
the deep recesses of her womanly soul—things she'll only release
when she's sure that you're the man she's been looking for.

It may take her some time to come around to this decision. Virgo
women are finicky about almost everything. Everything has to be
letter-perfect before they're satisfied. Many of them have the idea
that the only people who can do things right are Virgos.

Nothing offends a Virgo woman more than slovenly dress, sloppy
character, or a careless display of affection. Make sure your tie is
not crooked and that your shoes sport a bright shine before you go
calling on this lady. The typical Sagittarius male should keep the
off-color jokes for the locker room. She'll have none of that. Take
her arm when crossing the street. Don't rush the romance. Trying

to corner her in the back of a cab may be one way of striking out. Never criticize the way she looks. In fact, the best policy would be to agree with her as much as possible.

Still, there's just so much a man can take. All those dos and don'ts you'll have to observe if you want to get to first base with a Virgo may be just a little too much to ask of you. After a few dates, you may come to the conclusion that she just isn't worth all that trouble.

However, the Virgo woman is mysterious enough, generally speaking, to keep her men running back for more. Chances are you'll be intrigued by her airs and graces.

If lovemaking means a lot to you, you'll be disappointed at first in the cool ways of your Virgo partner. However, under her glacial facade there lies a hot cauldron of seething excitement. If you're patient and artful in your romantic approach, you'll find that all that caution was well worth the trouble. When Virgos love, they don't stint. It's all or nothing as far as they're concerned. Once they're convinced that they love you, they go all the way, tossing all cares to the wind.

One thing a Virgo woman can't stand in love is hypocrisy. They don't give a hoot about what the neighbors say if their hearts tell them to go ahead. They're very concerned with human truths. So if their hearts stumble upon another fancy, they will be true to that new heartthrob and leave you standing in the rain.

The Virgo woman is honest to her heart and will be as true to you as you are with her, generally. Do her wrong once, however, and it's farewell.

The Virgo mother has high expectations for her children, and she will strive to bring out the very best in them. They usually turn out just as she hoped, despite her anxiety about health and hygiene, safety and good sense. You must step in and ease her fears when she tries to restrict the kids at play or at school. The Virgo mother is more tender than strict, though, and the children will sense her unconditional love for them.

SAGITTARIUS MAN
LIBRA WOMAN

You'll probably find that the woman born under the sign of Libra is worth more than her weight in gold. She's a woman after your own heart.

With her, you'll always come first—make no mistake about that. She'll always be behind you 100 percent, no matter what you do. When you ask her advice about almost anything, you are likely to get a very balanced and realistic opinion. She is good at thinking things out and never lets her emotions run away with her when clear logic is called for.

As a homemaker she is hard to beat. She is very concerned with harmony and balance. You can be sure she'll make your house a joy to live in. She'll see to it that the home is tastefully furnished and decorated. A Libra cannot stand filth or disarray or noise. Anything that does not radiate harmony, in fact, runs against her orderly grain.

She is chock-full of charm and womanly ways. She can sweep just about any man off his feet with one winning smile. When it comes to using her brains, she can outthink almost anyone and, sometimes, with half the effort. She is diplomatic enough, though, never to let this become glaringly apparent. She may even turn the conversation around so that you think you were the one who did all the brainwork. She couldn't care less, really, just as long as you wind up doing what is right.

The Libra woman will put you up on a pretty high pedestal. You are her man and her idol. She'll leave all the decision making, large or small, up to you. She's not interested in running things and will only offer her assistance if she feels you really need it.

Some find her approach to reason masculine. However, in the areas of love and affection the Libra woman is all woman. She'll literally shower you with love and kisses during your romance with her. She doesn't believe in holding out. You shouldn't, either, if you want to hang onto her.

She is the kind of lover who likes to snuggle up to you in front of the fire on chilly autumn nights, the kind who will bring you breakfast in bed on Sunday. She'll be very thoughtful about anything that concerns you. If anyone dares suggest you're not the grandest guy in the world, she'll give that person what-for. She'll defend you till her dying breath. The Libra woman will be everything you want her to be.

The Libra mother will create a harmonious household in which young family members can grow up as equals. She will foster an environment that is sensitive to their needs. The Libra mother understands that children need both guidance and encouragement. With your enthusiastic input, the youngsters will never lack for anything that could make their lives easier and richer.

SAGITTARIUS MAN
SCORPIO WOMAN

The Scorpio woman can be a whirlwind of passion, perhaps too much passion to suit you casual types. When her temper flies, you'd better lock up the family heirlooms and take cover. When she chooses to be sweet, you're overcome with joy. When she uses sarcasm, she can shock even a blunt Sagittarius.

The Scorpio woman can be as hot as a tamale or as cool as a cucumber, but whatever mood she's in, she's in it for real. She does not believe in posing or putting on airs.

The Scorpio woman is often sultry and seductive. Her femme fatale charme can pierce through the hardest of hearts like a laser ray. She may not look like Mata Hari (quite often Scorpios resemble the tomboy next door) but once she's fixed you with her tantalizing eyes, you're a goner.

Life with the Scorpio woman will not be all smiles and smooth sailing. When prompted, she can unleash a gale of venom. Generally, she'll have the good grace to keep family battles within the walls of your home. When company visits, she's apt to give the impression that married life with you is one great big joyride. It's just one of her ways of expressing her loyalty to you, at least in front of others. She may fight you tooth and nail in the confines of your living room, but at a party or during an evening out, she'll hang onto your arm and have stars in her eyes.

Scorpio women are good at keeping secrets. She may even keep a few buried from you if she feels like it.

Never cross her up on even the smallest thing. When it comes to revenge, she's an eye-for-an-eye woman. She's not one for forgiveness, especially if she feels she's been wronged unfairly. You'd be well-advised not to give her any cause to be jealous, either. When the Scorpio woman sees green, your life will be made far from rosy. Once she's put you in the doghouse, you can be sure that you're going to stay there awhile.

You may find life with a Scorpio woman too draining. Although she may be full of extreme moods, it's quite likely that she's not the kind of woman you'd like to spend the rest of your natural life with. You'd prefer someone gentler and not so hot-tempered, someone who can take the highs with the lows and not complain, someone who is flexible and understanding. A woman born under Scorpio can be heavenly, but she can also be the very devil when she chooses.

The Scorpio mother is protective yet encouraging. The opposites within her nature mirror the very contradictions of life itself. Under her skillful guidance, the children learn how to cope with extremes and grow up to become many-faceted individuals.

SAGITTARIUS MAN
SAGITTARIUS WOMAN

You are in sync with your zodiacal sister born under the sign of Sagittarius. This good-natured gal is full of bounce and good cheer. Her sunny disposition seems almost permanent and can be relied upon even on the rainiest of days.

Women born under the sign of the Archer are almost never malicious. If ever they seem to be, it is only seeming. Sagittarius are often a little short on tact and say literally anything that comes into their heads, no matter what the occasion is. Sometimes the words that tumble out of their mouths seem downright cutting and cruel.

Still, no matter what the Sagittarius woman says, she means well. Lover or spouse, she is quite capable of losing some of your friends through a careless slip of the lip.

On the other hand, you will appreciate her honesty and good intentions. To you, qualities of this sort play an important part in life. With a little patience and practice, you can probably help cure your Sagittarius partner of her loose tongue. In most cases, you both will have to use better judgment, and you both will have to practice what you preach.

Chances are, she'll be the outdoors type of woman who likes sports, recreation, and exercise. Long hikes, fishing trips, and white-water canoeing will most likely appeal to her. She's a busy person. No one could ever call her a slouch. She sets great store in mobility. She won't sit still for one minute if she doesn't have to.

The Sagittarius woman is great company most of the time and, generally, lots of fun. Even if your buddies drop by for poker and beer, she won't have any trouble fitting in.

On the whole, she is a very kind and sympathetic woman. If she feels she's made a mistake, she'll be the first to call your attention to it. She's not afraid to own up to her own faults and shortcomings.

You might lose your patience with her once or twice. After she's seen how upset her shortsightedness or carelessness with money has made you, she'll do her best to straighten up.

The Sagittarius woman is not the kind who will pry into your business affairs. But she'll always be there, ready to offer advice if you need it.

The Sagittarius woman is seldom suspicious. Your word will almost always be good enough for her.

The Sagittarius mother is a wonderful and loving friend to her children. She is not afraid if a youngster learns some street smarts along the way. In fact, both of you Sagittarius parents may compete playfully in teaching the children all about the world from your various and combined experiences. You both will see to it that the kids get the best education and recreation money can buy.

SAGITTARIUS MAN
CAPRICORN WOMAN

If you are not a successful businessman or, at least, on your way to success, it's quite possible that a Capricorn woman will have no interest in entering your life. Generally, she is a very security-minded female. She'll see to it that she invests her time only in sure things.

Men who whittle away their time with one unsuccessful scheme or another seldom attract a Capricorn. Men who are interested in getting somewhere in life and keep their noses close to the grindstone quite often have a Capricorn woman behind them, helping them to get ahead.

Although she can be an opportunist and a social climber, she is not what you could call cruel or hard-hearted. Beneath that cool, seemingly calculating exterior, there is a warm and desirable woman. She happens to think that it is just as easy to fall in love with a rich or ambitious man as it is with a poor or lazy one. She's practical.

The Capricorn woman may be interested in rising to the top, but she'll never be aggressive about it. She'll seldom step on someone's feet or nudge competitors away with her elbows. She's quiet about her desires. She sits, waits, and watches. When an opening or opportunity does appear, she'll latch onto it.

For an on-the-move man, an ambitious Capricorn wife or lover can be quite an asset. She can probably give you some very good advice about business matters. When you invite the boss and his wife for dinner, she'll charm them both and make you look good.

The Capricorn woman is thorough in whatever she does: cooking, cleaning, making a success out of life. Capricorns are excellent hostesses as well as guests. Generally, they are very well-mannered and gracious, no matter what their backgrounds are. They seem to have a built-in sense of what is right. Crude behavior or a careless faux pas can offend them no end.

If you should marry a woman born under Capricorn, you need never worry about her going on a wild shopping spree. Capricorns are careful with every cent that comes into their hands. They understand the value of money better than most women and have no room in their lives for careless spending.

The Capricorn woman is usually very fond of family—her own, that is. With her, family ties run very deep. Don't make jokes about her relatives; she won't stand for it. You'd better check her family out before you get down on bended knee. After your marriage, you'll undoubtedly be seeing a lot of her relatives.

The Capricorn mother is very ambitious for her children. She wants them to have every advantage and to benefit from things she perhaps lacked as a child. She will train her youngsters to be polite and kind and to honor traditional codes of conduct.

SAGITTARIUS MAN
AQUARIUS WOMAN

If you find that you've fallen head over heels for a woman born under the sign of the Water Bearer, you'd better fasten your safety belt. It may take you quite a while actually to discover what this woman is like. Even then, you may have nothing to go on but a string of vague hunches.

Aquarius is like a rainbow, full of bright and shining hues. She's like no other woman you've ever known. There is something elusive about her—something delightfully mysterious. You'll most likely never be able to put your finger on it. It's nothing calculated, either. Aquarius do not believe in phony charm.

There will never be a dull moment in your life with this Water Bearer woman. She seems to radiate adventure and magic. She'll most likely be the most open-minded and tolerant woman you've ever met. She has a strong dislike for injustice and prejudice. Narrow-mindedness runs against her grain.

She is very independent by nature and quite capable of shifting for herself if necessary. She may receive many proposals of marriage from all sorts of people without ever really taking them seriously. Marriage is a very big step for her; she wants to be sure she knows what she's getting into. If she thinks that it will seriously curb her independence and love of freedom, she might return the engagement ring—if indeed she's let the romance get that far.

The line between friendship and romance is a pretty fuzzy one for an Aquarius. It's not difficult for her to remain buddy-buddy with an ex-lover. She's tolerant, remember? So, if you should see her on the arm of an old love, don't jump to any hasty conclusions.

She's not a jealous person herself and doesn't expect you to be, either. You'll find her pretty much of a free spirit most of the time. Just when you think you know her inside out, you'll discover that you don't really know her at all, though.

She's a very sympathetic and warm person. She can be helpful to people in need of assistance and advice.

She'll seldom be suspicious even if she has every right to be. If she loves a man, she'll forgive him just about anything. If he allows himself a little fling, chances are she'll just turn her head the other way. Her tolerance does have its limits, however, and her man should never press his luck.

The Aquarius mother is bighearted and seldom refuses her children anything. Her open-minded attitude is easily transmitted to her youngsters. They have every chance of growing up as respectful and tolerant individuals who feel at ease anywhere. You will appreciate the lessons of justice and equality that your Aquarius mate teaches the children.

SAGITTARIUS MAN
PISCES WOMAN

Many a man dreams of an alluring Pisces woman. You're perhaps no exception. She's soft and cuddly and very domestic. She'll let you be the brains of the family; she's contented to play a behind-the-scenes role in order to help you achieve your goals. The illusion that you are the master of the household is the kind of magic that the Pisces woman is adept at creating.

She can be very ladylike and proper. Your business associates and friends will be dazzled by her warmth and femininity. Although she's a charmer, there is a lot more to her than just a pretty exterior. There is a brain ticking away behind that soft, womanly facade. You may never become aware of it—that is, until you're married to her. It's no cause for alarm, however; she'll most likely never use it against you, only to help you and possibly set you on a more successful path.

If she feels you're botching up your married life through careless behavior or if she feels you could be earning more money than you do, she'll tell you about it. But any wife would, really. She will never try to usurp your position as head and breadwinner of the family.

No one had better dare say one uncomplimentary word about you in her presence. It's likely to cause her to break into tears. Pisces women are usually very sensitive beings. Their reaction to adversity, frustration, or anger is just a plain, good, old-fashioned cry. They can weep buckets when inclined.

She can do wonders with a house. She is very fond of dramatic and beautiful things. There will always be plenty of fresh-cut flowers around the house. She will choose charming artwork and antiques, if they are affordable. She'll see to it that the house is decorated in a dazzling yet welcoming style.

She'll have an extra special dinner prepared for you when you come home from an important business meeting. Don't dwell on the boring details of the meeting, though. But if you need that grand vision, the big idea, to seal a contract or make a conquest, your Pisces woman is sure to confide a secret that will guarantee your success. She is canny and shrewd with money, and once you are on her wavelength you can manage the intricacies on your own.

Treat her with tenderness and generosity and your relationship will be an enjoyable one. She's most likely fond of chocolates. A bunch of beautiful flowers will never fail to make her eyes light up. See to it that you never forget her birthday or your anniversary. These things are very important to her. If you let them slip your mind, you'll send her into a crying fit that could last a considerable length of time.

If you are patient and kind, you can keep a Pisces woman happy for a lifetime. She, however, is not without her faults. Her sensitivity may get on your nerves after a while. You may find her lacking in practicality and good old-fashioned stoicism. You may even feel that she uses her tears as a method of getting her own way.

The Pisces mother has, as you do, great joy and utter faith in the children. She makes a strong, self-sacrificing mother through all the phases from infancy to young adulthood. She will teach her youngsters the value of service to the community while not letting them lose their individuality.

SAGITTARIUS
LUCKY NUMBERS 2011

Lucky numbers and astrology can be linked through the movements of the Moon. Each phase of the thirteen Moon cycles vibrates with a sequence of numbers for your Sign of the Zodiac over the course of the year. Using your lucky numbers is a fun system that connects you with tradition.

New Moon	First Quarter	Full Moon	Last Quarter
Jan. 4	Jan. 12	Jan. 19	Jan. 26
2579	9402	2882	9670
Feb. 2	Feb. 11	Feb. 18	Feb. 24
6359	9074	4853	9146
March 4	March 12	March 19	March 26
8837	0172	2552	3681
April 3	April 11	April 17	April 24
1503	3947	7529	3572
May 3	May 10	May 17	May 24
5696	6142	2892	4615
June 1	June 8	June 15	June 23
5085	9931	0782	4632
July 1	July 8	July 15	July 23
0326	9745	5813	3704
July 30	August 6	August 13	August 21
4958	6634	7926	6185
August 28	Sept. 4	Sept. 12	Sept. 20
4310	0782	4610	5851
Sept. 27	Oct. 3	Oct. 11	Oct. 19
1728	9935	7269	9617
Oct. 26	Nov. 2	Nov. 10	Nov. 18
5236	6815	5039	9478
Nov. 25	Dec. 2	Dec. 10	Dec. 17
2569	2483	0637	7180
Dec. 24	Jan. 1('12)	Jan. 9 ('12)	Jan. 16 ('12)
3257	9408	3665	2357

SAGITTARIUS
YEARLY FORECAST 2011

Forecast for 2011 Concerning Business
and Financial Affairs, Job Prospects,
Travel, Health, Romance and Marriage
for Persons born with the Sun
in the Zodiacal Sign of Sagittarius.
November 22–December 21.

For those born under the influence of the Sun in the zodiacal sign of Sagittarius, ruled by Jupiter, the planet of wisdom and good fortune, 2011 will be an interesting mix of motivating challenges and idealistic motivations, bringing about a transformation of your personal value system and social perspectives. The area ruling your self-expression is especially highlighted, awakening hidden talents and potentials that could lead to a change in profession, in romance, or in leisure pursuits. You may experience the loss of someone or something that you have come to rely upon. Through a process of recovery you can develop new and more meaningful replacements, transforming your view of the world and your place within it. The negative influences that you should watch for is an easy come, easy go attitude and tendency to overindulge or to self-medicate your pain through the abuse of food, drugs, alcohol, or relationships. If you start to notice any of these tendencies creeping into your daily life, you would be wise to seek counseling and address these problems before they become ingrained.

Influences from Pluto and your ruler Jupiter put a strong emphasis on your money, your values, and your self-worth at the start of this year. You may experience a situation that threatens your security or your value system. This can have different effects depending on your individual circumstances, but is likely to prove a turning point. You may become more determined to amass money and material possessions as a gauge of your self-worth and success. Or you might go in the other direction and value those aspects of your life that money can't buy, then start to work building integrity and love in your daily life.

Your ruler Jupiter moves into Aries in January and is joined by ingenious planet Uranus in mid-March. This will give a positive charge to your self-expression through romance, art, study, travel, or friendship. This should also encourage you to explore and experiment with many different cultural, physical, or spiritual expressions of life. Adventure and risk taking will be more attractive, so there is a need for you to maintain your common sense in order to avoid mishaps.

Pluto, the great transformer, is visiting Capricorn all year and impacting your solar sector of personal finances. Regardless of your best intentions, this part of your life will undergo changes that are out of your control. Unexpected changes will not necessarily be major upheavals, but they will force you to adjust your attitude toward money and the things you value. You should manage your finances to ensure that you can survive through a drop in income. Those of you in business may experience a downturn in trade. Home repairs and improvements may incur heavy costs and clean out your savings. With Pluto in Capricorn, you might be tempted to get involved in illegal or risky businesses and eventually have to suffer the consequences.

Sagittarius individuals should practice moderation in all areas of business, investment, speculation, and credit, especially in the first half of the year. However, during February there is the chance of significant gains or rewards. Your desire to succeed and make your mark on society is sure to be strong. You also have the resilience and endurance to work hard and long to achieve your ends. There are good indications that you can achieve promotion and increased income over the course of the year. Some of you might discover that although your career path is highly respected and lucrative, it does not give you the satisfaction you crave. You want to enjoy your work and feel that your efforts are making a difference. So you might quit a highly paid job to work in an area that will give you personal rewards and satisfaction. Many Archers may consider returning to study or training in order to work in another field. Use the period between August 30 and December 25, when your ruler Jupiter is retrograde in Taurus, to review your goals and ensure that they are still relevant.

Health matters are likely to remain fairly stable all year. But during March and April you would be wise to pay extra attention to your physical and emotional life to protect yourself against infection and mental overload. Stress in the first half of the year could dish up some annoying conditions. Yoga and meditation help to ward off stress and anxiety. Physical exercise such as walking, jogging, or regular gym workouts will also aid your well-being. Put a healthy diet and physical fitness regimen in place early in the year. Then, when Jupiter moves into Taurus and your sector of health on June 4, possibly encouraging you to overindulge, you will have a healthy routine to fall back on. But Jupiter in Taurus in your sector of health usually gives your body physical strength and vitality. If your body has to heal or recover from an illness, Jupiter will assist the process. Emotions may be the stumbling block that detracts from your natural healing abilities. You might have to broaden your views and understanding of your problems. Be willing to embrace methods of natural healing that entail the spiritual aspects of life. If you seek help for a medical condition, try to avoid doing so during the Mercury retrograde periods. These are tricky times to obtain a medical diagnosis or to visit a doctor for the first time. Better wait until Mercury turns direct for an accurate diagnosis.

Electrifying planet Uranus moves into Aries, your romance sector, on March 9. Uranus will visit Aries for the next seven years, and will shake up your love life considerably. It could be a whirlwind for singles, with a new love every other week. Relationships can start amid much excitement and go out the same way. Such relationships are likely to feed off excitement and never settle down into a conventional pattern. Relationships between two people of quite different age groups are possible. And a sudden infatuation could break up an existing relationship. On-and-off relationships can keep you on your toes. Some Archers might be attracted to hotheaded, rebellious, or just plain difficult partners. The chances of falling in love with someone from another country are favored. Your ruler Jupiter is also in Aries from January 22 until June 4. During this period you will not lack love or adventure. You are more likely to be enjoying life itself and not looking for a permanent relationship.

Sagittarius couples are in for an exciting though somewhat disruptive year for romance. If you can add the taste of adventure to your love life, it will keep the excitement alive. Plan weekend trips to fun destinations. If you can't afford to travel on a whim, then put adventure into your life at home. Join other couples, learn new dance routines, play a sport together. Enjoy the passion ignited by the competitive spirit. You might go into business with a partner or work together for a humanitarian or environmental group. Find ways to stimulate the philosophical and spiritual aspects of your relationship. January, February, and late June are the best times for couples planning to wed.

Children will play a greater part in your life this year. Many couples might conceive quite unexpectedly, so be prepared if you want to avoid this. If you have children, you will not be able to take them for granted. Their development or activities will require that you pay strict attention and be very conscious of what is happening to them. They may be going through stages of growth that continually challenge you to adapt. Or they may be unusually rebellious or difficult. On the other hand, you may encounter very positive new and stimulating experiences through your children.

Creativity is starred in the first half of this year. Jupiter will imbue you with extra self-confidence to manifest your ideas and take a chance on achieving your dreams. If you work in any facet of the arts, crafts, or design fields, you will be better than usual at innovating and taking new approaches. New media and techniques will attract you to experiment with the plan and design of your work. Wild ideas could become profitable business ventures. You might return to study and push yourself to reach the goals of your childhood, regardless of a lack of money. Your quest for knowledge, understanding, and experience will spur you on. April and May will be a lucky time to set up a business, apply for finance, or sell your ideas. If you can get your venture off the ground, the second half of the year should provide the impetus to work hard, sustain your resources, and secure solid support.

Travel could play a large part in molding your future this year. Your desire to visit far-flung corners of the earth and to experience different cultures, perspectives, and experience can take you on many adventures. September to November will be a great time to set out on the adventure of a lifetime. You might head overseas to study or to further your research. You might join a group whose aim is to give aid or support to people in trouble spots around the world. You will gain valuable working experience while doing your part to bring about a better world.

Neptune, the planet of compassion and spirituality, visits Pisces, your home and family sector, from April 4 to August 4. Neptune here suggests that you might move away from your normal home life. This might signify a time spent in a foreign land or a period of pilgrimage where you leave the safety of your settled existence to seek a more meaningful one. There may be some confusion about your connections to your past, family, or home life. You will be more idealistic than usual when it comes to relationships with close loved ones. If you seek to balance your love of friendship and of adventure with periods of quiet and seclusion, you may be drawn to meditation and other spiritual methods as a means of self-understanding.

All year taskmaster Saturn moves through Libra, your sector of friends and of aspirations. You can build your social network, connect with people all over the world, and hopefully manifest your hopes and wishes. Some friends, who aren't really friends, can show their true colors. Some good friends can go out of your life. There may be problems with various groups, clubs, or organizations. Conversely, you may be elected to a leading role within such a group. You may gain promotion in a job that has you working with groups of people. Under Saturn's transit you are very likely to take on more work and responsibility.

Mercury, the planet of communication, turns retrograde three times this year: March 30 through April 22, August 3 through 26, and November 24 through December 13. These retrograde periods advise against major decision making, contract signing, purchase of transport and communication equipment, even general repairs. Such activities are subject to delays or mix-ups. However, these three-week retrograde periods are good for review, revision, and planning.

The year 2011 promises to be packed full of challenges for Sagittarius. Your understanding of the world and your part within it will grow. Adventure and refreshing changes will enable you to stretch toward your dreams in an innovative and creative fashion. You should learn much about your life, loves, and heart's desire.

SAGITTARIUS
DAILY FORECAST

January–December 2011

JANUARY

1. SATURDAY. Spirited. Happy New Year, Sagittarius! Take note of your inner desires because they will be your motivating force during the coming year. Finding the freedom to express who you are is likely to be high on your list of resolutions. You will be looking for adventure and entertainment and avoiding the mundane aspects of life. Many of you could be traveling with thoughts of home rattling around in your head. Stop and make a phone call or send an e-mail. The contact will clear your mind and set you free to enjoy the moment. A business proposition could look promising, but don't overspend on celebrations. Affection and kindness are expressed with ease. Tell someone you love them.

2. SUNDAY. Lively. All sorts of communications will keep you busy. If you're not on the phone, visitors could be knocking on your door. Sparks may fly as romantic Neptune and the dreamy Moon trigger passion in your life. Spontaneous Uranus and expansive Jupiter push you to move outside of your comfort zone. Breaking new ground can be exhilarating and challenging, broadening your knowledge and understanding of who you are at the same time. People will want to spend time with you. However, just because you are in demand doesn't mean you should have to please everyone. Go out of your way to please yourself. Indulge in the things that give you emotional satisfaction and peace.

3. MONDAY. Constructive. Your resources and the resources of others come into focus. You may be experiencing a power struggle of some sort. In any case, now is the time to put all your cards on the table. Be honest with yourself, then be honest with others. Many Archers will begin to reap the rewards of all your hard work. Whether you know it or not, you are in the prime position for success. Focus on the positives and take control. With understanding and forgiveness in your heart, miracles can happen. Be thorough and tidy up all loose ends, and you can finalize a project that has been a major cause of concern. Help can come from someone behind the scenes, and it renews your faith in the universe.

4. TUESDAY. Promising. This morning's New Moon in your Capricorn second house of personal values brings in a fresh annual cycle that will help you use financial resources more wisely. Some pressure is evident as the sensitive Moon and stern Saturn clash. If you're having money troubles, stay away from friends who urge you to spend. This is a good time to assess your budget, your values, and your priorities. If they are compatible and complementary, everything should be falling into place nicely. If not, it may be time to face reality. Surprises and upsets can bring sudden opportunities. Even a situation that looks dour will turn out in your favor. Face your fears and follow your heart's desire.

5. WEDNESDAY. Pressured. Listen to your thoughts and you may learn something about the subconscious complexes that motivate you. News from a loved one can bring peace and calm ungrounded fears. Protect your lungs today. Stay out of the cold air and start a daily practice of deep breathing. Prevention is better than cure. If you are a smoker, now is the time to call the quit line and get serious about breaking your habit. On a positive note, you could develop your singing voice with a few lessons. Surprise yourself as well as family and friends with your new talent for vocals. A community event in your neighborhood would be a great way to meet friends and to discover new interests.

6. THURSDAY. Restrictive. Your commitments could be holding you back. The feeling that your talents are being wasted or that you are not getting the recognition you deserve can upset your peace of mind and put you in a cranky mood. Ask an older, wiser member of your family or group for advice on a problem. They will give you helpful feedback toward a resolution. Your friends may have quite a lot to say, so make time for them. But don't get caught up in gossip, as it will backfire on you in the long run. Long-distance correspondence needs special attention, especially if you have loved ones overseas. There is a possibility you might have the wrong address for something important.

7. FRIDAY. Agreeable. Venus, the planet of love and harmony, now visits your sign of Sagittarius for the next three weeks, influencing your manner of self-expression. A desire to relate to others goes hand in hand with the ability to make personal compromises. Your personality is now filled with warmth, making a favorable impression wherever you go. Make good use of this phase to enjoy friendships and make new ones, take a vacation, or do whatever you enjoy. The Aquarius Moon makes contact with fuzzy Neptune in your sector of communication, so there may be some confusion over important details. Conversation is likely to get emotional, so leave important discussions for another day.

8. SATURDAY. Comfortable. This is a day when anything can happen, so go with the flow. Good things may seem to materialize from out of nowhere, but obstacles can crop up just as suddenly. Let your intuition guide you, and you will know exactly what to do. Enjoyment on the home front is your main focus. Tidy up and rearrange to maximize comfort and relaxation. Perhaps you might consider painting one of your inside walls a beautiful color to add ambience. Shopping could be a trap because extravagant Venus affects your whole demeanor and highlights your desire nature. If you are not blowing your budget on items out of your price range, you might blow your diet with rich foods.

9. SUNDAY. Demanding. An early morning call can disrupt your day off. Being a freedom-loving being, you might balk at some of the restrictions placed on you and renegotiate your plans. People love you, so you can get away with a lot. An outdoor music or art show will cheer your heart and make a great day for you and your loved ones. Your parents could be in the middle of moving or experiencing a change in lifestyle, and your help would be greatly appreciated. Go visit and surprise them. It will make their day. Childhood complexes can become apparent now. Pat yourself on the back for the positive way you respond to the present, but don't ignore your inappropriate, knee-jerk reactions.

10. MONDAY. Playful. Good feelings between you and everyone around you should make this a starred day. Set aside some time for hobbies or artistic pursuits that will allow your inner child to have fun and just play. Sagittarius parents are likely to enjoy playing with your kids. You might volunteer as a teacher's aide to become more involved in their schooling as well as develop your talents as a tutor. There is a danger that your idea of fun might not agree with someone close to you, which could instigate emotional power struggles. Be honest and face these issues head-on, and you will defuse any potentially explosive situation. Feelings of love can deepen, but be aware of possessiveness.

11. TUESDAY. Energizing. High energy is yours, Archers. You may feel strangely renewed, ready for a second round of challenges facing you lately. It seems that the stress of your personal difficulties is actually energizing you, moving you toward greater heights. A passing attraction may be irresistible. Perhaps you are simply enjoying the attention and missing the implications. Be careful if acting on a whim. The involvement that follows might not be what you are looking for. Social commitments could become a problem later in the day. Be sure that you don't overload your schedule. Make room to accommodate your innermost desires regardless of peer pressures.

12. WEDNESDAY. Eventful. Keep your mind on your work and stick to your timetable for success. Your mind is likely to wander all over the place if you let it. If you can keep the focus on one thing, brilliant ideas and inventions are likely. There is a danger of indulging and overstepping the budget, something you will regret tomorrow. People among your circle of friends may be more irritable than usual and disapprove of you. Don't take this personally. It says a lot more about how they feel about themselves. A friend might ask your advice and end up treating you like their therapist. Be very careful not to tell them what to do, as you will be the one they will blame if it fails.

13. THURSDAY. Profitable. Make sure you know exactly what you are doing today, as you may be asked to explain your motives. A personal reevaluation of the things you hold dear might surprise you. Lifestyle changes affect values, and you are likely to be experiencing a period of change at this time. Mercury, the planet of communications, is now in Capricorn in your second house of values and money, suggesting that it is time to focus on your budget and put your financial life in order. Business and commercial affairs come into the limelight, as do your spending patterns. If you have been overindulging, it may be time to start a detox diet to revive both the mind and the body.

14. FRIDAY. Manageable. Ideas and interruptions can disturb your rhythm. With the emphasis on your financial sector, it is a perfect time to concentrate on your budget. Important business negotiations can take up a lot of your time. At the end of the day you will know it has all been worthwhile. Job satisfaction will result from earnest effort, and the possibility of advancement is promising. If your work entails hours of driving, ensure that your seat is supportive. Balance your physical inactivity with an exercise regimen. The cost now will be less than future medical expenses and ill health. Anyway, being physically fit will benefit your job opportunities and make you feel fabulous.

15. SATURDAY. Empowering. Personal decisions may be weighing on your mind. Just remember that change is good, even though it may be painful. Your attitudes and behavior toward wealth—whether you are controlled by money and material assets, or whether you control them—is the essence of today's influence. You can share intimacy and understanding with your significant other. Plan an outing together to celebrate love. The Archer's social circle is likely to be expanding, including people from different walks of life. Don't refuse any invitations. Regardless of your comfort zone, you can learn something new about yourself. Singles might be surprised by love when you least expect it.

16. SUNDAY. Cautious. Mars, the planet of energy, moves into Aquarius and your third house of communication, turning up the tempo in your everyday life. Your enthusiasm for new ideas and your interest in humanitarian or environmental movements can be reignited. But do be careful not to start selling your ideas to others. Otherwise, you might end up in a situation of conflict and lose the battle completely. Playing group sports or getting active in a community effort will bring rewards for your efforts as well as personal enjoyment. Take the time to understand your own motivations in relationships, as well as your partner's, and you will be able to mend any rifts between you.

17. MONDAY. Sensitive. Pause before reacting to upsets. Reflection on the situation may show potential benefits that otherwise would be missed. Artistic and creative efforts will be rewarding. For those of you who are experiencing an emotional time, art therapy can bring peace of mind and forgiveness. You are very impressionable and could pick up on another's mood, so protect your peace of mind by avoiding negative people. Discuss joint finances with your partner before making a personal decision. Future misunderstandings and conflict will be avoided by defining each person's personal expectations with a legally binding agreement. A relationship can have karmic links. Be prepared for intimacy.

18. TUESDAY. Tricky. Your usual open and honest demeanor might have to be shelved if you want to sort through a business complication. Rather than draw your own conclusions, get a legal opinion and ensure you are following the law. Avoid all power struggles, and the opposition will simply fade away. This is a time for faith, not fear, and you will be successful. A personal problem might be the result of trying to control a situation or not letting go of your expectations. With faith, you can let go and allow the result of your efforts to come about naturally. A secret attraction to one of your associates can manifest in reality, and suddenly you lose interest.

19. WEDNESDAY. Revealing. Today's Full Moon culminates in Cancer, your solar house of sex, death, and money. Some of you might hit a financial jackpot, other Archers might discover a sexual attraction full of passion and intrigue. Luck in financial matters is significant. If you are thinking of purchasing a home of your own for the first time, now is the time to apply for the financing. If you have a family member or friend in the know, they will be able to help you also. Support in any other endeavor will give you the edge over rivals. A chance encounter could be the start of something passionate and permanent. Be spontaneous and put your trust in the universe. It knows what you want and won't let you down.

20. THURSDAY. Fun-loving. The Moon is now in Leo, your solar house of travel and adventure. Moon in Leo puts a spring in your step and love in your heart. An attraction to a foreigner could be the start of a love affair or a travel adventure. This is the perfect time to start looking at vacation specials and planning your next trip. The Sun moves into Aquarius, your solar house of communication, and boosts your interaction with friends, neighbors, relatives, business associates, and all the people you deal with every day. Focus on clear communication, which includes not only talking but also listening! A hectic pace could cause you irritation when you are expected to be in two places at once.

21. FRIDAY. Optimistic. Not one to be in a rut, you will try something new. Have lunch at an ethnic restaurant. Listen to new music groups. A change can be as good as a break, and will give you renewed interest and enthusiasm to stick to your goals. Misunderstandings or confusion about appointment times or detailed instructions may put you behind schedule, so double-check everything before you act. This is especially important with regard to legal matters. Be precise about the details. If you are unsure of a fact, ask for time to ascertain the facts. An opportunity to submit your resume to an airline or advertising company could be the start of a new direction in life.

22. SATURDAY. Interesting. Work interests and financial concerns come under the microscope. A pay increase or bonus might instigate an interest in the stock exchange. You may decide to start renovating and invest in your home. Personal satisfaction and recognition can be gained through being involved in a public event. Jupiter, your ruling planet, shifts into Aries today, bringing benefits and expansion to your solar house of fun, lovers, and children over the next four months. It is a good time to think about family planning whether you want a family or not. Artistic pursuits and fun-loving games and sports will be of more interest than usual. You may decide to go overseas for your next vacation.

23. SUNDAY. Surprising. Tension on the home front could be the result of outside activities dominating your time. Balance out your personal interests with your home life by making a few sacrifices. Remember, quality is better than quantity. Let the whole family decide on leisure and recreation pursuits. You might be surprised at some of the things that appeal to those near and dear. An interest in local politics may develop into a serious commitment after you attend a public rally in your community. Volunteering for a cause that you believe in can lead to full-time employment in an area that you never considered before. Unexpected things can happen, bringing positive outcomes.

24. MONDAY. Busy. Social activity surrounds Sagittarius today. There is plenty of opportunity to expand our network with new and interesting contacts. Extravagant tastes could lead you to blow your budget, and it would be wise to exercise restraint in this area. Make sure you have paid the monthly bills and expenses before you go on a splurge. An important social event demands that you dress the part, making you the center of attention. Single Sagittarius may meet an attractive potential lover. A sense of karma or déjà vu is a sign that you are right where you are meant to be, so relax and enjoy the ride. In fact, you can have success in love, money, and your career if you just let go.

25. TUESDAY. Meditative. Take pride in who you are and how the world sees you, Sagittarius. You aren't perfect, but no one else is. Reflect on the good you have done and the good you still can do. An issue you must confront involves your willingness to be of service to others. This may come up because it is the nature of your job, or because of your general willingness to extend your energy in the service of others. It's a good time to spend time with the parent who has influenced you most. Show your appreciation in small ways. Popularity is a double-edged sword. People who smile and show you a friendly face may secretly desire what you have. Guard against false friends and flatterers.

26. WEDNESDAY. Low-key. A somewhat laid-back day is promised. Although you will still be busy, you should find that you are left to work at your own pace. As the Moon wanes into the last quarter phase, it is an excellent time for Sagittarius gardeners to cultivate, harvest, transplant, and prune. Mowing your lawns now will retard growth also. If you are working in a team effort, you might experience some criticism. Don't get caught up trying to defend your ideas or actions. This will only fall on deaf ears and stir up your emotions. People's remarks will fade into the background as long as you don't react. Enjoy putting the finishing touches to a pet project.

27. THURSDAY. Nurturing. A quiet mood is likely to overtake you. A feeling of overload should be respected and treated accordingly. With the Moon residing in Scorpio in your twelfth house of secrets and solitude, you need to feed your soul with only the healthiest of offerings. Keep your feelings to yourself. Enjoy activities that will nurture your spirit as well as your physical well-being. An unexpected caller can liven the atmosphere later in the day, but don't let them coerce you into doing what you don't want to do. Romance is another possibility. Nurture the tender aspects. Scented oils, candles, and beautiful music moderate passion with love.

28. FRIDAY. Active. Get going early, and you can set the scene for the day. Mood swings could be the result of negative emotions coming from other people. Be selective about who you mix with and the conversations you get involved in. Confirm appointments early so you won't be stood up or arrive at the wrong time. Sagittarius salespeople may find your work harder than usual, as a multitude of complaints take up your time. Mental chaos can cause much disharmony. Time spent prioritizing and staying focused will be invaluable to the day's outcome. You are likely to be in the limelight with your social set, and may have to divide your attention to keep everybody satisfied.

29. SATURDAY. Harmonious. Socializing with a lot of people may not appeal now. Spending quality time with your significant other will bring complete satisfaction. Take advantage of the cooperative vibes to discuss the issues that are close to your heart. Show love and understanding. An artistic or playful event will be lots of fun, taking you on an adventure into an unchartered territory of emotion. Get started on a creative project, especially one that you have always dreamed of starting but never felt ready to begin. Now you can do it. All you have to do is start. A weekend away from your local area will give you new things to ponder and a change of pace from your normal routine.

30. SUNDAY. Fair. Don't get caught up wallowing in a woeful mind-set. If you let other people take advantage of you, you will resent it. This is your life, and it will be wasted if you try to please others instead of yourself. Forget the past and look after the now, and you will start to feel totally different. Write a gratitude list and remind yourself how good life is. Jupiter, your fun-loving ruling planet, could urge you on to extravagant spending. Satisfy the rebel adventurer in you with a trip into nature instead of to the mall. A large spectator event will imbue you with excitement and lift your spirits with every roar of the crowd.

31. MONDAY. Helpful. You may have many concerns disrupting your peace of mind. A supportive friend can give you their ear and advice, suggesting a simple way out. The message today is not to sit alone and worry, but to mingle and allow human interaction to lift your mood. Sagittarius students could be struggling with your comprehension of a subject. Call a fellow student and discuss your difficulties. Their explanation may give you the clarity you seek. Official responsibilities can weigh heavily. But once you step into the breach, a natural talent for leadership and for control puts you at your ease and makes a successful conclusion more likely. Don't give in to fear.

FEBRUARY

1. TUESDAY. Interactive. The tempo of your life is accelerating. A sense of restlessness may push you toward new and different experiences. Start by integrating travel into your routine instead of using it to get away from everyday life. Look at the big picture. Thinking small or getting caught up in minor details can distract you from important matters, especially during the morning hours. Put your mind to your budget and reflect on what really matters to you in your life. Then you can well decide on where your money should be spent. A secret desire to learn to paint, play the guitar, or dance should be brought out. Register for a class and let your spirit have some fun.

2. WEDNESDAY. Promising. The New Moon is in Aquarius and your third house of communication. The focus for the next month will be on siblings, friends, neighbors, correspondence, writing, electronics, and computers. Education features prominently. You might start to study a topic of interest and change the course of your life. The time is ripe for making changes within your local environment or getting involved in community affairs and events. With the added benefit of energy from Mars, you can expect a very busy month. Practice meditation with emphasis on breathing. You will be able to calm your mind and lessen the rashness of the Mars influence.

3. THURSDAY. Lively. Sparks may fly between you and a neighbor today. There may be a disagreement or some confusion, but this need not cause a rift. Focus on the positive qualities in your relationships in order to bring out the best in them. An unexpected revelation may catch you off guard, but it won't knock you off your feet. Take the advice of an older associate or friend. Benefit from their experience and understanding of your situation. Accidents are likely, so make sure you don't act impulsively. If you have any faulty electrical equipment, don't wait to get it repaired. The same goes for your computer. If you are doing important work, save it regularly.

4. FRIDAY. Stimulating. From today through March 1, Venus, planet of love and harmony, holds sway in Capricorn in your second house of values and money. This can be either good or difficult financially, depending on how you handle it. The good side stems from the power of Venus to attract material possessions and money, as well as people. Financial opportunities may come up. But difficulties may arise from your tendency to be extravagant. Venus makes your tastes more lavish than your budget can afford. Yesterday Mercury, planet of communication, moved into Aquarius in your third house of communication. Mercury here accents your intellectual abilities.

5. SATURDAY. Active. Four planes in Aquarius, your communication sector, suggest that you will be out and about today. Your family could be on your mind. It would be best to pay them a visit and catch up on the gossip. Sports activities will suit today's energies. Cheering your side on to victory will give you the benefit of expressing all your pent-up emotions in a safe environment. Cleaning up around the home might be a necessary chore. Get your visitors involved, and you will be done in half the time. Extravagance is also on the menu. A home beautification program might get a push, along with some new artwork or furnishings, and make home entertainment that much better.

6. SUNDAY. Exciting. Unexpected events can turn your plans upside down. You will enjoy the fun of spontaneous action, the new and interesting avenues of experience that open up. Impulse spending can exacerbate money worries, so leave your credit card at home. Just enjoy life's simple pleasures that money can't buy. Love is in your heart. For Sagittarius singles, there is a strong probability of romance. There is the possibility of a choice to be made. This may impinge on your freedom, so don't act rashly. Give it time. Too much talk and gossip can influence your thinking. Keep important matters to yourself for now. A group activity will provide a break from personal worries.

7. MONDAY. Creative. Your sense of adventure can bubble out into your daily routine, causing fun and joking on the job. Nothing will seem too much, so you do need to watch your workload and try not to take on more than is humanly possible. Artistic pursuits or study in metaphysical or philosophical subjects could override your other commitments, but will bring strong personal satisfaction. Dieters beware, as self-discipline could be lacking. In fact, overindulgence in romance, food, fun, and whatever else takes your fancy is highlighted. Your skills in the area of communication are strong this month. Writing, broadcasting, teaching, sales, advertising, or travel may give you the satisfaction you crave.

8. TUESDAY. Powerful. With lovely Venus and passionate Pluto together in the heavens, you can expect the focus to be on love and romance. Make a date for a candlelit dinner and nurture your loving relationship. With both Venus and Pluto in your second house of values and possessions, watch out for jealousy and possessiveness. Be slow to criticize or accuse. Then you won't have to make any apologies. You may be lucky enough to discover a hidden talent and the opportunity to direct it into a worthwhile endeavor. Group sports would be beneficial to you now. Not only would you gain from the exercise and training, but the companionship and connections will be invaluable.

9. WEDNESDAY. Fair. Get into your work and start to knock off the items on your to-do list. This is not a day for chatting. That will only hold you up and fill you full of useless gossip. A loved one may need your support. Anything you can do will help to prop up their self-confidence. If you are experiencing self-doubts of your own, get out your journal and write down your thoughts. You will be surprised how this process can clear away doubts. Maintain attention to detail on the job site, and you will be noticed for your thoroughness. This may or may not bring a pay increase, but you are likely to move up in standing and job satisfaction. Eat nutritious food for your energy needs.

10. THURSDAY. Fruitful. The First Quarter Moon in Taurus makes this a perfect time to get into the garden and plant your kitchen herbs and greens. Ban stress and anxiety from your daily life, and take up yoga or tai chi. The benefits will far outweigh the time it takes. You may feel as though you are being bombarded by the outside world, with e-mails, phone calls, and appointments. Burn some relaxing oils and remember to breathe, and your day will go more smoothly. Catch public transportation and save on parking fees and headaches caused by negotiating the traffic. Whatever you are doing, take time out to help a neighbor in need. The end result will be well worth your time.

11. FRIDAY. Sensitive. Environmental influences can play a part in your mood. Avoid negative or whiny people and give yourself a chance at peace. The subconscious is likely to hold sway over all and sundry, bringing up old prejudices and habits that can distort reality. Lunchtime meetings are in danger of being hijacked with adult beverages. Say no to the first drink, and you have the chance to seal the deal in your favor. A family reunion could cause old wounds to resurface. Reassess these hurts within your adult framework. Perhaps see a counselor before you do or say anything to family members. Partnered Sagittarius should plan an intimate evening with your lover.

12. SATURDAY. Delightful. Good communication will successfully mark this day. If you have an issue to discuss with your personal or business partner, now is the time to do so. An old friend may need your support in a marriage breakup; you can be a nonjudgmental listener. But do not give advice, or you might end up being the person that gets the blame if it doesn't work. In a sentimental frame of mind, you will enjoy rummaging through junk at market stalls. Explore the parts of town you have never visited; delight in the unexpected. Single Archers might be asked out on a blind date and be pleasantly surprised.

13. SUNDAY. Energetic. Set aside the morning to put all your loving intentions into practice. Pamper that special someone in your life. A massage followed by a home-cooked breakfast might be a lovely start to your day. Plans for the evening can run into obstacles, with too many people wanting to join in. You will have to stop trying to please everybody. Look after yourself if you want to avoid fights and problems. A family matter can intrude on your plans. If your family is making your lover feel excluded or inferior, you would be wise to simply leave rather than cause an argument that has a long-term effect. Hit the open road and get away from the usual routine.

14. MONDAY. Emotional. Strive for balance and healing no matter what the situation. You may come up against some very formidable opposition. But you can sidestep any threatening issues simply by not playing their game. Keep your mind on the big picture. Don't take other people's comments personally, and you won't have a problem. A business partnership may cause you some concern. If you feel that the balance of power between you and your partner is unfair, see a professional for advice before you attack. There may be more to the situation than meets the eye. Archers are often noted for the ability to say the wrong things, and you are in danger of succumbing today.

15. TUESDAY. Chancy. Keep your eye on your finances today. Ensure that business negotiations remain confidential and guard against gossip. Relevant facts could get confused and compromise your reputation. Communication via the Internet might not be reliable. Avoid giving out your personal information and credit card details. Doing so will eliminate the risk of fraud and theft as much as possible. Watch for computer viruses also, as they may be prevalent over the next couple of days. Conclude business dealings early. The danger of altercations, which can interfere with the finalization of agreements and contracts, is likely later in the day.

16. WEDNESDAY. Adventurous. Sagittarius creative forces are strong. Your sensitivity to innuendo offers new directions and potential. The urge to break out of your normal routine might entice you to register for a class on dance, drama, or photography. Travel is a strong possibility now. Regardless of your financial situation, you can come up with what you need to escape the doldrums of the mundane. The Sun nuzzling Neptune stimulates your awareness of other people. You might be more inclined to help your neighbors, siblings, or friends now. Be wary when it comes to making decisions. Allow yourself a good day to mull over the pros and cons, and be fair to yourself as well as others.

17. THURSDAY Diverse. Extra effort can bring better than expected rewards. A whimsical frame of mind can build castles in the sky or debate the fairness of relationship issues. But at the end of the day you will be no better off. Divert your thinking from the self to others, and your whole attitude can change. A busy schedule could cause confusion if you don't organize yourself before you set off. Plan your route for surefire success. Living or working among foreigners will be stimulating . Learning a new language to improve communication can broaden your horizons and outlook. A legal situation can challenge your sense of fair play. Stand up for your rights.

18. FRIDAY. Challenging. The Full Moon culminates in the fellow fire sign of Leo before dawn. This will set a theme of challenges throughout the day. Nothing will be usual. When it comes to balancing your professional and personal life, conflict can come into play. Think before you act. Always confer with those near and dear before making decisions that involve them. Starting a new job could be testing. Childhood complexes can be triggered through the behavior of people. Resentments, anger, fear are all emotions that are better examined in the light of your own motivations and expectations. Better let go of them rather than nurture them with constant attention.

19. SATURDAY. Empowering. Your standing in the community can get a positive lift now. A promotion could result in higher pay and better living conditions. Last night the Sun moved into Pisces, your house of home and family, and will visit Pisces until March 20. At this time of the year, psychological self-evaluation can be of enormous help in your personal growth. Memories from the past can be stronger than usual. An important family member may reappear in your life. A home renovation project to beautify and add value should be a lot of fun. Some of you might be considering the purchase of your first home along with the commitment and responsibilities this incurs.

20. SUNDAY. Demanding. With energetic Mars running into nebulous Neptune, your energy level could be at a low ebb. Worries might eat at your mind and take the edge off your fun. Guard against taking drugs to give you a lift or kill the pain. The confusion that might result will cause more pain and for longer. Social events can be uplifting. But be aware of how much you can give, then know when to stop. Choose your company carefully. This advice is especially important in matters of the heart. A very romantic and attractive stranger may not turn out to be what they say they are. So give yourself plenty of time to get to know them before allowing yourself to fall in love.

21. MONDAY. Helpful. Whether you actually get out of the house or not, your thoughts will be on others. Reach out to a friend in need. Give some support to heal a problem. A clash between the generations is likely. Take a deep breath and count to ten regardless of whether you are dealing with your children or your parents. Nebulous Neptune adds a dash of delusion to the mix, so it's important to try to understand another's point of view. Avoid making any hasty decisions or speaking out in anger. This afternoon, communicative Mercury moves into Pisces, your house of home and family.

Dinner with loved ones would be a great way to interact and sort things out.

22. TUESDAY. Variable. An opportunity to work from home would be right up your alley now. Energetic Mars joins the Sun, Mercury, and Uranus in Pisces, your sector of home and family; your focus is on this domain. Arguments might bring up issues that have long since been forgotten. But it is the general mood, not the issues, that will cause irritation. Put some positive energy into rearranging your home, imbuing it with ambience and calm. Meditation would also be a great help to you. It will allow you to let go of moods that are not appropriate at the moment. Nature will be very soothing. If you are finding it hard to cope with your job, take a long walk in fresh air.

23. WEDNESDAY. Quiet. Your home can be a haven. Take comfort under your own roof. Surround yourself with beauty by bringing fresh flowers inside. Scented candles, soft music, and fresh foods can also help you to relax. Your dreams could be trying to tell you something as the intuitive Moon moves through Scorpio, your twelfth house of subconscious matters. You may have a hard time understanding the language of your sleeping mind, so write down the details you can remember. A tendency to put your foot in your mouth by saying what you think, rather than what you want to say, could get you into trouble more than once. Pause before responding to people's moods.

24. THURSDAY. Favorable. With the Moon sailing into Sagittarius in your first house of personality, today is all about you. Enjoying a vigorous sport with friends and family or spending time at home should bring pleasure. Let the artist within have the floor. Encourage lateral thinking when it comes to problem solving. Time spent with children will be very rewarding. If Sagittarius parents have the time to help out at your child's school, you might discover an opportunity otherwise missed. Having people over for dinner might be just what the doctor ordered. Invite your favorite friends. They will enjoy your company, and you will enjoy playing host or hostess.

25. FRIDAY. Excellent. Starting a new business is favored. Clear thinking and positive vibes will make negotiations successful. Mental work is emphasized. Plans for the future can be laid intelligently and effectively. Beware of wasting time chatting with your friends or family. Although you might hear interesting gossip, you won't achieve too much. Travel is indicated. You may experience an inner restlessness that gets you outdoors exploring new avenues. A romantic liaison could become difficult to maintain due to expenses. Mixing with wealthy people can place monetary pressures on your already tight budget. There is a fine line between pleasure and pain.

26. SATURDAY. Tricky. Tension of all kinds, especially sexual, is very likely today. In fact, you may simply need sexual release. You can use this energy positively, but you may need to jog a mile or two before it is manageable. Take a few deep breaths and remind yourself to keep breathing each step of the way. This afternoon the Moon activates Capricorn, your house of personal finances, urging you to be more resourceful. Delay instant gratification and put away your credit cards for a while. You may have been blissfully overspending on pleasures. A feeling of guilt will overwhelm you if you are wasting money. Finish the evening on a love note with your significant other.

27. SUNDAY. Good. Alterations to your plans can leave you with time on your hands. Get into a creative pursuit around the home. Take the family out to the movies or an exhibition. Shopping should be avoided. There is still tension around finances, and buying on an impulse could set you back a pretty penny. Gambling won't help your bank balance. Romance is highlighted. You might meet a new love in the most unexpected places. Get together with your good friends and try partying in an unexplored part of town. The better care you take of what you have, the longer it will last you. It is important not to take anyone or anything for granted.

28. MONDAY. Comforting. With the Moon and loving Venus together in Capricorn, your house of money and values, you are likely to have warm and fuzzy feelings about yourself. Venus urges extravagant tastes. So be aware that you might be lulled into thinking you can afford a lot more than you can. Get together with family and friends for a feast of food and fun, music and dance, and all things artistic and romantic. Worries over child care costs could be on your mind. But you can still enjoy being with the kids and those you love. Sagittarius volunteering to do service overseas might have travel expenses paid by the aid organization.

MARCH

1. TUESDAY. Interesting. Communication of all sorts is starred. Financial commitments can put a strain on your sense of freedom, but won't stop you from traveling within your mind. Contact with family and friends overseas will inspire your own travel plans or get you going on a new creative endeavor. Get active in your local community now. Whether it is politics, local sports groups, or a local charity, it will broaden your horizons in more ways than one. Sagittarius parents might put some thought into your child's education. The right institution can solve a lot of adolescent problems before you get to them. It is very important to keep the channels of communication open.

2. WEDNESDAY. Friendly. Venus, the love goddess, has settled into Aquarius and your solar sector of communication, and will take up residence there until March 27. This will make your everyday surroundings and activities more pleasant and agreeable. Your social life will pick up as you get together with friends and neighbors to have fun or simply socialize and talk. You will not want to discuss serious matters, though. Venus keeps you interested in the pleasures of life. Sagittarius students should consider forming a study group with your classmates for extra help and support working on assignments. If you have a problem, seek out an older person for practical and immediate answers.

3. THURSDAY. Imaginative. Allow yourself to relax this morning. If you try to rush, you will probably only confuse issues and trip over yourself. Dreams could cascade through your memory and spark fantasies or fears, but they say more about your desires than anything else. If you do not already have a dream journal, now is a great time to begin. Then you can start exploring the glimmers of insight into your unconscious that these dreams provide. Concentrate on finishing personal projects and tasks around your home this afternoon. This afternoon the New Moon culminates in Pisces, your solar sector of home and family. Plan an evening to share fine food and affectionate moments with those near and dear.

4. FRIDAY. Revitalizing. The Pisces New Moon in your house of home and family signals a time of new beginnings. Whether you are purchasing a new house or just revamping, the time is right for a housewarming or a simple family get-together. Enjoy reminiscing about the past and toasting the future. If you feel that your partner is holding you back now, the best approach is to be honest yet kind and talk about the underlying issues. Insight and understanding can solve problems before they get out of hand. An interest in genealogy can open up a surprising episode in the family's past and give you plenty to research. Talk to your elders before it is too late.

5. SATURDAY. Emotional. The lesson this morning is not to have expectations. Take whatever comes in your stride and find enjoyment in doing so. Then your day will be marvelous. Visitors and phone calls are likely to interrupt private conversations or your need for privacy. Plans can change, putting extra pressure on you to find alternatives. If you are not careful, you might say the wrong thing or upset the wrong person. If you are feeling a little hot under the collar, remember to breathe before you speak. Get out to the countryside. Go for a drive and explore a local scenic spot. You will find the peace you desire even in a crowd. Music will be especially relaxing.

6. SUNDAY. Challenging. Difficulties can arise if you are trying to do everything your own way rather than taking advice from those who may be older and wiser. A person in your group might seem to pick on you, but your feelings could be misinterpreting their intentions. Love and romance are highly likely. Don't refuse invites from siblings or neighbors. They may be much more fun than you expect. Partnered Archers might invite your lover to do something totally different, such as visiting an amusement park or going to the races. Revive the spark by leaving your routine behind and experiencing something new. Lady Luck could be on your side, but don't invest more than you can afford.

7. MONDAY. Chaotic. There is a reasonable amount of stress in the air, so don't get hot under the collar. No matter how much preparation you put into something, changes can still take you by surprise. On a positive note, you can think laterally and come up with innovative ideas that might turn out to be better than your original ones. A change of career may not be part of your plans. But if the opportunity to branch out and turn a creative interest into a small business comes your way, take it. Don't worry about your confidence level. It will grow with the business. A casual romance or attraction could start to become serious as you hear words of love being spoken.

8. TUESDAY. Fair. A personal project can get off the ground and take up a lot of your time with the fine details. No matter what you do today, your mind is likely to be consumed with past memories or a difficult domestic situation. Going over and over the same details won't get you anywhere, though. Send it out to the universe and forget about it. Only then will a resolution become clear. An elderly parent might need your support. Take time off work if necessary to make sure they are okay. They may have something interesting to tell you, so listen attentively. Plan the vacation of your dreams now, and you are likely to find some great discounts to get you there in style.

9. WEDNESDAY. Bumpy. The planetary focus is on your home and family. Trying to balance outside interests with your family commitments is going to be difficult today. Concentrate on the things that are important. Otherwise, you could get sidetracked and let a loved one down. Trust your own intuition in decisions. Plans for a new home, renovations, or a simple rearrangement are starred. Practice caution when out in the car or using electrical equipment, as there is a risk of hasty actions that may cause an accident. Inventions and innovations are prominent. Make life a lot more enjoyable by revamping your diet and exercise regimen to put fitness and well-being first.

10. THURSDAY. Tricky. Confusion can result from denying your own intuition. You may try to please others, but in the end please nobody. Take care of yourself and everything will fall into place. Don't deny your softer, kinder side in any situation. Mercury, the planet of communication, is now in Aries in your house of romance and creativity, making this an excellent time for mental work. Your thoughts will turn toward fun and games as well as mischief. Practical jokes in the workplace are not a good idea. Speculation can be successful at this time as Jupiter, the planet of expansion, is also in Aries. Watch your gambling habits if you are inclined that way.

11. FRIDAY. Thoughtful. Good communication favors personal and business partnerships. You are now in a position to make positive new connections to further your business dealings. Don't be afraid to seek advice from a professional in problem areas. Their understanding can make difficult matters very simple. Shopping for communications and computer equipment can be cost effective. Listen to advice from neighbors and relatives for a lead on great secondhand options. Maintain healthy boundaries when it comes to helping others, lest others take you for granted. Plan a surprise romantic outing for you and your lover. The pleasure you both experience will fuel your passion.

12. SATURDAY. Significant. Uranus, the planet often called the great awakener, brings change and excitement to your solar house of fun, lovers, and children. Uranus has just moved into Aries. Uranus takes approximately seven years to move through a sign. Throughout this period you will seek new forms of self-expression and creative self-release. You might start to mix with different age groups. Relationships that begin during this period may not easily settle into a daily routine as previous relationships may have. Archers involved in a creative enterprise should find that new media and techniques will attract you. Try fresh approaches to the plan and design of your work.

13. SUNDAY. Cautious. Let go of the need to control if possible. A challenging situation between you and your partner, whether personal or professional, can test your patience. Back off and leave it alone. Any decisions or cross words may come back to hurt you down the road. Trust that the right solution will come on its own time, not yours. Joint finances may be under pressure, so watch your own spending and make sure you are not to blame. If you find the books don't balance, you might need to go back to the beginning. A mistake in the past could be the problem. Enjoy a social outing with your significant other. Don't get caught up in jealousy, either theirs or your own.

14. MONDAY. Manageable. Watch what you say, as your words might be misconstrued. Keep things simple and try not to let too many people get involved in your business. An interest in spiritual matters or the occult could lead to you taking a course in this area. You are likely to find that your intuitive powers are on the rise as a result. Don't let other people influence your ideas. Your own intuition knows what is best for you. Extra work pressures on you or your partner may be causing tension between you. Set aside some time to talk about your feelings to each other, and allay resentments and fears. If you find that you are time-poor, then work on a way to make time.

15. TUESDAY. Reassuring. If you feel let down by someone close to you, speak about it to them. It may just be a simple misunderstanding. Do not be afraid to ask for assistance if you need it. You have people around you only too happy to help you out at this time. You are likely to crave a bit of excitement to break the monotony of your daily existence, and a creative pursuit might fit the bill. Any avenue that will allow you to let your inner child out to play will lighten your mood and put pleasure in your heart. Get out and mingle with people your own age. There is promise of fun. Don't joke with the boss, who will not stand for tomfoolery.

16. WEDNESDAY. Opportune. Legal matters may seem to get out of hand. If you let go and trust the process, you will be surprised. Even if your bill is larger than expected, it won't break your bank. Think about taking a trip with your kids. Time spent together will allow you to talk without pressure, and the real problems may become apparent while discussing something completely differ-ent. Developing a relaxed and trusting relationship is paramount. You may be purusing available courses of study in an attempt to find a career that gives you more personal freedom and scope for your creativity. Visit various institutions for inspiration as well as information.

17. THURSDAY. Good. Accept an unexpected chance to move into the limelight. With your own unique flair you can achieve whatever you set your mind on. A change of profession or a relocation could be just what you are looking for. Be bold and send your resume out for job vacancies you normally wouldn't feel qualified for. One of those prospective employers might think differently. You might be inclined toward an extravagant lifestyle over the next couple of months while Jupiter is visiting Aries in your house of fun and so-cializing. Too much party food and drink can add the pounds before you notice. Cut out fats and junk food, then see the difference.

18. FRIDAY. Productive. Concentrate on the things that matter and don't let anybody sidetrack you from your goals. Work alone if possible and you can achieve the results you seek. Some of you might be in line for a promotion with a comfortable package to go along with it. Travel plans can go awry. Rather than stressing over it, relax. The time is just not right. Once plans fall into place, they might coincide with a fantastic bargain on a flight or accommoda-tions. If you are planning a family event, make sure you find all the relatives who have drifted away over the years. This will add inter-est and depth to the gathering. You may uncover a family secret at the same time.

19. SATURDAY. Auspicious. The Full Moon in Virgo connects your career matters with home and family, bringing changes to one or both of these areas. A sudden job opportunity, or some form of assistance with regard to career, home, or property matters, could be part of the picture. This can also produce an event that requires you to take charge and show your responsible side. Emotions run hot, warning of public displays that will affect your reputation. The rule to follow is to stop your first impulse with a pause. Then you can consider an appropriate reply to any accusation. It's a perfect night for dining out. Reserve a table for two, and enjoy the light of the silvery moon.

20. SUNDAY. Promising. As the Moon meets Saturn in Libra, it is necessary to be honest with your friends and family. You may be nominated for a responsible position on a committee of your

social club. Don't hesitate to accept, although it may seem daunt-
ing at first. Your self-confidence will grow with your competency as
you learn the ropes. This type of position is always a plus on your
resume. The Sun moves into Aries, your house of romance and creativity, promising a social and fun-loving get-together. If you are at
home alone, get an entertaining movie or book to keep you company because you won't want to be bored. A local concert or play
might be fun.

21. MONDAY. Variable. Romance, marriage, or any cooperative
venture involving a foreign country or someone of another culture
or race is foreseen. Issues connected with a second marriage or a
court decision might also arise. Discordant energies might build
between your house of friendship and your house of values. You
might want to guard yourself in personal relationships. Be generous when you can, but avoid being taken advantage of. If you are
having friends over, lock up jewelry to thwart the nosy. Retire early
tonight if possible, and be prepared for a few dreams.

22. TUESDAY. Misleading. Take off your rose-colored glasses and
accept that you are just human. You could be aiming too high and
putting yourself through hoops trying to achieve the unachievable.
The funny part is that you are the only one who notices, because
everyone else is too worried about their own imperfections to see
yours. Teenage children may have to be reminded of the tasks to
be done before they expect to go out socializing. Although it might
seem easier for you to do the tasks, it will not help them to be effective adults when it is their turn to take over. Your energy level could
be a bit low, so pamper yourself to recharge the batteries.

23. WEDNESDAY. Revealing. Rather than lie in bed tossing and
turning, get up and enjoy a project or hobby. Writing a journal
could be informative, giving you a chance to look back at thoughts
and feelings and get to know yourself a little better. Besides, if you
are struggling with indecision, this is a great way to discover what
it is you really want, which helps you to decide. You might take
up a new interest such as learning a musical instrument or pottery,
and enjoy the time alone practicing your techniques. This can be
another form of meditation that helps you to relax and understand
life's situations. Whatever you do, be kind to yourself.

24. THURSDAY. Dynamic. Today and tomorrow, the Moon visits your own sign of Sagittarius, which will boost your energy and
enthusiasm for life. The emphasis on fire signs suggests plenty of
action and creativity, and you are sure to find yourself center stage.

Take extra care with your attire before you venture out to ensure you will be noticed. Perhaps it is a good time to get your hair restyled, update your wardrobe, or simply lavish some love and attention upon yourself. People around you could seem a little moody. It might be wise to let emotional remarks or a backlash simply fade into nothingness while you maintain your composure. You will pick up vibes, so surround yourself with positive ones!

25. FRIDAY. Eventful. Good communication skills are highlighted. Get your correspondence and phone calls out of the way early. If you have an issue with a member of your family, a close friend, or neighbor, don't delay. Make sure you straighten out the misunderstanding. You are likely to be busy. If you run your own business, be prepared for customers. Satisfied or not, you will have your work cut out for you. It might be a good idea to work out a set response for each type of scenario to ensure you have the best response ready. A lover from the past could resurface, bringing back painful memories. Don't dwell on these thoughts. Instead, replace them with love for yourself and start healing.

26. SATURDAY. Intense. Suppressed emotions can resurface. The combination of the emotional Moon and hostile planetary energies can make you a good imitation of an erupting volcano. This can be a fine thing in the end, of course, as building pressure must be released. However, it may be best to spend time alone so that you can sort out your feelings without hurting anyone. It may not be you but the person next to you who experiences this emotion. It would be better not to interfere. Curb your urge to splurge. Unconscious desires can overtake your common sense completely if you are not careful. On a positive note, romance is bound to be hot.

27. SUNDAY. Mixed. Lack of tact and diplomacy could get you into trouble with those you love. Think before you speak and avoid the embarrassment. Likewise, watch your spending habits and avoid gambling. Some of you have been enjoying remarkably good fortune, but that doesn't mean you do not have to plan for the future. Take the time to organize and budget your finances. If you are resourceful, you can enjoy the good life and save for a rainy day at the same time. Venus, the planet of love and money, moves into Pisces, your house of home and family. Venus here highlights a desire for beauty in your living quarters and harmony among your loved ones.

28. MONDAY. Demanding. Circumstances may force you to change old patterns of behavior. Health problems can force a change in diet and limit such things as coffee, cigarettes, or alcohol, which will affect where you go and who you mix with. It only takes a few weeks to bring about a change like this. You just have to be committed. Someone in authority could push your buttons. If they are being abusive, the best response is to walk away and report their behavior to superiors. If they are making you accountable for your behavior, then you might consider this a fortunate situation and value the insight into your usually unconscious behavior. Mechanical problems with a car may arise.

29. TUESDAY. Difficult. Be aware that your words carry a lot of weight, especially in the workplace. You may have to deal with an evasive or unreliable coworker or employee at this time. Deception is in the air, so be on guard. Fall back on your good friends, especially those who are older and wiser. They will be able to help you to understand your role in any difficult situation and advise an effective response. Disputes on the home front could make your life unpleasant. If you are living in shared accommodations, it might be worth looking around for somewhere new. If you are among those near and dear, call a family meeting so that everyone can air grievances.

30. WEDNESDAY. Sensitive. Mercury goes retrograde today in Aries. And the Sun and Uranus are in Aries. This collection of celestial influences in Aries heavily impacts your sector of romance and creativity. You may long to have a permanent relationship, to start a family or add to it, or develop the artist within. Archers already in a relationship might desire more commitment, such as marriage or a deeper communion between you and your lover. Mixed messages can make for a confusing afternoon. Be careful to check all correspondence, orders, or business negotiations to ensure they are correct in all aspects. Don't believe all you hear. Double-check authenticity.

31. THURSDAY. Fruitful. Make changes on the home front to maximize comfort and ambience. Sometimes, rearranging the furnishings brings better relaxation and harmony to the whole mood of the family. Bring in some cut flowers and burn some essential oils to add to the atmosphere. Take time with those you love. Regardless of your hectic routine, you will find that you can manage to put aside at least half an hour to help a child with homework, cook a nourishing meal, or simply have a meaningful conversation with a loved one. You might be interested in antiques or genealogy, then start researching on your computer. Balance any obsessions with practicalities, and you are sure to enjoy your day.

APRIL

1. FRIDAY. Variable. Jobs around the home can hold you up. Instead of sticking to your schedule, you could waste hours chatting on the phone, grooming the dog, or watching the morning shows on TV. It is important to be quite conscious of what you are doing today. Otherwise, you may behave in a petty or irritable way that no one around you will understand or know how to deal with. Mercury, the planet that rules communication and commuting, is in reverse motion in the heavens now. You can expect all aspects of communication to suffer misunderstandings and delays until April 23, when Mercury starts to go direct. Contracts, business negotiations, and travel arrangements will also have problems.

2. SATURDAY. Spirited. A host of planets in Aries in your fifth house of fun, lovers, and children is joined by Mars, the planet of action. This strong influence should give freedom-loving Archers an extra incentive to develop your creative side as well as to be the life of the party. Your need for self-expression is strong. Any activities that are a bit different might seem like fun. But impulsive actions could get you into trouble. So pace yourself and know what it is you want. If you find that you can't get going with your plans, concentrate on finishing odd jobs and tidying up around your work space and living environment. You will appreciate this when unexpected visitors call.

3. SUNDAY. Sparkling. The New Moon is in Aries, making this the best time in the year to begin creative projects. Your wit is sharp, coupled with an eye for form and beauty. Romance will be a high priority this month. Mixing business with pleasure should bring positive long-term results, especially if you are building a network of retail and commercial contacts. A lifetime dream moves closer to reality. Taking a journey, beginning a new venture, or purchasing your own home is likely. A group commitment may become more of a nuisance than an enjoyment. If you find yourself doing things just to keep the peace, try doing things that make you happy and gregarious.

4. MONDAY. Challenging. If you have children, they may seem to be harder to handle than usual. Don't fuss or fret too much, because this will pass. The best results will come from allowing kids some independence rather than trying to suppress their self-expression. Find projects or entertainment that will keep you busy and use this excess energy in a positive way. Do be careful of rash or impulsive actions, as there is a very real danger of accidents at the moment. Speculation or an investment might be a winner. If you are considering the purchase of an investment property, now is the perfect time to start looking. Watch your health also, especially if you suffer from high blood pressure.

5. TUESDAY. Confusing. Neptune is the god of the oceans and rules the subconscious, eroding our boundaries and opening up our channels to the spiritual realm. Neptune has just moved into Pisces in your fourth house of home and family, bringing quite noticeable changes to your inner self over this fourteen-year period. You may become attracted to spiritual and occult subjects as a result of your own experiences. You will become idealistic about what your home should be like. That may bring disillusionment as you realize the difference between fact and fantasy. A parent may not be well and may need to be hospitalized. You can help by ensuring they get the best of care and respecting their wishes.

6. WEDNESDAY. Favorable. This is the perfect time to start a physical workout or exercise from jogging or bicycling. Make it part of your daily routine. If you are having difficulties with finances, you can work out a budget plan now that will give you the results you need. Focus on the small details rather than worrying about the big picture. Then you will find that all of the pieces fall into place without too much effort. Travel plans can be finalized also. You might like to check out homeopathics as a healthy alternative to fortify your system against germs. Romantic problems can be cleared away with the help of counseling so that you and a partner understand each other's value systems.

7. THURSDAY. Cooperative. Artistic Archers should focus on getting your creations out into the marketplace. Approach gallery owners about an exhibition, send your manuscript to a publisher, or apply for an audition. You will never know how good you are until you take a chance. A legal matter may reach an agreeable compromise and allay fears of court costs. Venus in Pisces in your house of home and family, combined with the Gemini Moon in your house of partnerships, can help create relationship harmony for you today. You can have a wonderful evening just hanging out at home with your closest companions. There is no need to search for anything that you can't find under your own roof.

8. FRIDAY. Lively. Social commitments can conflict with domestic matters. Leave your problems at home, knowing they won't run away, and enjoy connecting with personal and professional associates. A friend might be experiencing difficulties in their relationship and need your support. Don't hesitate to do what you can within reason, as you are sure to be a big help. A promotion to a leadership position would suit you well and give you the opportunity to develop your hidden potential. Don't be shy, accept graciously, and act spontaneously. A platonic relationship might transform into a loving commitment. Don't worry about what your friends will say. They probably saw it coming.

9. SATURDAY. Thoughtful. If you have something to say to someone and don't know how to go about it, write them a letter or send an e-mail. By writing out your intentions or feelings, you can make sure you say what it is you want to say without any interference or confusion. Plan to spend time with your loved one and enjoy intimacy and communication on a level never experienced before. Young lovers deciding to tie the knot might go shopping for engagement rings or start planning a celebration. Make sure your parents are the first to know in order to avoid upset feelings. Sagittarius psychic talents may emerge, giving you impressions or dreams that are worth your introspection.

10. SUNDAY. Bumpy. Tension over conflicting values can cause jealousy and power struggles. Consider your motivations in all your dealings and ensure that you are being honest. If there are any discrepancies, your conscience will be clear. A carefree approach to finances could put you into debt and cause future problems. Partnered Sagittarius might argue over joint resources. Instead of arguing, look first at what each of you expects and then find some common ground on which to base cooperation. A family reunion or get-together may bring underlying resentments to the fore. Perhaps you could all agree on an older relative who would play the part of mediator in order to air grievances.

11. MONDAY. Difficult. Be prepared for a few power struggles throughout the day. Be shrewd but honest, and don't believe all that you are told. This is especially important in all business or financial matters. If you are thinking of signing on the dotted line, make sure you have a professional check the legalities of the contract first. Your appetite for passion may increase. Try to keep your desires under control so that you don't regret anything in the morning. Play it safe. Stay away from dangerous people and places, and avoid temptation. A shopping spree or eating binge may threaten to get out of hand. Step back and ask yourself whether you really need something or are truly hungry.

12. TUESDAY. Manageable. The stresses of yesterday can give way to peace and understanding. If you find yourself going over and over the same incident or situation, you would be wise to change your thoughts. Pick up the phone, or get out into the great outdoors for a change of pace. Students might decide to alter your study plan and follow your heart rather than tradition. Studying the subjects that inspire and occupy your interest ensures that you end up with a rewarding career. Don't get too caught up in the pros and cons of any planned actions. If you let your mind beat up on you, then you won't get anything done. See a lawyer for advice on any legal matters that you are unsure of.

13. WEDNESDAY. Surprising. There is a positive influence of karmic energy in the ether. A good deed from the past can pay returns in the now. Watch out for any situation that exaggerates your personal pride and encourages you to make harsh judgments of others, or you might have to back down. Your creative energy is at a peak and will be best utilized finishing personal projects or preparing to showcase your talents. Don't be shy about letting your creations out in the light of day. The job of the critic is really to show you where you can improve. Sagittarius parents may be helping a child prepare for a performance or exam. The lesson for you is to allow them to make their own mistakes.

14. THURSDAY. Motivating. Check out your job opportunities. There is a possibility that you can earn a higher income and solve some financial problems. Be as clear as you can in all forms of communication, even when you are engaged in self-speak. Represent yourself to your superiors rather than let someone else misrepresent you. You need to find a healthy balance between work and home and to eliminate as much stress as possible for your health's sake. Working mothers could suffer from guilt over the lack of quality time you get to spend with your children. Instead of worrying, do something about it. You have to work to pay the bills. But when you are not working, plan fun outings.

15. FRIDAY. Opportune. Your personal power is on the up and up. Expect positive results in all your endeavors, and you won't be disappointed. A run-in with a female superior could give you food for thought. But rather than look at her faults, see where you have played a part in the situation. A friend or associate may give you some advice you might want to think about first. What suits another might not suit you. Be your own boss as much as possible, and you won't make mistakes. An opportunity for self-development may come through a friend. Even if you feel you have no spare time to follow up, do so anyway. You will find the time when you need it. A new romance could surprise lonely Archers.

16. SATURDAY. Unpredictable. Unexpected cancellations and alterations could disappoint the fun-loving Archer. Involvement in group activities might not bring you the friendship you had hoped for, but it will keep you busy and offer a chance to develop valuable skills. A friend in need may bring you down with their depressed mood. Rather than allowing them to go on and on about their problems, change the subject and take them outside for a different view on life. It will do you good, too. An interest in politics might inspire you to join a local political party and start work on the campaign trail, which will open up a whole new world for you to explore. Go out for fun tonight.

17. SUNDAY. Supportive. Love and romance are distinct possibilities. The Full Moon in Libra will make the perfect backdrop for a proposal. Archers with children should keep a close eye on them as they are more likely to need your attention now. As much as you would like to play, it seems you have been assigned the role of mature adult today. Plan creative entertainment that allows you to relax. The theater, a concert, or cultural event or exhibition may please. Adventurous Sagittarius will not be happy to laze around. Perhaps a trip away could be taking shape in your mind. See your travel agent and start the ball rolling. A lovers' quarrel will be short-lived, so don't do anything drastic.

18. MONDAY. Slow. The moody Moon slips into Scorpio in your twelfth house of the unconscious, suggesting it is time to take it easy and concentrate on your own needs. Problems may come at you from all angles. But rather than get yourself all worked up, put them aside and allow the answers to come in their own time. Have no fear, they will. Students should take the day off to catch up on assignments and study. If you have accumulated sick leave or vacation days, take the day off and treat yourself to a massage or simply lose yourself in a good book. Travel in the mind is often as good as physical travel, and a lot cheaper and less stressful. Be careful in conversation not to let out a secret.

19. TUESDAY. Rejuvenating. Good friends and confidantes contribute to your enjoyment. You may feel that you are lacking direction. Just by listening to the topics of discussion, you can get some interesting ideas. You should have the ability to motivate those around you also, and may get the opportunity to do some teaching. If you are already in the teaching profession, the desire to travel can coincide with job opportunities in countries of interest. A secret love affair might titillate your ego. But if you find that you have to deny important aspects of your life to maintain this secret, it may not be good for you. Talk to your lover about the prospects of being honest about your love.

20. WEDNESDAY. Enjoyable. It may seem as if everyone wants a piece of you. If there is not enough to go around, you might have to start thinking about putting some personal boundaries in place. Sagittarius creative urges are strongly enhanced. If you have been planning to beautify your home, today is the day to do it. A love affair that has been more about fun and good times could start to achieve a level of commitment, prompting a serious analysis of your feelings. The Sun moves into Taurus in your sixth house of health and work, prompting a much more practical approach to your daily routine and affairs. Take care of your throat and kidneys today. Drink plenty of water.

21. THURSDAY. Upbeat. Your natural love of life will pick up everybody who comes into contact with you. Don't be surprised if you receive more than one invitation to interesting social events. Do be careful not to gamble today. There is some luck around you. But it may simply encourage you to overextend yourself, and then it might desert you. Hard work and challenging situations are likely within your work environment. Rather than experiencing stress and fatigue, you are more likely to gain a deep personal satisfaction. The boss might notice your natural ability also and put you down for a pay raise. With Venus now in Aries in your house of romance and creativity, love isn't far away.

22. FRIDAY. Tense. Sudden fluctuations in your bank balance might be a cause for concern. Rather than beat yourself up over frivolous spending, work out a budget to get you back in the black from now on. You are likely to be easily led at the moment. Anything that adds interest or excitement might entice you to break your routine or budget. Instead, plan fun among your work and commitments to balance out your day and alleviate the danger of breaking your budget. Problems of boredom might arise in your relationship also. This can be easily remedied by doing something different together. Do not fall into a pattern of recriminations or resentments, or the situation could become explosive.

23. SATURDAY. Productive. This is an excellent day to roll up your sleeves and take care of the boring and menial tasks that have been left on the back burner. By sorting through your paperwork, taking care of your to-do list, and clearing out the bygone and ir-relevant clutter, you will experience a wonderful sense of freedom. Mercury, the ruler of communication, is now moving forward in Aries, your sector of creativity and romance. So stalled plans for fun and personal enjoyment can be reignited. An attraction to someone who seemed aloof and out of your league may surprisingly be recip-rocated. Don't hinder your progress with negative projections. Start manifesting your desires.

24. SUNDAY. Fair. No matter what happens today, you may feel you have missed out on something better. A lack of funds could hold you back from joining in on a fun outing. You might not be feeling one hundred percent. The day will be far more construc-tive if you concentrate on sorting out your program for the com-ing week. Make sure you have plenty of snacks available, though, because unexpected guests are bound to drop by. If you live near the beach or a scenic spot, get out in the fresh air and enjoy nature and the gentle exercise of walking. You'll be surprised at the ideas that come to you, giving inspiration and a sense of adventure to your plans.

25. MONDAY. Smooth. Although the pace gets hectic, with the phone running hot and more jobs than the time in the day allows, an inner peace can prevail. Find a comfortable pace for yourself and refuse to be overwhelmed. If you need to, let the answering machine pick up calls. Delegate minor tasks and responsibilities to others. The role of teacher could be thrust upon you with new em-ployees, awakening a talent that you never knew you had. Some of you might start teaching a creative skill and find yourself earning money doing the things you like. Follow your dreams. Don't be too shy to try something you have yearned to do since you were a child. You may be a natural.

26. TUESDAY. Stressful. Don't be too quick to jump into litigation. The costs may far outweigh the benefits. You should watch that your mind doesn't move so fast that you end up doing things you don't know you've thought of yet. A health problem might get sorted out simply by studying up on the causes and applying natural products along with the healing effects of positive thought. If you suffer from undue worries or even heartache, a class in meditation will do won-ders for your health and peace of mind. A prudent investment is likely to pay off. If you are considering becoming involved in the stock market, call a friend in the know. They might have some ex-cellent information for you.

27. WEDNESDAY. Auspicious. Unusual dreams may hold the key to problems you've been having lately. Share them with someone who is objective. Time spent resting at home is well spent today, but don't be surprised if frequent disruptions keep you from relaxing completely. The urge to travel is strong, and you should start to check out the destinations your income will allow. Search the Internet and read up on these countries in the blogs of travelers. You are likely to find a route that suits both your wallet and your desires. A job opportunity in the arts could give you the adventure you crave. Or you might start a journal and plan an e-book to make some extra cash. Nothing is impossible now.

28. THURSDAY. Erratic. Stop running around trying to please everybody. You are just twisting yourself up like a pretzel and not achieving anything positive. Sit down with your family and be prepared to hash out concerns and worries that are causing conflict. Even if you can't find an answer this time, you will start to understand your options and everyone will feel included. If you live in an extended family situation, start plans to reorganize the living space to allow for privacy for each individual. Home renovations could get under way. With the strong planetary emphasis on your creative sector, you won't do anything halfway, so budget well.

29. FRIDAY. Intense. Self-confidence and high energy levels may give you a devil-may-care attitude as you approach life with gusto, regardless of the consequences. Lady Luck is on your side, but there is only so much bad planning that she can save you from. Watch the tendency to preach about your beliefs. What you see as giving advice might sound like a lecture to your listeners. Seek balance in your life as the Aries Moon triggers disruptive Uranus. If you don't take good care of yourself, you are likely to fall ill. Be sure to get plenty of vitamins and the proper amount of sleep. Avoid alcoholic beverages. Accidents are likely to happen, so slow down and take precautions.

30. SATURDAY. Eventful. Good vibes give this day a positive charge. A flurry of invitations to different occasions could make decision making very hard. Whatever you do is bound to be fun. Some of you are likely to be on the road, enjoying new places and meeting new people. Be prepared for sudden urges that will take you on a totally different route from the one planned. A sports event would be a great outing for your group, with the opportunity to let out your frustrations to the roar of the crowd. In fact, if you are having an argument with a friend and neither of you can give in, go bowling and let the winner take all. Love will nicely complete this upbeat day.

MAY

1. SUNDAY. Carefree. The high intensity of planets in Aries in your fifth house of romance, creativity, and children is excellent for any kind of physical activity today. Your energy level is high, but you do need to watch out for overconfidence leading to risk taking. Sagittarius parents should plan a day of fun and play with your kids. Visit a theme park, go exploring your neighborhood. Actors and artists will be in your element. If you are shy about expressing your natural talents, take in an art gallery, the theater, or a cultural exhibit and revel in the creativity of others. Love is also on the menu. Singles should get out and mingle. Couples should take the time to express their love verbally.

2. MONDAY. Constructive. The New Moon is in the practical and financial sign of Taurus, highlighting your sector of health and work. Prospects for earning extra cash or getting a pay increase look very good. A new business venture can take off now. Your ability to concentrate on the daily tasks and to take care of the small details is enhanced. Wholesome eating habits can be introduced if you are concerned about your weight or your health. Extra supplements available from your local health foods store are a cheap and effective form of treatment. Romantic conflicts can be avoided with a straightforward and honest approach. Just remember to be tactful.

3. TUESDAY. Positive. A little fussy about the practicalities of daily life, you won't let others string you along or mess up your plans. Make the most of this assertive mood to broach a sensitive subject with a loved one. Progress can be made in all matters of the heart. The New Moon in Taurus is in your sixth house of health and work, highlighting any health problems that have been slowing your enthusiasm or causing discomfort. See your local naturopath for some dietary guidelines and natural remedies. Take charge of your well-being in order to avoid future pain and financial expense. This is the perfect time to start new projects. Stop putting off the inevitable and start getting active.

4. WEDNESDAY. Confusing. Mixed messages are bound to make life difficult today. If someone else isn't holding you up, it might be your own indecision. Your sense of personal security may be under threat. But instead of falling prey to unfounded fears about the future, concentrate on the present and the things you can rely on. Write a gratitude list and change your focus toward the positive. Surprise your lover with plans for a romantic evening. Celebrate being alive and in love. Business partners might want to make changes to the structure of your joint venture. Before you object, take a look at their proposal. It might be far better than what you expect, with benefits for both of you.

5. THURSDAY. Spontaneous. Fun and creativity are starred. Your mood is likely to be punctuated with episodes of mirth and amusement. Romance can overtake you in the most unlikely places, opening you up to some unique possibilities. You do need to practice some restraint, though. Today's abundance of fire signs suggests the chance of leaping before you look. A lovers' quarrel can escalate into an out-and-out war, as tempers run hot with impetuosity. The creative influences are perfect for artists and writers. If you have accumulated sick days or vacation leave, it's a great day to take off work to express your creativity or simply have fun.

6. FRIDAY. Tricky. This is one of those days when the heavens seem to have their own plans regardless of what you are thinking or feeling. Take advantage of the romantic edge to let your lover know you care. Plan a surprise for the evening, something you know they will appreciate, and enjoy watching their delight. With the Moon moving in harmonious aspect to psychic Neptune, you should trust your instincts when dealing with others. Sagittarius businesspeople will have a nose for a good deal and be able to hustle a bargain in any negotiations. The catch is to do your homework and know the ins and outs of the deal, rather than go with the good vibes, or else you might fall prey to a con artist.

7. SATURDAY. Intense. Try not to involve others in a lovers' quarrel as their interference could make the situation worse. Although you might look for help to understand your motives and your partner's, the best advice you can get is from your own heart and a co-operative attitude toward your mate. It always takes two to tango. If there is a difficulty with your intimacy and understanding, seek counsel from a professional who you can trust to be impartial. Watch the urge to splurge. You may be trying to fill an emotional hole with physical things that will not make any difference to anything except your bank balance. Plan to have fun and let your inner child play.

8. SUNDAY. Varied. This looks to be a fun day for enjoying your loved ones and odd jobs around the home. Creativity is highlighted, as is romance and entertaining. Ask family and friends over for social bonding. A home beautification project will inspire you to stretch your capabilities. You could end up taking on a major restoration job and recycle some of your old junk into artistic and useful things. A new romance can go through a bumpy phase. If you are finding trouble communicating, or even getting in touch with your true feelings, it is better to leave it alone until you are clear. Otherwise, you can confuse matters more and create the problems that you are trying to avoid.

9. MONDAY. Exciting. Unexpected events can bring good luck and change a normally boring day into something special. A vacation could be in the pipeline and travel plans are being made. Sagittarius students might be off overseas on a scholarship or exchange program, or simply to learn the language. If you are stuck in a dead-end job and yearn for broad horizons, you could be tempted to book your passage and make your own luck. Chances are you will find a niche where your skills are appreciated. Keep in touch with your parents. There may be some issues that you can help them with. Reassurance may be all they need, especially if they worry about you and you are away a lot.

10. TUESDAY. Testing. The first half of the day may be exceptionally busy as the powers that be expect certain deadlines to be met. Find something fresh and interesting to break up the routine. The purchase of a big-ticket item could be busting the budget. If you are thinking of going to a loan shark, think twice. Try the auctions on the Internet, and you might find what you are looking for at half the price. Think about what you are buying, too. Do you really need it? Or are you simply trying to keep up with the Joneses? Today's aspects suggest a need for a change of plan. If you are honest with yourself, you may agree. Don't put off until tomorrow what you can do today.

11. WEDNESDAY. Busy. You'll need to be more focused as the Virgo Moon activates your tenth house of career and status. Try to keep your eyes on the prize. Get everything in order so that you will look good while the rest of the world is stuck in low gear. With Mars now in Taurus in your sixth house of work and health, you'll need to be as organized as possible. This is a perfect time to start an exercise program that strengthens your inner core and improves your health overall. With Mars in this house, you will enjoy getting physical. A strenuous workout will be best as long as it is compatible with any physical ailments you may have. Employ a personal trainer for the perfect option.

12. THURSDAY. Pressured. Go with the flow and conserve your energy as much as possible. Otherwise, nervous tension may threaten to give you a migraine or indigestion. You could feel like you're being pulled in several different directions at once, making it difficult for you to remain balanced. Listen to your heart rather than the opinions of others. If you feel you are unable to be objective about a certain situation, give yourself time to step back and think about it more carefully. You may have to deal with a friend, partner, or family member who's in need of attention, but it's nothing a little love won't cure. Make your family your top priority, and you will find that good things follow.

13. FRIDAY. Cautious. There is a need to be careful and ascertain that the information you have is based on fact. If someone is telling you a suspicious-sounding story, then you might end up looking foolish. Making decisions could be harder than usual. You are likely to put off the important stuff while you get sidetracked by the TV or computer games, so be mindful. Keep your eyes and ears open at meetings and social gatherings. You could make a valuable connection in the business world now. A strong attraction might be the beginning of a significant romance for single Archers, but beware of repeating the past. Childhood complexes can be outgrown if you practice conscious awareness.

14. SATURDAY. Social. This is a nice day to have lunch with a friend or coworker, so take the initiative. The emphasis is on teamwork, so do what you can to foster good relations. Although a light and friendly mood lifts your spirit for most of the day, finances may fluctuate to an alarming degree. Keep your wits about you. Nothing can go wrong if you pay attention to the details and don't allow your mind to wander. You may feel like pursuing a newcomer to the scene. The Moon and Saturn both in Libra create sparks, so don't go overboard. Intense, passionate types are likely to get your attention. Light flirting could be taken more seriously than you intend.

15. SUNDAY. Variable. Get up early and get your chores done. Plan a morning game of golf, or whatever sport turns you on. If socializing is more your scene, organize a champagne breakfast somewhere gorgeous and enjoy relaxing with close friends and family. Children should be a lot of fun. Sagittarius parents might consider starting a new sport or pastime that you can do together and that will bring you closer and foster friendship. At noon the Moon moves into Scorpio, your twelfth house of secrets and solitude. The next two days are perfect for recharging your spiritual batteries.

Pamper yourself with your favorite foods and perhaps a long hot bath with aromatic oils.

16. MONDAY. Fair. If you can take this day off and concentrate on what is important to you personally, you will benefit immensely physically, mentally, and spiritually. Adventurous Archers might enjoy a class in meditation and learn to travel in the mind while relieving built-up stress and anxiety. Some of you may book a vacation to get away from it all. Communicative Mercury and luscious Venus move in tandem into Taurus in your sixth house of work and health, suggesting that you are inclined to rich foods and overindulgence in more ways than one. On the other hand, you might be so engrossed in becoming the body beautiful that you will be a sucker for slick advertising.

17. TUESDAY. Motivating. Spend the morning tieing up any loose ends and finalizing business negotiations. The Full Moon in Scorpio highlights your twelfth house of secrets. So you need to be careful that you are being totally honest with yourself in whatever transactions you engage in. You also should be sure to run any contracts or agreements past a professional to protect yourself from fraud. A loved one may not be well, and your care and attention will aid in their recovery. You might even check out natural therapies to speed their recovery. The Moon will move into your sign of Sagittarius at noon, putting you in the spotlight. Don't be surprised if you receive an invitation to a gala event.

18. WEDNESDAY. Fortunate. You're ready to face the world again, so welcome fresh challenges and new faces. You are especially charming and magnetic today, so don't hesitate to ask for what you want. An intense encounter with someone will have an impression on you for better or for worse. But your generous personality will ensure that the outcome is a win-win situation. Coworkers are sure to be by your side if you need help. Don't hesitate to ask, especially if you have just started a new job. One of your new associates is likely to become a friend for life, perhaps even the love of your life. You have good luck at the moment. Follow your dreams realistically, and your fears will disappear.

19. THURSDAY. Lucky. This is another good day for financial success and business negotiations. Get out and about as much as possible. The great outdoors will be good for your thoughts, enabling you to understand and digest new experiences. A health issue could be caused by an allergy or the wrong diet. See a naturopath or nutritionist to give your system a boost, and you will be top-notch in no time. The opportunity to study or travel overseas may come your way unexpectedly. Don't let doubts or fears hold you back. You can achieve your dreams now. Archers who are looking for work should dress as if you already have the job of your choosing. Then you will automatically fit in.

20. FRIDAY. Misleading. Juggling your professional life with your personal life could become problematic. Make sure you are honest with those near and dear. Don't say you are going to do something when you really are planning to do something else. You might simply be trying to please everyone at the same time, but this can backfire and do the exact opposite. The same will hold true if you try to wrangle a day off by telling the boss an untruth. It could even be the end of your job. The desire to throw your energy behind a good cause could instigate a change in profession. Instead of working for a living, you will live to work. Inspiration for change is in the air.

21. SATURDAY. Bright. The focus changes as the Sun dances into Gemini and shines its ever-loving light onto your personal and professional partnerships. Good vibes abound. You do need to watch that you don't get careless, or you might lose something of value. This is not a day for a lot of activity but for savoring your inner comfort and cheer. Lazing around the house with your loved ones will give you all a chance to review the week and talk of dreams for the future. This intimate environment allows you to discuss any issues that may have caused discord and to find forgiveness and understanding without pressure. Put aside any worries about your home or finances. Those worries will fade.

22. SUNDAY. Pleasurable. The Moon visits zany Aquarius, sparking your communication zone and relating to chatty Mercury, saucy Venus, and energetic Mars. So you can expect plenty of unusual social activity. Single Archers might mingle with someone gorgeous. Engage in a dance of desire with tantalizing suggestions and teasing of all sorts. Some of you might get caught up in a challenging situation of jealousy and possessiveness, something you freedom lovers don't enjoy. You may need to consider whether you are chasing love or lust. Don't expect to follow your usual routine. Instead, plan to do something different. If you are stuck at home, make a few changes and add our own loving touch.

23. MONDAY. Interesting. Tension between you and a coworker might be the result of a simple misunderstanding. Be willing to apologize, regardless of whose fault it is, and a friendship is likely to result. Archers who are involved in legal proceedings may find that today is not the best time to meet in court. Be happy to wait a few more days, and a resolution might come to light that you hadn't thought of. Keep your patience as you sit in traffic. Keep your eyes out for speed traps also, and take something to read in anticipation of delays. A neighborhood project might capture your imagination. Check all the ins and outs before you join in. There may be costs you don't know about.

24. TUESDAY. Sensitive. Your sensitivity to your surroundings and your empathy to those near and dear will be increased today. A friend may need to discuss their problems with you. Or you may discuss your own problems with a friend. Either way, the sympathy and understanding are far more important than finding any real answers. Your mind is likely to fantasize and daydream, making it hard to focus on your work at hand. So involve yourself in the chores that don't need your sharp intellect. Later in the day, you can finish more difficult work when your clarity returns. Relationship problems might cause depressed feelings, but worrying won't solve anything. Be present in the moment and let tomorrow worry about itself.

25. WEDNESDAY. Intuitive. Initiate contact with like-minded people and start building a positive network of friends. If you are in a business partnership and feel unhappy about some of the arrangements, you might need to work on self-assertion skills. You could be trying too hard to please and have allowed your boundaries to disappear. Get clear on your direction and please yourself for a change. It will bring happiness. A romantic alliance might be developing into a deeper commitment, as you realize your daily lives have become intertwined. This is a good time to talk about your personal goals and move into the next phase of your relationship with awareness, love, and understanding.

26. THURSDAY. Eventful. Attend to your household chores before you head out into your day. There is likely to be so much going on for you today that by the time you get home, you will just want to relax and will appreciate order. A forthcoming event can take up most of your thoughts as you finalize your plans. Make sure you also take notice of those near and dear and include them in your life. Otherwise, the harmony in your home might be sadly lacking later in the day. Don't be surprised if you just know things all of a sudden. You may be a little nervous and highly strung with this energy. But you can harness it safely if you surround yourself with understanding and loving people.

27. FRIDAY. Spirited. A lively atmosphere prevails today. Don't let your nervous energy get used up in a talkfest, but motivate yourself with your new ideas. If you can think outside of the box, you will be able to turn many situations to your advantage. When it comes to finances, it's not what you know but who you know. Contact friends or family who may be able to help you, and you can solve your problems in no time. Set a direction toward which you channel your energies, and you can achieve much more. Misunderstandings between you and your significant other can be cleared up now. Plan a romantic outing together. Without even trying, you may experience a profound sense of intimacy.

28. SATURDAY. Nurturing. Enjoy the little things in life for inner contentment. With a bevy of planets in the financial sign of Taurus hitting your sector of work and service, you might prefer to save your money and do things yourself. This is an excellent time to start a vegetable garden to grow fresh herbs and salad greens for your diet meals. Throw old veggies in the patch, and their seeds might grow naturally. Join an art class to enable your artist within to express hidden emotions and unconscious feelings. You might discover more about your psyche this way than countless sessions with a therapist can uncover. A gathering of friends can bring warmth and romance.

29. SUNDAY. Erratic. The Moon joins Mercury, Venus, and Mars in Taurus, your sector of work and health, intensifying a thoughtful mood. Your emotions are likely to be up and down. Your need to finish off a project could override any other considerations. If the people around you seem a little disgruntled, talk to them about it but don't let them tell you what you do. Power struggles can only occur when both parties want to struggle, so don't give it the time of day. Some lucky Archers are likely to be packing for an overseas trip. You may want to shop for the right luggage to make your journey comfortable. Make sure you take out insurance and eliminate the grief.

30. MONDAY. Demanding. Various situations can test your willpower. Although this may be trying, the results will be rewarding. Hasty actions can put you into more trouble with a loved one than you would like. But if looked at in a positive sense, this will give you a chance to discuss an issue that has been avoided. Pay attention to your health. If you are suffering from pain, get it checked out. Don't wait until it gets worse. See a natural therapist for tips on maintaining your health, and save on future medical bills. An exercise plan may be a good remedy for ill health and depression. Now is the perfect time to start a new routine. Not only will you feel better, you will look fantastic.

31. TUESDAY. Diverse. Make sure you have a healthy breakfast before setting out for this very busy day. Your mind is likely to work overtime, making it hard to keep your mind on the job at hand. Write lists of what you have to do and employ your thinking on practical issues as much as possible. Conversations in the workplace may be irresistible. While you are trying to work, snippets of gossip can take your mind away again. Make sure you have a map if you are out on the roads making deliveries or keeping appointments. There is the possibility of confusion, and directions are especially susceptible to mix-ups. Check your cell phone regularly so you do not miss an important message.

JUNE

1. WEDNESDAY. Constructive. Today's eclipsed New Moon in the sign of Gemini indicates the ending of one cycle with a significant fresh cycle beginning. It's time to revamp your methods of relating to allow you true freedom of expression. Business partnerships may need to be overhauled. A reappraisal of efficiency and success will give you a clearer picture on what should be changed. A legal matter may need your urgent attention. Don't just leave it all up to your attorney. Do your own research as well. A difficult relationship could come to an end. If there are built-up resentments on either side, it will make the divorce proceedings messy. Address these resentments for a positive outcome.

2. THURSDAY. Interactive. The Moon in Gemini accents your seventh house of relationships. Be extra sensitive to your partner's feelings. This extends to business partners, superiors, and best friends. Stop worrying about what you want to say and really pay attention to what others have to say. This can help you get ahead in many ways. You can't change the way others behave, but you can alter and gain an understanding of your own reactions. You may have quite a few social engagements to attend. As you wend your way through each, there is likely to be one particular individual who makes a strong impression on you. Karmic connections are highlighted.

3. FRIDAY. Helpful. Mercury, the planet of communication, has moved into Gemini, your relationship sector, and joins the Moon in Cancer, your sector of joint resources and commitment. Even if you and your partner are not connected financially, discussing your daily stresses can give each other insight into moods and undercurrents and nurture a deeper intimacy within your relationship. See that you are covered by insurance so that losses won't cause so much pain. There is a possibility that someone close to you is not telling you the truth. Or perhaps you are not being honest in return. If you are involved in legal matters, revise all aspects of the matter to make sure your claim is airtight.

4. SATURDAY. Beneficial. Jupiter, your ruling planet, moves into Taurus in your sixth house of work and health, and will visit Taurus for the rest of the year. This is a very good time for any kind of work and for fulfilling duties that contribute to your personal growth. You can look forward to an improved job situation, better working conditions, or even a new job with better pay or opportunities for self-fulfillment. This is also an excellent period for health. Jupiter gives your body physical strength and vitality. However, you do need to be careful about gaining weight, so try to avoid any overindulgence. Some Sagittarius may enter into a business partnership with your life partner.

5. SUNDAY. Adventurous. Philosophical and cultural interests may make this day unusual. Get the weekend newspaper and check out the entertainment section for events of interest that you can attend. A political rally can introduce you to new schools of thought and offer opportunities to get involved in the public arena. Connections made via various social media could offer accommodations and instigate your plans to explore other cultures. Even if you're an armchair tourist and only watch travel shows, you can enjoy learning about far-off places on this pleasant afternoon. This a great day for a little daydreaming, so allow yourself to go as far as your mind will take you.

6. MONDAY. Restless. Your spirit may be itching for some adventure. Because of your daily duties you may feel stuck in a boring routine. Your need for some excitement might entangle you in other people's dramas, causing problems you don't need. Stay focused on your own creative projects, then your inspiration and enthusiasm will return. Watch out for irritability later in the day. Avoid taking your frustrations out on those near and dear. Plan a social activity for after work. Let off steam playing sports or philosophizing with your friends. If you work in the import-export trade, difficulties caused through faulty translation may be avoided with an upgrade to your computer program.

7. TUESDAY. Testing. If you get the opportunity to take off on a road trip, the break would do you a world of good. Disagreements on the job or with family and friends may put you in the position of having to defend your own ideas and opinions. Although challenging, this test can uncover a few doubts on your own part. In-laws can be especially troublesome for you, especially if you are trying to justify why they should babysit for you again. Legal issues may be a thorn in your side also. Religious discussions are likely to deteriorate into ideological brawls, so avoid them. In fact, try not to discuss anything more serious than the weather if you want to avoid a scene.

8. WEDNESDAY. Difficult. Tension may exist between your private life and your public persona. Both your family and your career may be vying for your attention. It seems like you can't please anyone today. The harder you try, the worse it gets. Family arguments or difficulties at home may affect your job performance. Be extra careful if you are out in the public eye with your family. Any emotional outbursts can affect your reputation negatively. On the other hand, with your ability to intuitively grasp an understanding of business issues, you might be recommended for a promotion or higher pay. Find a way to release stress and relax to avoid unnecessary arguments.

9. THURSDAY. Distracting. Luscious Venus slips into Gemini, your seventh house of partnerships, and adds the law of attraction to all your social interaction. There is a slight suggestion of envy. So be careful not to leave a loved one in the dark about your business or whereabouts, lest they get the wrong ideas. A flattering business proposition may not be all that it seems to be. Do not get bedazzled by the generous-sounding offer. Just get professional help to interpret the fine print and see the realistic picture. Positive working associations point to good teamwork. If you work in sales, there may be a good commission coming your way. Greed may be the only problem.

10. FRIDAY. Promising. Persistence is the key to success today. Sagittarius businesspeople may be disappointed with your net profits at the moment. But don't rock the boat with changes at this point. The profit margin may turn around sooner than you think. As a member of a social club, you could be asked to take on an official role. Even if you feel skeptical about your abilities, accept the job with appreciation. You may find that you have a natural talent for your role, which will build self-confidence. Love and romance are on the horizon. If you are looking for someone new, be open to instant attraction and you may be swept off your feet. Couples might plan a romantic interlude.

11. SATURDAY. Varied. With all your commitments, there might not be enough of you to go around today. A new romance could bring a child into your life and awaken the kind and nurturing aspect of your soul. Be careful not to promise more than you can give, though. The road to hell is paved with good intentions, and you may let down those you care about. Whatever you are doing, you won't want to leave anybody out. Your creative side can find a fun way to include everyone. If you have to work today, you are likely to rush your job in the hope of finishing early, which might only slow you down. The lesson is to enjoy where you are and love the ones you are with.

12. SUNDAY. Quiet. Stay in bed and enjoy languishing. If you are smart, you will have a stack of movies to watch and won't need to go anywhere. Some of you might be worn out from frenetic activity the last couple of days. Make sure you have a nutritious breakfast, then eat lightly all day. This is a time for regeneration and reflection, so make the most of this traditional day of rest. Do what you can to recharge your spiritual batteries. Attend a worship service, go for a long walk in the park, or spend the evening curled up in bed with a good book. Or start a class in yoga and meditation and get fit while relaxing.

13. MONDAY. Demanding. A lot of small problems can add up into one large frustration if you are not careful. Don't take the worries of the world upon your shoulders. Especially don't blame yourself for other people's behavior. Otherwise, you might explode and end up saying or doing something you regret. This is your lunar low period, and you should be kind to yourself. Cross off the list some of your chores and visits, then relax. Nothing will run away, and you will be able to get them done tomorrow. If you are in a position of not being able to take time off, see if you can work behind the scenes and limit the amount of contact you have with others. The solitude will soothe your soul and settle your nerves.

14. TUESDAY. Pleasant. The Moon sweeps into your own sign of Sagittarius, lifting your spirits and boosting your popularity. Yesterday it may have seemed you couldn't get any help. Now people may fall over one another in the need to please. Good aspects connect the Moon, lovely Venus, and sensitive Neptune. So embrace romantic and compassionate moments. Being in the right place at the right time is your specialty today. You are likely to run into that special

someone and rekindle the romance. A family member might be unwell and ask for some of your time. Interesting gossip will work
wonders in taking their mind away from their illness.

15. WEDNESDAY. Hopeful. The eclipsed Full Moon falls in your
sign of Sagittarius and promises positive change, even travel. You
have extra energy and confidence to achieve your goals. Have lunch
with someone special to add pleasure to your day. Plan a brisk walk
or bike ride this afternoon. Some of you may be stuck in the office,
but it doesn't have to be a tedious day. Keep a positive attitude and
you will find it is highly contagious. Life is good, so celebrate. Your
charm and grace are at an all-time high. Even Archers suffering
from depression or frustration will find it is easier to open up and
be hopeful. Embrace love and other little miracles.

16. THURSDAY. Challenging. Serious business discussions or
negotiations concerning finances or property can stall over a disagreement. Be prepared to wait rather than agree to something you
really don't agree with. There is a possibility of underhanded tactics.
Finances need to be protected today, so don't leave your credit card
details with anyone you don't know can be trusted. Issues around
power and control can surface in your personal relationship and
limit your freedom. Instead of trying to play the game, step out
and get some professional advice. Abuse comes in all forms. Verbal
abuse is a strong but subtle weapon that will wear away self-esteem
before you know it.

17. FRIDAY. Strategic. Today may be very hectic and busy for you,
so take a few deep breaths and pace yourself. Pause and consider
your own motivations before entering into any delicate negotiations. Mercury, planet of communication, is now in Cancer, your
eighth house of power and control. So you should ensure that you
have clarity on all aspects of an issue that concerns you. Passion
can grow over the phone, as this mode of communication gives the
voice and inflection much more power. Don't be surprised if the
calls between you and your lover start to heat up over the next
three weeks. Unusual artwork can boost your assets, so make sure
you insure it adequately.

18. SATURDAY. Uncertain. Your social life can get a shake-up with
invitations to unusual events and the necessity to make a choice between them. You can't please everybody, but you will fret anyway.
Ask yourself what it is that you feel like doing, and the choice will
be easy. You do need to be careful of the company you keep today.
Don't visit dangerous, poorly lit neighborhoods. Your partner may

unexpectedly confront you over joint finances and question your values. Be honest and defend your values if they are important to you. This type of issue is quite normal in relationships. It is only through compromise, not control, that harmony is achieved.

19. SUNDAY. Auspicious. Social interaction and group activities are starred today. Your natural good humor attracts people to you, and your social circle is likely growing. Phone calls, e-mails, and social engagements can fill up your time and keep you from doing any of your chores. Make sure you don't leave your loved ones out of the action, and all will go smoothly. Partnered Archers will enjoy an intimate getaway to rekindle the passion and commitment. End a lovely day under a sunset far away from prying eyes. Some Archers may be getting married on this day. The good vibes coupled with powerful communication will make this event memorable for you and your guests.

20. MONDAY. Chancy. Fantasy and daydreams can infringe on clear thinking. This is not a day for making important decisions. It is better to allow a problem to work itself out than risk making a bad call. Steer clear of advertised sales at the shops. You could get talked into buying an expensive lemon that you will regret for a long time. The stars are ominous for illegal activity or dishonesty of any sort. What goes around will come around. This can work positively, too. A helping hand to a friend in need will be greatly appreciated. You might receive help when you most need it. Buy a gift for your lover to let them know how special they are.

21. TUESDAY. Variable. Mars, the planet of action and energy, has moved into Gemini in your seventh house of relationship, bringing a certain amount of tension into your life over the next month. Mars rules assertiveness, the seventh house rules the area in life where compromise is necessary, and Gemini rules the mind. The trick is to use dynamic energy to work through your differences. Then you can find grounds for compromise. Excessive physical strain should be avoided as your body is more subject than usual to minor infections, chills, and fever. Stay close to home and rely on personal comforts. Drink plenty of nourishing liquids.

22. WEDNESDAY. Introspective. The life-giving Sun is now domiciled in Cancer, your eighth house of sex and power, and turns up the volume on joint resources, investments, and deep commitments. An interest in the occult and psychic phenomena could entice you to fork out more of your hard-earned dollars for something that with a little instruction you can do for yourself. Start meditating and join a psychic development circle. Learn to tap into the psychic potential of your soul's inner knowledge. Memories of the past could bring up long-forgotten resentments and remind you of the history you are carrying around in the cellular level of your body. Practice forgiveness for inner freedom.

23. THURSDAY. Suspenseful. The level of tension you are living under is likely to be extreme. Practice deep breathing. If possible, have a massage to relax your joints and aid the elimination of toxins from your body. Whether you have to meet a friend or are awaiting the finalization of an important business deal or even exam results, you will be kept in suspense. Except surprises. A sudden attraction could turn into love at first sight and spark the beginning of a whirlwind romance. Or you might have a fling that only lasts half a day but stays with you forever. Partnered Archers should be brave and try an exhilarating sports activity.

24. FRIDAY. Emotional. Arguments over who deserves what and who has worked the hardest can bring out your tactless side and rile the emotions further. Refrain from pettiness. Put what is really important first. Fun-loving Archers would much prefer to plan your next adventure and leave the boring details far behind you. Before you do anything rash, remember to listen as much as you talk. Then you might understand a lot more about your family dynamics. An unexpectedly large bill might incite insecurity and the blues, putting worries in your mind that don't need to be there. Get a payment plan and start budgeting. Thinking on a practical level will placate heavy emotions.

25. SATURDAY. Playful. Enjoy a fun-filled day as the Aries Moon lights up your fifth house of romance and creativity, urging you to express yourself. Enjoy some time playing with children. If you haven't got children in your life, find a way to get in touch with your inner child. Watch a comedy or play miniature golf for a fun change of pace. Creative endeavors that also have a practical purpose move forward, including home renovating and the teaching of children. It is a good day to put a lot of odd jobs behind you. If you are looking to buy an investment property, tour the local area and talk to neighbors.

26. SUNDAY. Passionate. Loving relationships can heat up as the Sun draws close in aspect to powerful Pluto. Attraction turns into sexual ardor, which turns into deeper levels of intimacy and demands total surrender. Handled wrongly, attraction can become a need to control and lead to power struggles. Stay away from dangerous places in order to keep yourself safe. This applies to drugs and alcohol as well. Your system is apt to be weaker than usual as Neptune saps the Mars energy. Mistakes and confusion could be the result, not to mention potentially harmful effects to your health. Stay close to home. Enjoy the warmth and comfort of old friends and those near and dear.

27. MONDAY. Fair. Stick to your normal routine no matter what interruptions occur, and you will have some time to yourself later in the day. All sorts of unusual happenings can make a normally boring day quite interesting. Singles might run into an attractive stranger and feel as if you have known them all your life. Couples are likely to experience a situation of déjà vu that makes you wonder about the spiritual bonds in life. Keep to yourself at work. No matter how juicy the gossip, don't get distracted. An early night with your family will do your energy level a lot of good. Whip up a nourishing meal for all to share.

28. TUESDAY. Bumpy. The tension in the air will affect everybody today. Don't expect others to be agreeable to your ideas. People are likely to oppose you. The trick is to accept that each person is an individual with different ideas, then find the middle ground. If you try to convince another to accept your views, you will only end up in a fight. Compulsive or obsessive behavior will also be pronounced, and you might notice your bad habits seem ten times worse. Physical exercise is a great way around your difficulties. It will release tension and calm your mood. Stop thinking about yourself. Do something thoughtful and kind for someone you love.

29. WEDNESDAY. Fortunate. A more harmonious vibe returns, accentuating social engagements. Hang out with the people you love. If you have to attend a social function, take someone with you. Your phone is likely to ring nonstop, and visitors will make for a fun day. Business negotiations that have stalled can start to move again. Call a meeting of all relevant parties and the problems may now be resolved. Watch out for the green-eyed monster in your romantic sphere. A rival for the object of your affection could arrive on the scene. Stand up for yourself. Competing for a person's affection isn't a good start for a relationship. As soon as you let go, the right person may appear.

30. THURSDAY. Rebalancing. Just when you thought life was settling down, the tension and excitement return. You may have overloaded your agenda and now can't focus on any one thing for fear of missing another. Trying to please others will only run you ragged and end up pleasing no one. Forget about the big event tonight. Start ordering the present moment for your maximum enjoyment and efficiency. You may or may not be at peace with the great cycle of life. If you're not at peace, it's time to review your beliefs and the feelings they are based upon. Look at the glorious sunrise, flowers in bloom, children at play, old folks reminiscing, and the serenity of the sunset for your answers.

JULY

1. FRIDAY. Complex. This morning's eclipsed New Moon is in Cancer, your eighth house of sex and power. The lunar eclipse forms part of a grand cross with the Sun, Saturn, Uranus, and Pluto, signaling restrictions, power struggles, and a need for flexibility. This powerful aspect suggests that forgiveness is a necessity. Holding resentments or playing the victim will only result in health issues and pain. Stick to your daily routine and give an honest day's work. Care for those around you and lend a hand with kindness when needed. These simple rules will enable you to find peace and avoid the competitive struggle for power. Take time for loving, cultivate tender intimacy.

2. SATURDAY. Thoughtful. All sorts of idealistic plans could take up a large part of your thinking. Mercury, the planet of communication, cruises into Leo in your house of the higher mind and travel, and makes aspects to philosophical Jupiter, inventive Uranus, and idealistic Neptune. Write down your plans. You are likely to come up with some original and worthwhile ideas that you can work on in the future. Travel is likely to be on your mind, even if it is just to get away from your daily surroundings for a few days break. Some of you might decide to go back to college and brush up on your education for career purposes, or for your own philosophical or spiritual interest.

3. SUNDAY. Adventurous. Today has the potential for being absolutely lovely as the Moon moves into Leo in your ninth house of travel and adventure. Some may even find romance with someone from a far-off place or different culture. Trying something new will be good for your soul, so be open to new experiences. In-laws and other relatives at a distance are feeling generous toward you, so make an effort to communicate. If you can't afford to take a trip, get out of the house and go for a drive in the country. Exploring little towns and the local history might be a lot more interesting than you thought. Start tracking your ancestors in the country and explore your roots.

4. MONDAY. Powerful. Your powers of attraction get a boost from Venus, the goddess of love, as she moves into Cancer in your eighth house of sex and power. Loving relationships will gain greater intensity now. Money can come through personal or professional partners, inheritances, or public financial institutions. Obviously, this is a good time to seek a loan or other financial support. Many of you are likely to be experiencing a major change in your values or in your home life and family. Such changes may ultimately give you more freedom to express your individual creativity. This could result in relationship problems, but with the help of a counselor these can be overcome.

5. TUESDAY. Good. The emphasis is squarely on your career. If you are applying for a promotion or a new job, your chances of success are considerable. If you are already in a secure position, your abilities could be such that your employer is happy to grant a pay increase to keep you. Although you are feeling confident with your achievements, some of you might have a partner that keeps nagging for you to do more. Instead of avoiding the issue or getting cranky, speak honestly about how you feel. You need to nurture yourself at this time. Meditation and yoga are excellent forms of relaxation, and will ease tension and give clarity of mind.

6. WEDNESDAY. Helpful. Creative inspiration is enhanced today. Problems and disappointments can be turned into positives by changing perspective. Turn situations around objectively in your mind and solutions will become simple. Partnerships, whether personal or professional, may have been hard work lately, but today you have the chance to enjoy some rewards through good relations. A legal matter that is in danger of becoming very expensive can be defused through a face-to-face meeting. Take the approach that there are two sides to every story, and the middle ground becomes obvious. Plans for a trip overseas may need to be postponed. You will know when the time is right.

7. THURSDAY. Restless. The Moon in Libra hits off a major planetary configuration today. The overriding influence on you is your need for personal freedom. You might find yourself wishing others would leave you alone to do your own thing. Responsibilities can seem to be that much heavier. If you feel depressed, take heart that this will pass and instead of wallowing in self-pity, get outside and help someone else who is worse off. Listen compassionately to the complaints of another. Playing sports will be wonderful for your state of mind. Go for a walk on the beach or in a park, letting the fresh air and nature calm your mind.

8. FRIDAY. Fair. You have a natural charisma today, and may discover new friends and admirers. Any opportunity to practice your people skills at work will give positive feedback to your employer. An opening for you to move into another area of work might be promising, just like a natural thing for you to do. There is a tendency to the dramatic at the moment. In the area of relationships you could experience painful intensity. Passion and attraction are strong for you. If you are attracted to someone that you can't have, you need to find something to avoid obsession. If someone is obsessing over you, steer clear of them and let someone else know.

9. SATURDAY. Imaginative. An introspective mood can trigger personal creativity. Be careful of pushy people and give their advice a wide berth. Your intuition is capable of steering your course in the direction that is right for you. What started out as a strong sexual attraction may start to ease into a loving and committed relationship. This is a perfect time to get away to an exotic destination where you and your lover can be intimate without interruptions. Check out the deals on the Internet. You may not have to go very far to find a secluded resort that fits the bill and your budget. For some Archers, solitude to fantasize and dream is apt to be more attractive than the real thing.

10. SUNDAY. Interesting. Put your problems aside for the day and just enjoy whatever comes your way. Interruptions can put fun and excitement into otherwise boring situations. A friend might be in a tight situation and need your help. Before you know it, you are out and about, having lunch at a café with new friends talking about interesting things. If you have a relative or friend in the hospital, go for a visit and cheer up their day. Take some flowers and fruit, and your good wishes will linger after you have left. If you are feeling guilty about something that you have done or said, give the person a call and let them know you are sorry. It will make all the difference to both of you.

11. MONDAY. Sensitive. You might be like a human sponge, picking up the emotions and moods of the people around you. If you are feeling confused, get out on your own and go for a walk. This will enable you to get in touch with your own feelings and gain clarity of mind. Sagittarius who have moved may find yourself in a neighborhood quite different from anywhere you have lived before. The best way to find comfort is to talk to your neighbors and explore the community groups and events for an opportunity to get involved. Disagreement over joint resources could be of your own making. Be prepared to listen to your partner and consider their argument.

12. TUESDAY. Energetic. Get up early and make the most of high levels of energy to catch up on your chores. With the optimistic Sagittarius Moon boosting yours self-confidence and charm, you can achieve a lot today. Turn your attention to your appearance. It might be time to purchase some new clothes and enhance the impression you want to make. Do be mindful of your budget. There is an indication that you could spend more than you can afford. Likewise, any leaning toward gambling isn't advisable at this time. Investments in real estate could be an exception as long as you do your research thoroughly. An inheritance might be in the pipeline for some lucky Archers.

13. WEDNESDAY. Focused. Business matters demand extra attention. Spontaneity is not a good attitude when it comes to big bucks or your livelihood, as you might tend toward trusting your instincts now. Remember that if someone is trying to pull the wool over your eyes, they are going to give a very convincing spin to their venture. The best attitude is caution. Have any contract or agreement you are thinking of signing checked out by a professional first. Self-starters could be looking for financing to get your project off the ground. This is a positive time to approach financial institutions for a loan. If you are ready to start trading, get professional help with your advertising for success.

14. THURSDAY. Encouraging. Review your values and priorities before the Moon becomes full overnight. What can you spend less time doing, so that you can spend more time with the ones you love or doing what you love? Remember, love often involves many little sacrifices. Draw up a budget that will allow a comfortable lifestyle and also allows you to save. If you can't currently afford the lifestyle of your choosing, it might be time to change jobs or study for a new career. If you have an addiction, such as smoking or gambling, that is draining your funds, seek help. Follow in the footsteps of those who found a cure.

15. FRIDAY. Positive. Before dawn the Full Moon culminates in Capricorn, your second house of money and values, and highlights issues of self-worth. Your ability to see the big picture can work in your favor. When people try to bog you down with the fine details, you can point to the things that matter. With benevolent Jupiter giving you luck in the workplace, this is a very good time to look for personally satisfying employment or apply for a promotion. Sagittarius students could have luck getting into your preferred institution, and you might even gain admission to an overseas college or university. Don't hesitate to apply for scholarships or exchange programs as your luck is good right now.

16. SATURDAY. Eventful. Pace yourself and avoid becoming frazzled. This is likely to be a very busy day, with a thousand and one things to be done yesterday. Sagittarius is noted for enthusiasm and not looking before you leap. Be warned to take care, and you will avoid unnecessary accidents or mistakes. Your managerial skills come to the fore, and teammates may look to you for guidance because of your nonjudgmental manner. Don't be surprised if your phone runs hot as friends seek your advice. A social function can give you and your significant other a chance to socialize and enjoy fun and laughter. Single Archers are likely to meet someone new tonight.

17. SUNDAY. Diverse. Sagittarius is renowned for foot-in-mouth disease, and this is a day when you need to watch what you say. Practice tact and diplomacy as much as possible. A philosophical or spiritual gathering will be inspiring, giving you a different slant on things. Your views on life and your daily routine are changing. Different belief systems can attract your intellect. Some of you living in an ethnic neighborhood may decide to learn the predominant language in order to facilitate communication. Attend various community events. Get involved in activities such as fund-raising for charities, schools, and clubs, and it won't take you long to become bilingual.

18. MONDAY. Fulfilling. Home and family come under the spotlight today. If you wake up feeling sleep-deprived from endless dreams, think about starting a dream journal. The unconscious is expressed through dreams. After you record your dreams for a while, their meaning will start to become apparent. There might be a family get-together for a special celebration, and you may receive something of value. Whether it is information or an heirloom or something else, it will be important to you. Home renovations can get expensive, but you could meet someone who is willing to show you what to do and how to eliminate the cost of paying a professional.

19. TUESDAY. Bumpy. A family disagreement should be worked out before you leave home. Otherwise, it will play on your mind all day and disrupt your routine and efficiency. Double-check all your figures during the day because there is the chance of a mistake or misunderstanding. This is not a good day for automobile repairs or driving tests. Your lover may be dealing with a difficult situation, which leaves you worrying all day. Instead of staying in the dark, send them a message reminding them to call. Love and romance are indicated. For hopeful romantics this could be your lucky day. Dress up and go out to your favorite venue with a few friends.

20. WEDNESDAY. Easygoing. Watch out for the tendency to let opportunities slip by simply because you are enjoying yourself. You will kick yourself tomorrow if you do. Attend to any family matters early in the day. Then you will have the time free for your creative expression. Your fun-loving mood is likely to rub off on your co-workers, improving teamwork and boosting production. If you are self-employed, you might decide to take on an employee to give you more free time as well as lighten your load. A romance with a fellow employee may take you by surprise. After you soak up the flattery, watch the signs. You might end up in a situation that is not of your making.

21. THURSDAY. Demanding. The influences are such that no matter how much help you receive this morning, you may still feel abandoned by all. Try not to wallow in self-pity, just get on with your work. Stick to your guidelines and do a good job. By afternoon you will be laughing again. Sagittarius folk love freedom and adventure, but you do have to toe the line some days and today is one of them. A relationship breakup might inflict pain and heartache. If you write out a list of the positives and negatives, you could be glad to be free again. Your health would benefit from moderation. If you go to extremes in regard to personal action or physicality, slow down and smell the roses.

22. FRIDAY. Mixed. Problems can arise through thoughtlessness. Take note of the people close to you and be willing to compromise. Then your relationships can reach new heights. If you notice that the people around you seem more argumentative than usual, consider your own attitudes. You may be a little more idealistic about your aims and aspirations than usual, and expect a bit much from others also. Vacations may be due, and now is the time to start planning a trip abroad. See your local travel agent for all the tips and advice on airfares, times, and destinations so you can be sure to enjoy the trip. Devote your evening to the kids, and let your inner child romp.

23. SATURDAY. Revitalizing. This looks to be a truly lucky day for the adventurous Archer. A new creative project around the home can give you the chance to break out of routine while still living in it. Stretch your imagination. Get out and about to new and interesting places. An invitation to escape the usual and go camping in the wilds might be lots of fun and break the daily grind. Overindulgence is the one thing that might be harmful to you. If you are on a diet, be vigilant because your willpower may not be as strong as usual. The shining Sun moves into Leo, bringing warmth and creativity to all while highlighting your ninth house of travel and adventure.

24. SUNDAY. Industrious. Rest and relax on this sweet vibration, as life is too short to spend worrying about little things. Your health will improve if you spend time in the sun with your loved ones. Get some fresh air and exercise if you can. If you are planning to tidy up the house, gather everybody together, turn on your favorite tunes, and make it a party. Invite the neighbors and enjoy a multicultural experience. Sagittarius parents who are planning a large party should get a nanny early so you don't miss out later. A desire to travel and forge a career can be achieved in the armed forces. If you are leaving for duty, make sure you contact everybody you love.

25. MONDAY. Uncertain. Young Archers might be experiencing disapproval from your parents. If you are moving out and can support yourself, then you must be firm and understand that your parents are grieving for you. Once you are on your way, they will get over it. But in other situations, Sagittarius may be subjected to persuasion and interference. No matter what, stick to your own ideas. You are likely to be confused easily now. Instead of getting into an argument, just bow out of the discussion. Turn your thoughts to what's in front of you and change the topic. If you are leaving on an overseas trip, chances are you might already be feeling homesick.

26. TUESDAY. Bright. Having Gemini, the sign of the Twins, in your partnership sector suggests that you have more than one significant commitment. Perhaps your social life is as important to you as your home life. Just for today focus on your lover, pamper them with affection, and remind them of your love. Make sure they know it is real. A business partnership is likely to be booming, and your teamwork second to none. Take advantage of the good times to lay down a legal framework for the division of the profits; don't leave anything to chance. A new acquaintance may attract you in such a way that it seems you have known each other in a past life.

27. WEDNESDAY. Emotional. The sensitive Moon joins forces with action-oriented Mars, causing impulsive and emotion-driven actions. This influence is subjective, and can make compromise and cooperation hard. It is a good time to avoid any sensitive discussions with your mate. On a positive note, this influence gives you the willpower and control to break down otherwise formidable barriers. Your creative ability can come up with a valuable invention. Make sure you patent your idea because you might be able to sell it to the public. Confusion and misunderstandings are still probable as Mercury opposes dreamy Neptune. Enjoy the fantasy world of a best-selling book or popular movie.

28. THURSDAY. Upbeat. Harmonious Venus joins the Sun in Leo, your house of travel and adventure. Foreign cultures, politics, and religion can be of interest to you. Buy your ticket and go; you won't regret it. Some of you are likely to start a new romance with someone from a foreign shore. Or you might meet their family for the first time today. Whatever you are into, you will want to study up on it and become an expert. You could start teaching a subject at which you are expert. Sagittarius actors may get a part in a foreign film that gives you your big break into stardom. The chance to follow your dreams is possible. Luck is on your side.

29. FRIDAY. Distracting. Disagreements between you and your mate can focus around joint finances. The cosmos suggests you should decide to disagree right now. Mercury, the planet that rules communication, moves into Virgo, your tenth house of career, and is in a tough aspect to cloudy Neptune. This will complicate matters. So just wait until things become clear. On the other hand, the mysteries of life can fascinate you. You may find yourself thinking of someone you haven't seen for a while, then be pleasantly surprised to hear from them. Meaningful coincidences could color your day. Dreams can be especially insightful. Pay attention to subtleties.

30. SATURDAY. Exciting. New and exciting opportunities are likely. The Moon joins the Sun and saucy Venus in Leo, your house of travel and adventure. So plans for the future may include an overseas jaunt. Don't stay at home, even if you have a large family. Take them out for some fun. Do something different such as attending a concert, a play, or an exhibition. Go for a picnic to a recreational site that features swimming and sporting activities. Go kite flying with your lover, or sign up for skydiving. Anything that gets your blood pumping and the adrenaline flowing will be lots of fun. Singles can meet someone out of the ordinary and enjoy a delightful affair.

31. SUNDAY. Variable. Take precautions to let someone know where you are going and when you expect to be back before you leave the house this morning. Your impulsive mood may put you in spots that are more dangerous than usual. So it is wise to play it safe. You might prefer your own company. If you are staying at home, take the phone off the hook and bar the door. A backlog of work or study could bog you down early. But if you get into it, you will have the afternoon free and a clear conscience. A political rally or a cultural event might be interesting, and inspire you to start getting involved in the community. Joining up with volunteers abroad could appeal to you.

AUGUST

1. MONDAY. Manageable. Mondayitis could hit this morning. A sleepless night due to an overactive mind can leave you feeling like anything but going to work. Take a day off if you can and catch up on your chores at home. Put all the ideas that kept you awake down on paper and do something about them. If you have a burning desire, then it will probably manifest. So you should start laying plans to make sure you get exactly what you want. Concerns over the health of a family member may be eased after a medical assessment. If they are struggling to make ends meet, help to pay the bill or take up a family collection. The good news will speed up the healing process.

2. TUESDAY. Satisfying. Avoid taking or seeking advice. There is a friend or associate who may not have your best interests at heart and gives you the wrong advice. You know in your heart what is right for you, so listen to your conscience and you can't go wrong. Step up to the challenge if a leadership job is offered to you. Your ability to see the big picture will be invaluable to all those who come under your influence. There is an emphasis on healing now. Sagittarius who are suffering some minor physical ailments should perhaps seek a recommended therapist. You may gain a fresh and more objective view of your situation with an understanding of how to reach your goals.

3. WEDNESDAY. Stressful. Action-oriented Mars moves into Cancer, your eighth house of sex and power, and turns up the volume on passion and the desire for control. The Moon also moves into a major planetary configuration and poses power struggles with friends and associates. Your need to be independent is strong.

But your need for the support of others puts you in a dilemma of either pleasing others or pleasing yourself. It doesn't matter which you decide on. Just make sure you are conscious of your decision, and don't fall into emotionally manipulative tactics. If you do, they will come back to bite you. The best course of action is to do nothing, just concentrate on the work at hand.

4. THURSDAY. Reflective. Mercury, the planet of communication, is retrograde in Virgo, your house of career, through August 26. During this period you can expect all sorts of mix-ups, delays, and misunderstandings. Contracts and agreements can stall. Use this time to reflect on the matters of importance, and you might discover more about your inner motivations than you do now. Plans can change and disrupt your day. Some of you might get a call from work to let you know you are not needed today, causing concerns about your income. A close friend could let you down, but don't take this personally. They are sure to have a lot going on in their life and didn't mean to upset you.

5. FRIDAY. Healing. Hurts and disagreements from yesterday can be resolved today. The heavens suggest that you take it easy and do something to pamper yourself. Neptune, the planet of spirit, now goes retrograde in Aquarius, your house of communication. So a course in meditation and yoga would be very beneficial for your nerves and physical well-being. Anything that nurtures your spirit will bring joy to your heart. Take a walk out to a nature reserve and commune with wildlife. Escape the worries of the world however you choose, then reap the benefits on body, mind, and spirit. If you are stuck meeting a deadline, lock out any interruptions and clear your mind with deep breathing.

6. SATURDAY. Erratic. This is one of those days where nothing goes according to plan. It doesn't have to be a bad thing. In fact, it might be better than you could have planned. The trick is to go with the flow and don't try to be rigid. Sagittarius artists should make the most of the creative vibes and immerse yourself in your work. Home lovers might gain inner rewards from tending to your family and home. Matchmakers will have fun trying to get the potential lovers together as plans change unexpectedly. Health nuts could purchase exercise equipment so that you can work out at home anytime you feel the urge. This will be great for working off your frustrations and avoiding what is in the fridge.

7. SUNDAY. Renewing. Your new lunar cycle begins today as the Moon slides gently into Sagittarius. Concentrate on the things that you want and feel. You can implement new habits and get personal projects off the ground. Your popularity is likely to be on the rise also. Expect visitors and invitations to interesting social engagements. Issues of control within your personal relationship might come to the fore. If you find it hard to express who you are without thinking first, you may want to escape on your own. Be careful of confiding in friends who want to give you advice, which is only what they would like you to do. Take your own inventory and get professional counseling.

8. MONDAY. Motivating. Mercury, the planet of communication, retrogrades back into Leo, joining the Sun and Venus in your ninth house of travel and adventure. Plans for fulfilling a dream that may have failed can be reviewed and revised. Knowing what you know now means you're much wiser and therefore capable of creating a successful plan for the future. Use your spare time to reflect on past mistakes and experiences. Get to know yourself better. Business negotiations can become problematic, with the prospect of settlement moving farther and farther away. Don't fret. Realize it is out of your control. Instead, leave it behind and get on with work that is moving. Let time take care of it.

9. TUESDAY. Problematic. Emotions run hot today. Try not to take on other people's feelings. You can only control yourself. If someone else is not happy, and you are doing your best, then it is their problem. Remember, you are not the center of the universe. Take care of your own needs and wants, let others take care of theirs, and your day will be simpler. Conflict over joint resources might simply be caused through misunderstanding. Don't enter into accusations or heated arguments, which will not solve anything. Take the issue back to its beginning and try to work through what has occurred. Then you may find a resolution that will suit both of you. If that doesn't work, try mediation.

10. WEDNESDAY. Focused. Concentrate on what is most important and urgent. Financial and business problems can be very complex. The egos of everyone involved will complicate matters even further. Stay out of any power struggles to make your day easier. Taking baby steps is the best approach. Fix things up one by one, and get the simplest matters out of the way first. Retail therapy is dangerous. Stay away from the shops and don't start looking at big-ticket items lest you impulsively sign away the next few years of your life. Concern for the law is highlighted. All business negotiations should be researched to make sure your legal obligations are met. Then you won't have anything to answer to in court.

11. THURSDAY. Expansive. Self-expression through creativity and relationships is starred. A new love interest may enter your life, bringing new and interesting views. Someone may be foreign and introduce you to customs you have never known about. An individual from another walk of life can show you a whole new approach to daily living. Get out and socialize. Make new contacts and friendships that will be valuable in the future. Watch the urge for extravagant or self-indulgent purchases. You could easily fritter away your hard-earned dollars on something that doesn't mean that much to you. Avoid conflict. Seek instead the possibility of compromise and resolution.

12. FRIDAY. Optimistic. Today's aspects point to the benefits of expanding your mind through philosophical debates, studying, or travel. Spend the morning getting organized, straighten out your appointments, and make sure you haven't overscheduled. You will enjoy the afternoon and make considerable headway toward achieving your goals. Conversations can be misinterpreted. So be extra careful that you have the correct information, and speak clearly in any business matters. When it comes to your mate or steady date, misunderstandings could be more subtle and long lasting. Refuse to enter into any mutual accusations, as they will not be helpful in resolving the problem.

13. SATURDAY. Sensitive. Irritations and frustrations can take the edge off fun times. The Full Moon in zany Aquarius can frazzle the whole planet, so keep your eyes and ears open and take care of you and yours. Be alert on the roads, especially as tempers fray and road rage kicks into gear. A personal project might be frustrating, since you can't get the bits and pieces you need to finish it. Perhaps you are trying to contact someone and all you get is the answering machine. Just leave your message and get on with something else. Try to cut a bad habit. If you eat or smoke or drink too much, you will have to live with the consequences.

14. SUNDAY. Pleasant. Enjoy sleeping in and hanging out at home with your ever-loving family. If you live away from home, you might go back for a visit and enjoy reminiscing about the days gone by. Country dwellers planning to move to the city for work may be sorting through your possessions, with pangs of homesickness already hitting, and you haven't even left. Some of you might be out and about looking at houses, hoping to purchase the house that will suit your family's needs. Consider renovating. You might find an older house that fits the bill and makes the costs more affordable.

Some of you may be packing for a trip overseas and answering calls from well-wishers and friends.

15. MONDAY. Active. The energy and motivation to get things done will bring success to your endeavors. Don't waste the morning on the housework. Get out and get the ball rolling. This is a good time to apply for a loan. If your home is in need of renovations, now is a good time to get started. A business associate may confide in you, giving you information that will put you in front of your competitors. You can carry the deal off without stepping on toes or upsetting the wrong person. You yearn for travel and adventure, and now is the time to arrange your trip. Apply for your passport and start budgeting. Once your trip is arranged, you will be amazed at how smoothly everything else falls into place.

16. TUESDAY. Fruitful. Get the day off to a good start by writing a gratitude list. Your appreciation of your environment and the people in it is heightened, and this will remind you how lucky you really are. An exciting event could be in the pipeline, making it hard for you to relax and concentrate on your work. Practice breathing and meditation to get back on track. A close family member may be returning from a long sojourn overseas, and you are busy with preparations for a celebration on their arrival. Parents of a child who is going through a difficult stage might consider enrolling them in a sports group and giving them a healthy avenue for releasing stress.

17. WEDNESDAY. Favorable. An unexpected and exciting new romance can set your heart alight. Good vibes and a sense of adventure are highlighted. Sagittarius couples might discover a hobby or interest that you can do together, sparking passion and romance again. Don't be afraid to do something new. Take a risk or invest in a venture close to your heart. Doubts can hold you back forever, and you'll never know what you can achieve if you don't try. You do need to watch out for risks when they are physically dangerous, though. Electrical problems and accidents might occur. Foreign cultures or philosophy might inspire your intellect and get you back to school to broaden your knowledge.

18. THURSDAY. Spirited. Fantasy and imagination can distort the true reality of a situation. Be aware of your desire for love and romance, and don't confuse it with your daily life. Otherwise, you might put someone up on a pedestal who will eventually fall off. Looking through rose-colored glasses, you will miss the pitfalls ahead of you. Have fun while you work. Your creative urge may

surface through a personal hobby as a talent you never knew you
had. Sharpen your knowledge of it. Then you may be able to earn
extra cash teaching others who want to learn. Take note of a promise that you have made and make sure to keep it. Otherwise, you
might never make it up.

19. FRIDAY. Beneficial. You may have so much work, you don't
get time to take a break. But the dollars will add up and your pay-
check will reward you. Perhaps there will be a bonus to encourage
your good work. Your financial position looks better than usual,
and it might tempt you toward extravagance. With your love of
luxury highlighted, spending could skyrocket and destroy your finances, so try to find the middle of the road. If you are working for
yourself, business is likely booming, and you may have to take on an
employee. Make sure you make the conditions clear, as you could
tend to be too easygoing for your own good and allow someone to
take advantage of your goodwill.

20. SATURDAY. Buoyant. The good vibes continue, and you
should enjoy your daily routine even more than usual. Good friends
may come around, and you could all end up partying into the night.
Sagittarius dieters will need to watch your diet. Overindulgence
in rich foods will detract from the fun you are having. If you are
too carefree, you might let out a family secret or repeat gossip to
the wrong person. Keep your overindulgence to the good things in
life. Enjoy fun and laughter with friends. Cook a nourishing home-
cooked meal with a delicious salad of nuts and greens, and go to
bed with a clear conscience. When it comes to love, remember to
maintain boundaries.

21. SUNDAY. Interesting. Being the life of the party should not
mean that you wake up with empty pockets, a wild hangover, and
no memory of what you did. An opportunity to do something you
have only ever dreamed about might be possible now. A very attractive foreigner who has been the object of a secret desire might
ask you out on a date. Surprises are in store for you, so brush up
and be ready. A spiritual gathering can be very uplifting, giving you
an understanding of the mysterious and divine. You will enjoy any
gatherings of people where you can broaden your understanding
and knowledge of life and the universe. Start saving for an extended
journey.

22. MONDAY. Auspicious. Venus, the goddess of love, has cruised
into Virgo, your tenth house of career and long-term goals, and will
visit Virgo through September 14. Make the most of this beneficial

influence. Venus brings favorable circumstances into your business
and professional life, attracting persons and circumstances that facilitate your work. People in authority are favorably inclined toward
you, and most activities in your professional life will run smoothly.
You may be involved temporarily in artistic work such as design, lay-
out, office decor, and public relations. A new love relationship with
an older person who acts as a guide can help you get ahead in life.

23. TUESDAY. Ambitious. Today the life-giving Sun joins Venus
in Virgo in your tenth house of career and long-term goals. This
next month is the time of year when you should turn your attention to the most outward aspects of your life: your career, your role
in the larger society, and your standing and reputation within the
community. You could come into the limelight. You may be called
upon to take over the direction of a task or project that gives you
considerable power. Success is much easier now. But you do need
to be aware of your capabilities, and don't pretend to be what you
are not. This is also a positive time for Sagittarius couples to start a
joint business venture.

24. WEDNESDAY. Uncertain. Be very careful what you say and
do because there may be ramifications for a long time to come.
Intense emotions will infuse any personal encounters with added
meaning. Whether what you are picking up is from the other person
or from your own unconscious drives is the problem. So it is better
to keep your feelings to yourself until you have had time to reflect.
Sexual attractions will be stronger than usual. You might end up
in a hot steamy affair with someone unsuitable or deceptive. Your
parents might need some assistance from you, even if just to hear
that you are okay and think about them. Give them a call and put
their minds at rest.

25. THURSDAY. Difficult. Problematic areas in your life might
start to ease. Don't relax too much, because your conscious attention is still needed. Conflict over finances between you and your
partner may start to ease also as you discover compromise and
cooperation. This will demand as much from you as your partner,
so don't expect them to do all the work. Sagittarius students can
experience problems memorizing and understanding important aspects of your subjects, making an upcoming exam a worrying thing.
Use rosemary oil to fortify your memory while writing and reading.
Very soon, clarity of mind will return.

26. FRIDAY. Successful. A powerful and positive planetary configuration hits off your areas of finance, work, business, and career

over the next couple of days, and portends good results with any activity in these areas. Archers seeking employment should get your resume out to as many people as possible. Don't be too shy to call in person about your favored positions. Business mergers should be profitable and build your reputation in the business world. You would be wise to have your accountant or lawyer go over all the details before you actually put your signature to any documents in order to ensure the legality of the venture. Get a health checkup to ease your mind.

27. SATURDAY. Cheerful. A cheerful intellect can steer you toward new and interesting people, places, and things. Contact with foreigners may whet your appetite for travel and the study of foreign cultures and trade. Mercury, the planet of communication, is now moving forward in the sky. You will find that delays and misunderstandings clear up, and contracts and agreements can be finalized successfully. You might escape the mundane with a movie or novel. Enjoy this easy relaxation. Love is in the air. Whether you are in a relationship or meeting someone new this evening, the time is ripe for romance and intimacy. Buy tickets to the theater or a concert to impress your date.

28. SUNDAY. Promising. Lying in bed with your lover or a good book may attract you far more than getting the chores out of the way or running the children around to their functions. Nevertheless, the day will unwind in its own way and take you along with it. Tonight the New Moon culminates in Virgo, your tenth house of career and long-term goals. This signals the beginning of a new lunar cycle, and bodes well for new enterprises in the business and professional realm. Social engagements might put you in a leadership role or even up front with the microphone as a celebrity in your own hometown. Be genuine, avoid false pride, and your reputation will blossom.

29. MONDAY. Uplifting. You're looking good and feeling good. Popular should be your middle name. With the favorable focus on your house of career, you can achieve more than usual. Luck is on your side also, although your reputation for good work, kindness, and generosity contributes to this. Some Sagittarius job seekers may get an opportunity to work through your partner or lover. If you are part of a large company, have a talk with your supervisor and they will give you some tips on how to advance faster. If they take a liking to you, it will be even better. Relocation due to career opportunities might upset your family. Sit down and discuss the benefits, and they will probably give their blessings.

30. TUESDAY. Mixed. The tension of the last couple of weeks is starting to ease, but don't get complacent or you will step on the wrong toes. It is important that you watch what you say and use tact at every opportunity. You may suffer from a tendency to worry about a certain situation, and could be simply making a mountain out of a molehill. Be in the present, and you will notice that everything is fine. It is usually only fear that makes tomorrow or yesterday not so fine. Involvement in sports will be good for your health and well-being. Don't sit inside. Get outside and use your muscles, and your whole approach to life will lift. You might also lose a few pounds and feel fit.

31. WEDNESDAY. Cautious. Teamwork will demand that you rein in your enthusiasm and inclination to speak before you think. Although you think that you know how it is meant to be, your companions may not agree. If you are having a problem, seek the counsel of an old and trusted friend who has the wisdom of experience. Sagittarius businesspeople experiencing a slowdown in trade and income should use this period to drum up business. Get a professional to help with your advertising and set up a Web page, and you can expect a marked improvement. Relations with women could be more difficult than usual now. Leave it alone. Anything you do to remedy the situation will only make it worse.

SEPTEMBER

1. THURSDAY. Caring. A strong love of nature is apparent at this time. The desire to give something back to the human race might incite you to join forces with an environmental or humanitarian group. With your constant yearning for travel and adventure, the idea of becoming a volunteer abroad could suit you completely. Check out all the options on the Internet as you may be able to build up your career at the same time. Sagittarius is definitely lucky when it comes to career, promotion, and pay increases. If you are not happy in your present position, start applying for positions that do appeal, or ask your boss for a promotion with better pay. You could be pleasantly surprised.

2. FRIDAY. Low-key. Take it easy and get plenty of rest and relaxation. If you have to work in a hectic environment, move behind the scenes and stay away from the high-traffic zones. Any work without interruptions will be enjoyable. You will especially enjoy research and study projects, which makes this an excellent day for students to catch up on your assignments. Emotional irritations could be prevalent. You are apt to be in a subjective frame of mind and take other people's comments personally. Don't judge yourself harshly. Curb self-criticism. When it starts to beat you up over little imperfections. Turn your perspective to the positives.

3. SATURDAY. Deceptive. What you see is not what you get today. Your mind could be playing tricks, using romantic notions to glorify the stark reality. Before making any important decisions, weigh the pros and cons as realistically as you can. Forget about what you hope for and look at the facts. If you are going away this weekend, ensure that your property is protected with a reliable security system. Likewise, don't leave valuable property in your car in a dark street, and you won't be a loser. By the evening, the ever-changing Moon will cruise into your own sign of Sagittarius and put you in the mood to party. Your popularity is on the rise, and you are likely to make some exciting new contacts.

4. SUNDAY. Independent. Mix with positive people, and the day should be a success. Social functions, entertainment, and new experiences are on the horizon, and you won't want to be bothered with the chores. Get out early so you don't waste any time. Your generous nature tries to look after everybody today, so you might have to practice tough love. Otherwise, your family could suffer. If you give too much to those outside the home, there won't be any time left for those at home. Be mindful of the things near and dear, and you can find a balance to suit your needs and those of others. Travel plans may be on your mind. You can use spare time to shop around for bargains on flights and accommodations.

5. MONDAY. Uncertain. Changes to your work hours, job description, employment conditions, or implementation of new technology might cause insecurity. Speak to the supervisor or your boss, and get the rundown on what is going on. It is probably just a new system designed to boost productivity and has nothing to do with you personally. Many of you are likely to be enjoying your employment conditions, and could consider extra study to improve your rate of pay. You can discuss this with your employer for extra feedback. They may even offer to pay for your extra training. Watch out for negative propaganda in your workplace and you will avoid getting caught in a corporate power struggle.

6. TUESDAY. Uncomfortable. Guard your savings. Hearty feelings and good vibes may lull you into spending more than you can afford, putting you in the unpleasant situation of having your credit declined. A friend or associate could be spreading rumors about you that are creating undue stress between you and your coworkers. Question behavior that makes you feel uncomfortable. If you are open and honest with others, they are likely to reciprocate. Challenging underhanded tactics is the best way of dissolving any suspicion others may have about you. If you are planning to ask your boss for a promotion or pay increase, do so before lunch and you are likely to get a favorable response.

7. WEDNESDAY. Impulsive. A certain level of irritability is likely to prevail in the current atmosphere. Try not to react to the jibes and insinuations of others, and you can avoid unnecessary clashes. There is a possibility of accidents or mishaps. The best advice is to pause before reacting emotionally in any situation. You may be in a conservative mood today, which is favored for planning a workable budget. Start to work toward your dreams, and set up a savings account that can turn into a valuable nest egg for the future. Your generous nature might inspire you to sign up as a volunteer for a local charity. If you care for others in your spare time, you will save money that would otherwise be spent on entertainment.

8. THURSDAY. Confusing. The pace of life picks up as the Moon slips into zany Aquarius and your third house of communications. Traffic jams are likely this morning and this afternoon. Drivers may be confused and distracted, causing minor accidents and big delays. If it seems like you will never get your work done, don't worry, it won't run away. Remember that life is what happens while you are busy making other plans. Slow down and enjoy what you are doing in the here and now. Archers tend to be future oriented and miss the small details. But if you start to take stock of the present, you might reach your goals faster. Practice breathing exercises for better focus.

9. FRIDAY. Demanding. Plan your agenda before you start today and try to keep yourself within this guideline. Otherwise, you may take on more than is humanly possible and run yourself ragged. Besides, the boss might notice that you are not doing your intended work and reprimand you, which would not be pleasant. If you are experiencing some doubts about an important decision, talk to someone older and wiser and benefit from their experience. You are going to have to draw the line when others ask for favors. Learn to strengthen your boundaries. Remember that helping another can sometimes enable them to be helpless, and can be quite detrimental to them in the long run.

10. SATURDAY. Dreamy. As the Moon cuddles up to mystical Neptune today, out will come the rose-colored glasses. There is a lovely mood for lazing around and enjoying the fantasy of a good book or a movie. Lovers can enjoy romantic vibes also, and find a secret love nest to whisper sweet nothings in each other's ears without interruption. There is a strong possibility of misunderstandings, though. Messages can become very unclear and colored by various hopes and fears. Leave anything important until tomorrow. Revel in some rest and relaxation. Just be sure your choices are not based on a wish to escape your responsibilities.

11. SUNDAY. Relaxing. Stay at home and enjoy finishing odd jobs and not having to run to a timetable. Family-oriented Sagittarius will enjoy the quality time with your loved ones. If the weather permits, you might enjoy a picnic at the beach or some other scenic spot. Good food and fun and games will put pleasure first and renew your love of life. Home renovations could be turned into fun by getting the whole family involved. Ask some friends or neighbors over as well and make it a party. Everyone has their own special skills to contribute in order to feel useful. Young lovers who were secretly planning to tie the knot may decide to announce and so surprise the family with the good news.

12. MONDAY. Hectic. Today's Full Moon in Pisces highlights your sector of home and family. Juggling your private life with your professional life could become a problem. No matter how important a family commitment is, your job is also important. If you are required to work, then you should talk to your family and find a compromise. If you take the approach that you are all in this together, the major decisions can be made collectively and alleviate blame on your behalf. Moving to another residence could be the result of a promotion. If you have to relocate, make sure you check out the neighborhood so that you know what to expect. Hopefully, there won't be any unpleasant surprises.

13. TUESDAY. Sparkling. The Moon and erratic Uranus create an atmosphere of excitement and expectation. Your creativity is at a peak. Budding Sagittarius artists might register for a course to get you going with the right techniques for your craft. Nervous tension can be high, especially if you are preparing for an important event. All the signs point to success in any venture you undertake now, so practice relaxation and enjoy the excitement. An unexpected surprise may turn your plans for the day upside down. But the spontaneity will give you a delicious sense of freedom. You might

202 / DAILY FORECAST—SAGITTARIUS—2011

cancel out of other engagements to let go and simply enjoy doing the things that you never get the time to do.

14. WEDNESDAY. Focused. Take it easy today. Make sure you can give the time and effort needed to attend to what is important. You have the ability to put out some impressive work if you can stay focused. A new romance or a relationship issue could keep interfering with your concentration. Rather than fight it all day long, pick up the phone and make a date so that you are not stuck in the anticipation of not knowing what will happen next. You have the ability to think outside of the box and come up with inventive ideas, which will impress business associates or employers. Be careful to whom you show your work. There are rogues who will brazenly steal your ideas.

15. THURSDAY. Exciting. Lovely Venus moves into Libra in your eleventh house of friends, hopes, and wishes. Venus bestows positive influences on these areas of your life. This might be the spark that lights an unexpected romance between you and a good friend, heightening your self-confidence and artistic ability. Make the most of what is on offer over the next three weeks as Venus brings a cornucopia of life's treats your way. Sagittarius artists may get the opportunity to exhibit your work and start earning an income from your passion. Writers also should send your manuscripts to the publishers. A favorable response is foreseen. Be careful what you wish for now, as it can come true.

16. FRIDAY. Fortunate. Advancement at work could come your way today. You are naturally good in a teaching or supervisory role because you can grasp the big picture and help other people to understand with kindness and empathy. Work in one of the caring professions may also attract you at this time. Practice constraint if you find that your popularity means friends are calling you all through your working day, as the boss is sure to notice your unprofessionalism. Overindulgence is a trap, especially if you use food or alcohol to medicate your feelings, as emotions are likely to be strong now. Perhaps if you are having trouble with your emotions, you could see a counselor instead.

17. SATURDAY. Satisfactory. Nervous tension could result from a stressful career. There are natural methods for eliminating stress from your everyday life. Check out the Internet for clues. Try yoga, meditation, and tai chi. See a nutritionist and enrich your diet with calming vitamins and minerals. Make sure you drink plenty of water; being properly hydrated eases many symptoms. If you have been asked to make a speech at a social function, put aside a couple of hours to outline what you want to say. Your seemingly spontaneous good cheer will benefit from added meaning and structure. A job offer to work overseas should not be scoffed at. Accept the offer, then start planning.

18. SUNDAY. Restless. The need for thoughtfulness is highlighted today. It is often said about Sagittarius that you are a careless talker. Today is no exception. Words spoken in jest or a simple throwaway line might spear a friend or loved one through the heart. Archers who are feeling bored should include your significant other in any plans for fun. If you leave your mate at home, you might never hear the end of it. Those of you who like to collect antiques or some form of artwork may discover a real prize for a bargain-basement figure. Set out to explore various consignment shops and thrift stores run by local charities.

19. MONDAY. Eventful. Mars, the planet that rules action and energy, shifts into Leo in your natural house of travel and adventure. Be willing to take a few risks to get a venture up and running, and you should not be disappointed. Your energy levels are likely to be good over the next six weeks, making this a great time to implement your plans. Many of you will make arrangements for an overseas adventure. Some of you may even quit your job to break out of the mundane in order to experience the excitement of new and different cultures. A romance with someone from a foreign shore could be the direct result of your interest in their culture and different way of life. This is also a good time to learn another language.

20. TUESDAY. Chancy. This is one of those days when the odds can go either way. Keep your wits about you and plan well ahead. Your romantic inclination might lead you into an entanglement with power and control. Enjoy the moment, but take what people say with a grain of salt. Reserve a decision or a commitment until a later date. Legal matters could become quite complex. You should leave nothing to chance and have your attorney deal with all aspects of the case. Those of you going through divorce proceedings and the resultant property settlement might be able to reach a compromise now. But if you do, get it in writing just in case your ex-partner changes their mind and reneges on the deal.

21. WEDNESDAY. Auspicious. Speculation and financial arrangements are favored. Don't expect the day to follow its normal routine. Changes in mood and differences of opinion could upset even the best plans. An interest in metaphysics might inspire you to visit a psychic or to study one of the occult sciences. You will enjoy an opportunity to philosophize with others now, but you must curb the strength of your convictions. You don't want to browbeat others with your opinions. You need to discuss all interpretations of the topic. Work in the import-export industry could hit a few snags due to changing political policies. The best way to overcome this is to study the ins and outs thoroughly.

22. THURSDAY. Pleasant. An opportunity to escape into the countryside or to travel for business may be a pleasant break in your routine. Be alert at work. A change in your direction is indicated. Expect surprises along the way. If you are driving, keep your eyes on the road and your hands upon the wheel. Intimacy is favored. If you can plan a romantic evening with your significant other, you will gain a better understanding of each other that allows for compromise. If you find that your partner has a different goal in life from your own, this doesn't have to be a problem as long as you are both willing to allow each other some personal freedom. This is probably easier to say than to do.

23. FRIDAY. Cooperative. The Sun moves into Libra, joining saucy Venus and serious Saturn there in your eleventh house of associates, hopes, and wishes. Benevolent Sagittarius is likely to think of others more than usual during the next month and perhaps put your friends first in many of your endeavors. Team sports will be a lot of fun, offering a great way to exercise and get fit. You will not enjoy rough sports, though. You will prefer sports that get you out into the great outdoors, perhaps surfing, skiing, or golfing. Students might be struggling with your cost of living and have to get an evening job. The improvement in finances and elimination of stress will far outweigh the loss of study time.

24. SATURDAY. Creative. Fantasy and imagination are highlighted, allowing you to tap into your unconscious creativity and be free from any hangups or childhood complexes. A major social event such as a masquerade ball or wedding could have you in a frenzy of preparation all day. Your ability to come up with unique ideas and jokes and keep everyone laughing will make you the center of attention in any social setting. An idea for a novel should be acted on. You can do this without heavy financial costs, just your computer and you, free to explore all the recesses of your mind. You will know what you want to say and how to say it. Follow your hunches and you can't go wrong.

25. SUNDAY. Lively. Mercury, the planet of communications, joins the Sun, Venus, and Saturn in Libra, accentuating your house of social groups, hopes, and wishes. Mercury here puts the focus on your communication and social intercourse. A younger person can attach themselves to you and put you in a mentor's role. This will have its benefits for you as well as for the younger person. Passing on your experience and wisdom will put many aspects of your life into a clearer perspective. A reexamination of some of your goals may occur at this time, perhaps because of a new relationship or simply because you are not achieving anything meaningful in your present course of action. Talk it over among friends.

26. MONDAY. Transforming. Be prepared for new insights that will bring up the need for change in an important financial or business venture. If you are worried about your financial situation, have a talk with your bank manager and see what can be worked out. The changes that are likely to occur today are those important to the harmony and balance within your life. Archers new to stepparenting might feel challenged by this unknown and untested relationship. The trick is to be willing to become friends with a stepchild. Do not vie for the attention of their parent, who is your lover. Sagittarius parents might be surprised by the news that another child is on the way.

27. TUESDAY. Insightful. This morning's New Moon is in Libra in your eleventh house of networking and future goals. The focus is on making contacts and reaching out to others in both a social and professional sense. It's a time to turn inner restlessness into fruitful contact with others. Get things back on track again. This New Moon influence may also inspire the launching of amazing work projects and health regimens. Be open to new ideas and suggestions. There is the possibility that some Sagittarius may resist change. This applies to your relationships, too. If your partner wants to discuss dissatisfaction, don't be oversensitive. A balance can be obtained as long as both of you are willing to compromise.

28. WEDNESDAY. Good. Life might start to get back to normal after the extra excitement and stress of the past week. Enjoy tidying up your office, sorting your correspondence into coherent piles, and answering your e-mails. That way you won't miss a great new offer from a club you belong to, or an advertisement about a community event you want to attend. Returned travelers may be surprised to get a call from friends overseas who have some very interesting news. You might receive an invitation to a celebration on a foreign shore and start planning your trip. Sagittarius salespeople are likely to make an impressive commission on a sale, which will boost your savings.

29. THURSDAY. Disruptive. Sudden upsets can thwart your ambitions and send you back to the drawing board. Stay away from the rat race. Give your nerves a peaceful environment in which to calm down. Archers love adventure and the great outdoors. Try to arrange a weekend adventure trekking in the mountains or relaxing in a seaside resort. It might stretch your budget, but it will improve your health. A new relationship can take on a more committed glow as you both give each other support to achieve your aims without a possessive need for control. Life should be getting better. You may find that upsets will open the way for a positive transformation in your life.

30. FRIDAY. Fair. It is easy for you to get worked up over an imagined slight. Watch your thoughts and don't get caught up in self-pity or a guilt trip. The facts of the matter are that most people are so caught up in their own dramas that they don't take any notice of what you are doing. Forgive yourself for any imperfections, then get on with the task of enjoying your day. Consider learning meditation. Or experience a guided meditation from an expert. Strive for mental peace and physical relaxation. Starting a journal would be a good idea also. You can look back over this period and gain enormous insight into your inner workings. Never doubt the value of hindsight.

OCTOBER

1. SATURDAY. Cheery. An early morning sunrise can set the pace for a magical day. Lots of celestial influences suggest social activity. Friends calling for advice, organizing a special celebration, visitors dropping by from a sports or social club are just some of the possibilities you can expect. Your own objectives are likely to be reliant on what other people are up to. But the harmonious aspects suggest you will have a lot of fun along the way. A tendency to overindulge or to take on too much is the only negative that might detract from your fun. Contact with people from foreign countries is indicated. You might actually be traveling or interacting with someone who is journeying abroad.

2. SUNDAY. Mixed. Practice self-love. Reinforce self-confidence that way. Remember to smile when you look in the mirror. Remind yourself of all the things you like about being you. A club meeting might take up more time than you had expected, making you late for the rest of your day. Be assertive and stand up for yourself in situations where people want to prattle on. Pull the topic back on track and enjoy what you are doing without having to watch the clock. Companions discussing philosophical or spiritual topics can become quite belligerent if you all stubbornly hold to pet peeves. Practice as much tolerance as possible, and try to eliminate prejudice or bias from the conversation.

3. MONDAY. Tricky. There is a danger that antagonistic situations can arise. Don't put yourself in an uncomfortable situation, and this will help you avoid trouble. Discussions over a property settlement or some other matter can blow up. So make sure a mediator is present to steer the conversation away from emotional issues. There is a likelihood of obsessive tendencies becoming obvious now. The positive side is that your ability to concentrate on your work and to achieve impressive results can open up new opportunities for advancement. The message today suggests that if you stick to your own business, the day promises success. But if you get caught in other people's business, it might not.

4. TUESDAY. Problematic. There are people around you who may be trying to exert influence over your ideas. This could have something to do with a business deal. You should not sign any agreement or contract without first double-checking all aspects with a legal or financial adviser. Someone might want you to take sides in a political dispute. Perhaps you will be asked to give someone a character reference when you really don't think they are of the best character. Two close friends going through a breakup may both seek your support. This is not a good time to enter into a business partnership. Trust what your own intuition tells you and support your own interests first.

5. WEDNESDAY. Wistful. A heightened sensitivity makes this day perfect for developing a creative talent or project. Any humanitarian endeavors are well suited to your energies as well. You may be totally disorganized and running around in circles, madly trying to get a thousand and one things done. But there will be those moments when serendipity steps in, and you find yourself in the exact right place at the exact right time and you couldn't have organized it better. A short but sweet romantic interlude can remind you that magic does happen. Just stop and let it in. Spiritual and philosophical pursuits will give your inquiring mind plenty of food for thought. Take time for study.

6. THURSDAY. Disconcerting. Strive for a friendly, cooperative attitude today. There may be times, quite unexpectedly, when someone decides that they know better, even after you thought you had discussed the ins and outs and everyone agreed. These irritations will contribute to a feeling of uncertainty. Life can be hectic, and there is a small chance of accidents. So watch any hasty or impulsive urges in order to avoid mishaps. Mechanical or electrical problems can also arise, so make sure all electrical equipment has been checked for safety. It might be time to take your car in for service. Student Archers may experience frustrations with your application to a learning institution.

7. FRIDAY. Sentimental. This is a day when art, poetry, and love will feel at home. Attempting to pay bills, meet a deadline, or keep your mind on business matters just won't fly. Mix-ups and misunderstandings may arise if you become absorbed with feelings and undercurrents instead of practical matters. Sagittarius artists should concentrate on your work. Your imagination is likely to conjure up some great ideas and impressions for you to transform. But students are advised to take the day off rather than try to get your mind to focus on facts and figures. Thoughts of someone who is grieving or unwell could spur you to visit, or at least to pick up the phone and call this dear one.

8. SATURDAY. Easygoing. Work around the home today and enjoy a break. Home renovations could get under way. You are sure to have some friends with special skills willing to come and give you a hand with any technical aspects that you aren't sure about. Don't be shy about asking. They will enjoy being helpful. You could supply lunch and make it a fun day for all. Read the price tags if you are shopping for an outfit to wear tonight. Your taste may lead you into the designer section and out of your financial comfort zone. A friend who recently returned from an overseas trip might call and entertain you with travel stories, encouraging you to arrange your own trip as soon as possible.

9. SUNDAY. Helpful. Sophisticated Venus slips into secretive Scorpio, your twelfth house of the unconscious. Selfless acts of compassion and empathy are foreseen. Your inclination to assist someone worse off than you could influence what is on your agenda for today. A secret love affair can move up a notch in passion and intrigue. Consider what you are doing here. The fact that it is secret means you don't want certain consequences. If this could be hurtful to another, it won't sit right on your conscience either. A new group of friends may enhance your self-image and introduce you to new experiences. Don't be surprised if they unexpectedly turn up for an impromptu party.

10. MONDAY. Innovative. You begin the new workweek with spontaneity and creativity working for you. Don't be afraid to have your say. Chances are your ideas will bring some fresh air into a somewhat stale situation. Invent new ways to get your work done and impress fellow employees. In fact, there may be an opportunity for you to get into a teaching role. If you are already teaching, you could receive an award as recognition of your talent in this field. Sagittarius parents might have trouble with a child who is not co-operating with your plans. Either discipline them or find out their reasons for this behavior. Don't fall into the trap of bribery. This will not be helpful to them or you.

11. TUESDAY. Spirited. Today's Full Moon falls in Aries, your fifth house of fun, lovers, and children, and heralds fresh beginnings among lovers and friends. It's a fun-filled day when facts and figures will be at the bottom of the list. Volunteer work could be at the top of your list. Volunteering could create a strange situation in which you have to pay someone to clean your house while you give your services freely to help someone else. Your brain might seem like scrambled eggs after a weekend of romance with a new love. All you can think of is hearing their voice over the phone. Electronic equipment can be unreliable, so don't be surprised if your phone or Internet connection refuses to bend to your will.

12. WEDNESDAY. Erratic. Quirky behavior is the order of the day. Stay out of arguments over social arrangements as they are likely to be reorganized at another date anyway. Cooperation may be almost impossible. A strong independent influence suggests too many chiefs and not enough braves. Competition between you and an associate can make working together very tense. If you focus on what you are doing and forget about anyone else, you are likely to achieve your desired goal. Remember, you are only as good as your competition. So wish them well, too! A legal matter may have to go to court, and this will cause concern over the cost. Don't worry about something that hasn't happened yet. Let go.

13. THURSDAY. Positive. Mercury, the planet of communication, joins lovely Venus in Scorpio to further accent your twelfth house of unconscious drives and compulsions. Childhood complexes can sabotage your plans and intentions. Listen to your thoughts. If you are suffering from any fears, dig deeper and find what you stand to lose or gain. Understanding the fear will ease its hold over you.

Gossip and power struggles should be the order of the day. If you feel that someone is denigrating your reputation, just turn your back. Unless you have foolproof evidence of their behavior, simply ignore it. Your good nature and reputation will outlive their underhanded manipulation.

14. FRIDAY. Interesting. The Sun meets Saturn in Libra and suggests that professional advancement is a possibility. It will definitely be on your mind, and can entice you to work even harder at your job. There may be new responsibilities now, or an unfinished matter from the past could resurface. Mixing with older people can be to your advantage if you listen to advice. One in particular may take a liking to you and have a word with someone important in your favor. If your employer asks you to represent the company, make sure you know exactly what to wear and what outcome you are trying to achieve. An opportunity to travel comes through work, but you won't get to pick your destination.

15. SATURDAY. Sensitive. Misunderstandings between you and your partner should clear up after lunch. Be prepared to say you're sorry, and it will make a difference. A spiritual influence in the heavens today could soften the materialistic aspects of life and put a whole new light on your problems. Don't plan to do too much, and you can get a lot achieved in a relaxed atmosphere. If you are not feeling well, make sure you are as loving toward yourself as you are to others. Enjoy nourishing food and rest. If you are worrying about a brother or a sister who seems to have disappeared, relax. Bad news travels fast. If you haven't heard anything, they are sure to resurface eventually.

16. SUNDAY. Surprising. This can be a busy day even if you haven't made any plans. Couples might decide to head out for a drive in the countryside and visit a relative you haven't seen for a while. When you arrive, another relative you haven't seen for ages may be visiting. Strange coincidences can remind you of things left undone and of some of the consequences of the choices you have made. The fickle finger of fate has its own agenda. The best you can do is to become more aware of your identity. A chance encounter with a group of friends may sweep you along to a social function. This promises to bring exciting new contacts into your life, perhaps even a new best friend.

17. MONDAY. Opportune. A significant celestial configuration promises success and opportunity in love and money. Plans to form a business partnership with someone who can complement your skills and talents with a multitude of their own are starred. Expect luck when it comes to financial decisions as long as you make sure they are aboveboard and fair to all parties involved. Corporate Archers might be involved in a secret merger to form a monopoly, and this too needs to be checked to make sure it is totally legal. Screen all employees involved in such secrecy. A leak would blow the whole deal wide open. Make it an early night for improved performance at work tomorrow.

18. TUESDAY. Frustrating. No matter how hard you try, the goal-post keeps shifting and you can't seem to get any closer to your prize. Do not lose heart. Your hard work is still making ground. You just can't see it yet Perhaps you could be a little kinder to yourself and use the steady approach instead of the all-or-nothing approach. Communication is your ace in the hole. Concentrate on putting your words to work for you. Get the people who matter on your side for extra help. Archers looking for work or fighting for a cause should write letters to the powers that be. Advance your case by outlining you credentials. Let that special someone know you care.

19. WEDNESDAY. Productive. As the Last Quarter Moon wanes, it is a good time to go back over your work to see if you have been thorough. Anything that needs adjusting can be done now to ensure that the new lunar cycle next week begins on a solid foundation. Relationship difficulties can also be reviewed, perhaps with the help of a counselor, to bring to light those blind spots that keep causing discord. Conversations between friends may be instrumental in manifesting a childhood dream. Build up your network of friends and associates who can be beneficial to you. Send out e-mails outlining your ideas. If you have worked it right, your dream will take on a life of its own.

20. THURSDAY. Restless. Vacations may be due, and plans to escape overseas might become a reality. Be organized when it comes to packing. Get advice from a fellow traveler on the necessities that should not be left behind. Sign up for insurance and avoid worrying about accidents or losing your luggage along the way. Your imagination is a positive attribute, especially when it comes to solving problems and finishing creative projects. Writers and artists can get your work out to the public with the benefit of a manager to advertise your unique style. You are open to learning new ideas and will enjoy all aspects of your life. You can see the usual with a new and unusual perspective.

21. FRIDAY. Misleading. Don't take anything at face value today. An offer that sounds too good to be true probably is. The same goes for an attraction to somebody new. Although you might feel that you are communicating wonderfully with each other, only time will prove that this is a fact. A bevy of conflicting influences warns that caution should be taken in all new endeavors. Your energy level is strong, suggesting that this is a good time for physical work or exercise. Sagittarius sportspeople should move your training routine up a notch or two. Stretch your abilities and move into the professional sphere. Sagittarius parents might be training a child, and finally start to see improvement.

22. SATURDAY. Eventful. Misunderstandings can cause all sorts of problems and delays. Be extra careful with neighbors who may be from a different cultural background. You might insult them without meaning to, and you'll have to live with the repercussions. Tread carefully in your local neighborhood because gossip will spread like wildfire. A focus on work and employment will enable you to use some overtime and catch up on a backlog of work. Salespeople will have creative new ideas for selling your product. Get ideas down on paper and make sure you don't forget anything important. Sagittarius in a committed relationship might escape for the weekend to reignite the passion and excitement with your mate.

23. SUNDAY. Reflective. Concerns over your reputation and professional advancement can put a damper on your social life. If self-improvement is your main objective, you may prefer to stay in the background, away from distractions and people. Disillusionment in love could be a product of your own making. If you idealize your partner and put them up on a pedestal, they will sooner or later fall off. Before you break it off, reflect on the fact that they are simply human, too, with all the faults this entails. The Sun moves into Scorpio today, and joins communicative Mercury and saucy Venus in your twelfth house of solitude and personal limitations. Sun in Scorpio signals a period for self-analysis.

24. MONDAY. Demanding. Group activities such as meetings could be very stressful. Agreement and compromise could be obvious by their absence. Decision making may have to be delayed until another day. Traveling could be equally frustrating in that your plane, bus, or train does not run on time, making you late for appointments. You may even miss one because you are too late. Your generous and kind nature makes you a very thoughtful person. But you do need to find a balance between what you do for others and what you do for yourself. Ensure that your needs are met and you aren't run ragged, or you won't be any good to anybody, let alone yourself.

25. TUESDAY. Challenging. High ideals can demand a superhuman performance, leaving you open to disappointment or even depression. Be practical and accept that some problems can't be resolved just by you. Forget about guilt and blame. They will only make you sick. If you are in an abusive situation, get some support to help you get out. The nature of abuse is such that it saps your self-esteem. Without any support or hope, all you have is despair. Remember that you cannot control others. They have their own free will. Start a journal and give yourself a chance to review your thinking. Or try a meditation retreat to discover the spiritual assets of love and peace within your own soul.

26. WEDNESDAY. Moderate. Today's New Moon hides in Scorpio and intensifies your twelfth house, which rules the unconscious inner drives that have power over you simply because you are not aware of them. Contemplation and inner reflection are favored at this time. A business lunch could be successful. Listen to your colleagues rather than try to sell your ideas. By tuning in to the emotional sensitivities of others, you can instinctively know the right response. Any time you can spend by yourself will be gold. Without any interruptions or the moods of others to accommodate, you can get in touch with what you are feeling and come up with truly original ideas. Meditation and yoga are starred.

27. THURSDAY. Varied. Although you are likely to shun the outside world, don't take the day off if you think your boss or teacher will find out. The repercussions of your deceit will be far worse than dealing with your normal routine. Romantic intentions can lead to a weekend hideaway that will give you and your mate the chance to get to know each other and enhance intimacy. An elderly parent might have reached a stage of not being able to stay in their own home. Investigate the options for nursing homes. If you have siblings, do not do anything without talking to them and reaching agreement. Work from behind the scenes if possible, and you will be surprised at what you can get done.

28. FRIDAY. Insightful. The Moon is now in your own sign of Sagittarius, boosting your popularity and putting the focus squarely on you. Your moods could be up and down and depend very much on the moods of those around you. Pamper yourself as much as possible. Perhaps you might get the time for a massage in order to boost your immune system and physical well-being. A creative project or hobby might be too expensive for you to keep up. Consider all your options before you quit. Remember, all work and no play is very unhealthy for any person. Sagittarius students may be able to win a scholarship if you push yourself a little harder. Join a study group with classmates.

29. SATURDAY. Buoyant. Good vibes and good friends should make this day one to remember. Acknowledge your own magnetism and allure, but avoid sounding arrogant or bossy. Although you may feel like staying at home on your own, the phone is apt to heat up and people might knock on your door. A local market with stalls selling knick-knacks from foreign cultures could inspire your thinking. Keep going and visit a museum, a cultural exhibition, or some other artistic play that strikes at your core. Your energy level may be a little flat. So this is a good time to implement a new diet and exercise plan. Join a local gym and engage a personal trainer to get the best workout.

30. SUNDAY. Peaceful. Hanging out at home alone or with your lover is starred. Pay bills. Ensure that you are up to date on all your repayments, credit cards in particular, so that you can avoid late fees and even higher interest. Sagittarius folk who live in a busy household may decide to fill up the gas tank and take a drive to wide-open spaces. Head for a scenic spot where you can walk and observe the ramblings of your mind while you enjoy nature and gentle exercise. Concern for a young friend might prey on your mind. Pay a visit and give them the benefit of your experience and knowledge. The role of mentor is a natural for Archers.

31. MONDAY. Trying. It may seem as if obstacles face you no matter which way you turn. Stop trying too hard, and put one foot in front of the other. If you focus on what is happening in the moment, the future will end up taking care of itself and will do a much better job than all your fussing and fighting could achieve. Conversations, especially gossip, should be ignored. Things are not what they seem. A teaching role might fall into your lap and before you know it, you're speaking to a crowd of enthralled students. Just let it flow. You know all the information you need. Otherwise, you wouldn't have been given the job. Boost your energy level with multivitamins taken along with meals.

NOVEMBER

1. TUESDAY. Deceptive. What you think and what you do can be quite different. Examine what it is that causes this dishonesty in your actions. Often, there is an underlying fear that you won't get what you want if you act true to your thoughts. Stop second-guessing others and find true freedom. You have support from behind the scenes, and may be tempted to manipulate a situation to your advantage. As long as you have the main players on your side, you should be successful. Plans for travel and adventure may be delayed. The current political climate can interfere with where you can go and what you can do there. Be practical, accept that there are powers stronger than you, and let it flow from there.

2. WEDNESDAY. Agreeable. Saucy Venus moves into your own sign of Sagittarius, adding charisma and charm to your attributes. You should make a favorable impression with others. You will be a valuable asset in business meetings and negotiations. You can make peace among others and pay the mediator effectively during this Venus influence. A certain amount of restlessness may interfere with job satisfaction or your daily routine. Try all avenues. Get involved in social pursuits and volunteer work, and you might find what you are looking for. A desire to help others should be strong. Any involvement in humanitarian or environmental issues can revive your inspiration for life, love, and adventure.

3. THURSDAY. Entertaining. Mercury, the planet of communication, joins Venus in your own sign of Sagittarius and stimulates your mind and ideas. Talking and socializing are your forte now. You will gain great enjoyment from mixing with different people. You do have to keep a watch on your focus. Your mind can jump from one thing to another and confuse you as well as others. There is a fortunate aspect for business negotiations and contracts, which adds to your normally adventurous nature. You may find yourself getting around your local area far more than usual. As you travel around, keep your eyes and ears open. You may encounter profitable and interesting experiences along the way.

4. FRIDAY. Distracting. The responsibilities of home and family can seem like lead weight restricting your sense of adventure and inhibiting your dreams. Talk to your loved ones, and you may be able to organize time for personal freedom. Finding the balance between work and play can be achieved with a cooperative approach. You are probably in a chatty mood, and may not get off the phone for most of the day. In fact, you could end up being an impromptu counselor to friends, neighbors, or siblings. Avoid getting involved in other people's drama. Doing that will bring problems you don't need. This is a positive time for a business venture. Collaborate with colleagues over the next move.

5. SATURDAY. Lively. Your creative use of imagination and ingenuity can win you lots of brownie points from those around you. Your mind may tend to be overactive, but you're highly inventive. When anyone has a problem, you are apt to work out ways to fix it. Your artistic urge won't let you down. Get out the tools of your trade and amaze yourself with what you produce. Make your own holiday cards. With your talent, you can make each card a unique message of your love. Social gatherings will be very enjoyable, but watch what you say. In your gregarious mood you could talk to the wrong people about the wrong things and give away important secrets.

6. SUNDAY. Impulsive. Patience is a virtue, but it may be very hard to find in today's celestial climate. Watch your words. Archers can be very tactless at times, and you don't want to hurt someone's feelings inadvertently. If you are not feeling one hundred percent, make an attempt to look after yourself. You are likely to push yourself to the limit and make things worse. Sagittarius parents may have worries about a child. Any attempt at discussing the situation with them now might turn into an argument. Do something exciting together. Break down the barriers through friendship rather than discipline. Shoppers can get a good deal on linens and other fine fabrics.

7. MONDAY. Pleasing. Regular daily happenings can turn out to be full of romance and mystery. A brief encounter with someone who captures your mind and imagination, not to mention setting your heart racing, might dominate the rest of the day. Your thoughts will be focused on engineering another meeting. If you are about to receive an award or honor, don't let the jitters hinder your experience. Chamomile or valerian are calming herbal teas, and a splash of lavender oil will also help. A very helpful colleague may give you a lead on a promising new investment, all the while feathering their own nest. Find out what their expectations are before you get wildly excited.

8. TUESDAY. Disillusioning. All things being equal, your life should be sailing along pleasantly enough. Still, your mood could plummet into a dark and depressed place. This is a good time to sit down with pen and paper and let all your thoughts out so that no one else has to hear. Before you know it, the mood will pass and sunshine will light up your life. Worries over a child could take your thoughts away from your job. Going over and over a problem will not help you solve it. Practice some breathing exercises and relax as much as possible. Concentrate on the work at hand. The future will fall into place. If you try to take control, all you'll do is create more problems.

9. WEDNESDAY. Lucky. Awaited news can bring cause for celebration. Simple plans can lead to important new opportunities. Keep your eyes and ears open. Serendipity treads quietly. Your finances should be in good shape. If they are not, then perhaps you might hope for a lottery win. Luck is yours, so purchase a ticket. Do not procrastinate when it comes to an important meeting, deal, or investment or you might miss out. The mood is such that you may just expect results without putting in the hard effort. This attitude will let you down now. You have to help luck along. Archers looking for work should get an early start and show up first at an audition or interview. It will make a difference.

10. THURSDAY. Irritable. Restlessness on the job may be because you are not being fulfilled and have little job satisfaction. Take a look at your options. Compare them to what your heart desires and what are your long-term goals. If these are not compatible, then it is time to question your values and priorities. Perhaps be prepared to let go and welcome a change. The Full Moon in Taurus shines its light on your sixth house of work and health. If you aren't happy with your daily work, your health is bound to suffer. Consider returning to study. You might be surprised at the options available to you. Sagittarius adventurers might find a course out of the country that fits your budget and fires your mind.

11. FRIDAY. Motivating. Mars, planet of assertiveness, has moved into Virgo and lends energy and action to your house of career. Mars here arouses your ambition to achieve, and you will be willing to work very hard to reach your goals. But you won't tolerate too much authority over your initiative and independence. This is a perfect time to get a business venture off the ground and start working for yourself. Dealings with government officials can be testing. Watch out for competitors in your chosen field. Don't become angry or resentful if anyone achieves more than you do. Any attempt to defeat a challenger could just hold you back from your own objectives in life.

12. SATURDAY. Renewing. Stop thinking about the future and enjoy the present. Cultivate companionship with your significant other. With good insight and fundamental instincts, you can intuit a partner's needs. Renew the deep love that each soul yearns for so much. Cultivate the passion and the supportive commitment that belong to you. Single Archers are sure to be dressing up in your glad rags to meet someone and hoping for subtle cues and magical openings, which are bound to arise. It is all about being in the right place at the right time. If you stay at home, you will miss out. You might be named as a speaker at an important social function this evening, so dress to impress.

13. SUNDAY. Harmonious. The celestial influences favor family get-togethers and reunions. A celebration for a christening, wedding, or anniversary can renew the ties that bind and uncover parts of family history you were hitherto unaware of. Listen to your elders and hear some valuable advice. Charity work will be well rewarded today. Some of you might be caregivers for someone less fortunate, and will discover a friendship and love worth far more than gold. If you have recently experienced a marriage breakdown, make the most of your friends and family ties. Human contact heals pain. It doesn't take long for love to creep back into daily life. Positive thoughts will bring positive outcomes.

14. MONDAY. Helpful. Whatever the cause for concern, don't worry, it will pass. The morning starts off with vibes of competition, financial losses, or a personal setback. But by the evening there should be cause for celebration. A large bill may arrive in the mail and threaten your feelings of personal security. If you call the company and arrange a repayment plan, your fears will drop away. Budgeting will be good for you anyway. After the bill is paid off, you can start saving for something you hold dear. You have good friends and plenty of support around you, so call in a favor if you need some extra help. Don't borrow money to pay back a debt, though, as this is simply moving sideways.

15. TUESDAY. Prosperous. Your career looks to be on the up and up, and you may celebrate with the purchase of a big-ticket item. Do be sure that you have insurance for all your property and you can live worry free. You may be surprised at what you will end up doing. Inventive Archers might start an Internet business and enjoy the freedom. If you are a fund-raiser for a local charity, put forward your ideas and you may come up with a real winner. So good, in fact, that you might end up with an opportunity to start your own business and build up valuable equity. You may have to take time off work to care for an ill child or a parent. See your employer and ask if you can work from home.

16. WEDNESDAY. Complex. There may be so many things to attend to that you don't know where to start. Begin by changing your attitude from worrying about your abilities to being thrilled by the chase. You will do what you can do. But how you think and feel about it is the difference between enjoying life or not. You may be suspicious if your partner seems to be preoccupied with people and activities outside your home and family. Rather than jump to conclusions, try explaining your feelings and asking your partner. There is likely to be a much simpler explanation than what you are imagining. Many of your problems could be of your own making. Relax and stop fretting.

17. THURSDAY. Upbeat. Good fortune presides over this day. If you are not happy with the usual run-of-the-mill routine, you may initiate change at every opportunity. Playing the prankster should keep people laughing, but might get you in trouble with your supervisors, teachers, or employers. A sudden interest in New Age subjects can introduce you to another perspective on the meaning of life, the universe, and everything. But over time, this might open doors into areas of employment not known right now. Anything that expands your understanding of the world and all its peoples will be of major interest. A course in martial arts might get you fit and give you a spiritual understanding.

18. FRIDAY. Disquieting. A lack of exercise or an excess of rich and fatty foods can cause irritability and discontent. Start drinking plenty of water and taking a walk each day, then watch the improvement. Those near and dear will be the first to notice and cheer. You have many possibilities open to you. Whether it is job advancement, travel, or love, it is up to you. Don't be your own worst enemy and look for all the negatives. With that sort of attitude, you will lose before you even start. Think positive and the world is your oyster. An offer of a leadership role will be beneficial. Feeling shy is normal. Accept the offer and take it as it comes. Your confidence will grow day by day.

19. SATURDAY. Good. A social role or activity might put you in the public eye. You may have the gift of oratory. Your empathy and ability to read the moods of others will endear you to them. Your busy schedule and willingness to take on even more may be the cause of physical lethargy. But while your mind races, you may not want to get off the couch. Delegate others to take care of your most pressing engagements, then relax for a change. Go for a swim or play in the garden. Anything that grounds you and that lets the soothing vibes of nature slow your brain and bring a little bit of peace will be the order of the day. Make sweet love to your lover and sleep well.

20. SUNDAY. Fair. Take a backseat and get as much rest and relaxation as possible. You may want to do a bit of work on your health. Throw out all the instant snacks that are really junk food. Shop at a farmer's market for local fruit, vegetables, and nuts. The nutrition in fresh food will boost your energy and your immune system, and you'll be more alert in no time. A secret attraction to a friend or neighbor could make you feel awkward around them. Come clean and tell them of your feelings. Ask them out on a date and you may not be disappointed. Those of you already in a relationship would benefit by focusing on your lover and letting go of all your other cares and woes.

21. MONDAY. Inspiring. Plans for a new project need your whole-hearted attention if you are going to get it off the ground. Shut yourself away from interruptions and finalize your ideas. The peace and quiet will do you good at the same time. This is one of those days when contemplation will allow your intuition to speak to your heart. Start a journal if you don't already have one, and let the pen have a life of its own. You'll be amazed at what comes to light without censoring or editing. One of your friends might ask you for a sizable loan and put you on the spot. You may want to help, but are unsure whether you can trust them to pay you back. Find out if you can get a guarantee.

22. TUESDAY. Energetic. Happy birthday, Sagittarius! Today marks the beginning of your annual celebration. The life-giving Sun rolls into your sign and adds its warmth and creativity to everything you do over the next month. This is a great time to do a personal inventory, assess how far you have come toward your goals, and be grateful for all the good things in your life. This could be a busy day, so make sure you eat a good breakfast. Treat yourself with love, and you will always have a smile on your face. Your ability to make friends and influence people is on the rise. A cherished goal might start to look achievable. Romance will also be a highlight this month.

23. WEDNESDAY. Restless. A chronic case of itchy feet might drive you out of the house in search of adventure. If you have a sick day to use, now is the time to take advantage and hit the road for a change of scenery and a spontaneous adventure. Visit a museum or an exhibition heretofore unseen. Take a drive to a town or cultural spot that you haven't visited before and give your mind something new to think about. If you don't get out, you are likely to stay at home alone and surf the Net or watch television all day long. Beware of retail therapy. Instead, examine your thoughts in order to understand what is creating this inner need for self-gratification.

24. THURSDAY. Unsettling. Beware of the temptation to gloss over bad behavior. Even white lies can have powerful repercussions. You may want to make a situation look better than it is. Or you may fool yourself into believing what you want to believe. But at the end of the day the truth remains the same. Your denial simple enables what is not kosher to keep on keeping on. The Scorpio Moon signals that you are at a low point in your lunar cycle. Look after yourself now more than ever. Finish those odd jobs and personal projects that are holding you back from going forward. Clear out what is not needed. Then make room for something new and refreshing to come in and take its place. Practice love, and that is what you will get.

25. FRIDAY. Refreshing. The New Moon in Sagittarius today heralds the start of a new lunar cycle, promising happy and creative vibes. Single Archers might have a new romance on the boil, and start to feel that something more will follow. Your love of life gives off a charisma that attracts all sorts of good things into your life. Mercury, the planet of communication, has just moved retrograde in your sign and will stay retrograde until December 14. This will cause misunderstandings and delays to all forms of communication. Contracts and agreements can fall through or get held up during this time. Travel plans are best left until after Mercury moves forward again. Use this time for reflection.

26. SATURDAY. Favorable. Attractive Venus cruises into Capricorn, your second house of values and money, adding love and generosity to your daily life. Loving relationships are apt to intensify and bring you closer to your significant other. Singles looking for love might get more than you bargain for, so watch out for possessiveness and dominating types. You should find plenty of bargains to make your shopping trip worthwhile. An incredible deal on finance can allow you to refurnish your home, with no interest or repayments for years. But don't let this justify the purchase of something way beyond your means. You will eventually have to pay for it.

27. SUNDAY. Dramatic. Watch out for childish acts that say you are not getting enough of what you want, or that reveal your need to please because you don't feel good enough. Resentments are the first sign that something is not right inside. So rather than look at others, take a hard look at yourself first. Your partner might be flirtatious and belittle you in front of others. Do not make a scene about your partner's behavior. This will only put you in the same boat. Instead, you might be better off to state your feelings and simply leave. This will put the ball firmly back in their court. You might be undecided about a work-related decision. Stop thinking about it. When you least expect it, the answer will come.

28. MONDAY. Variable. Work prospects look excellent, as does your earning capacity. Be willing to make changes if you are not satisfied with your current employment. Go back to school, or sign up to volunteer abroad. Even volunteering in local institutions will give you work experience as long as it is compatible with your chosen career. This is a great time to apply for a loan for the purchase of property or a business. Gather up all your references. Before you put in your application, research which financial institution gives the best rates and is reliable. Personal concerns may be your main priority. Perhaps you need time off work to deal with things.

29. TUESDAY. Intuitive. This is one of those days when you need to turn off your mind and let yourself act spontaneously. Trust that your inner instincts know what is right for you and go with it. The more you question yourself, the more paralyzed you will become. A secret attraction to a coworker could come out into the open when they ask you for a date. It might surprise you to know that while you have been slyly checking them out, they have been doing the same to you. The universe is on your side if you just relax and let it flow. Tidy up your paperwork. Then you won't overlook a bill or some other correspondence that also needs attending to. Gossip sessions can have negative repercussions.

30. WEDNESDAY. Harmonious. Despite your current busy schedule, you can remain remarkably cool, calm, and collected. Make the most of your charisma to win friends and influence people, and you will be amazed at what you can achieve. A role as a representative for your workplace or for teammates will bring out the best in you. Don't refuse to do your bit for the group. Sagittarius writers can rely on today's intellectual stimulation to finish a manuscript for publishing. Your material should be welcomed warmly. Those of you home from school can put in valuable study time now. Get assignments ready for submission in order to earn high grades. Just be sure to address all questions.

DECEMBER

1. THURSDAY. Useful. There is an intensity in the air that will set everybody's passion meters on high. Shoppers are bound to find an expensive piece of apparel that you just have to have, although you don't know where you will wear it. In fact, it might just hang in the closet, but you will always love it. Home renovations will come to the fore with renewed inspiration to beautify your home and make your everyday life that much more enjoyable. You will want the very height of fashion now, so shop around for the best prices before you buy. Your energy level could be a bit flat. You might have to bring work home with you so that you can catch up before your deadline is due.

2. FRIDAY. Challenging. The competition is likely to stretch your abilities and bring out the best in you. Delays can be very frustrating. You may be waiting for a check to arrive, a contract to be signed, or word about a job application. Yet nothing is happening. With Mercury, planet of communication, and Jupiter, planet of abundance, both in retrograde motion, these two aspects of life can't move forward. Meanwhile, concentrate on your preparations for the festive season and be prepared ahead of time. It will take all the pressure off in the final week when the whole world seems to operate in a frenzy. Spend time with your loved ones. Perhaps you could take them out to dinner and have a laugh.

3. SATURDAY. Manageable. Today's message says not to take yourself for granted and don't let precious resources sit idly by when you can put them all in play. Think twice before running out to buy something new. You may already have what you want in the cupboard. Don't be a slave to fashion. Use your creative style and flair to create your own world the way you like it. Give yourself a break from your fantasies and be happy being normal. Play in the garden, visit friends, throw an impromptu party, or just laze around your home. You can do as you please. Romance is not far away for lonely hearts. Put on your Sunday best and visit new locales. You never know who you will meet.

4. SUNDAY. Stimulating. Prepare for an exciting day. Romance is high on the agenda for most Archers, whether you are sleeping in late with your nearest and dearest or out early visiting your favorite club. Nestling up close and feeling the nurture of love and desire will be your main aims. Parents should take your kids out for fun at a theme park, or for an adventure in the countryside. Be reserved about bringing along friends, as this may make for mischief and interfere with intimate contact. A burning ambition might override all other plans. Even while out with your loved ones, you are plotting and planning your rise to power. Keep a notebook with you for writing down ideas.

5. MONDAY. Enthusiastic. Incorporate fun into your routine day and put a smile on everyone's face. Don't be afraid to put your reputation on the line with a new idea. Your creative abilities are heightened and your career prospects look very positive. You may even have some excess cash that you would like to invest. A broker will have some great ideas for you to think about. Don't delay. Call and become a client while the aspects say go. Business plans could be held up until after the holidays. So spend this time refining your ideas and perfecting all the ins and outs. Young and single Archers may meet a stunning new love who not only looks gorgeous but also has money in the bank!

6. TUESDAY. Frustrating. Try not to rush. Then you won't have to redo as many things. The Taurus Moon makes a strong aspect to Mercury and to Jupiter, which are both in retrograde motion. This means slow down. Reflect, review, reorganize, reapply, redefine, re-examine, repair, reassess. If you are trying to do one hundred things at once, stop, then start with one at a time. Your day will be so much more enjoyable. The amount of work you manage to plow through will be impressive. Enjoy the camaraderie of coworkers and a long lunch. It will eliminate stress and give you a new outlook on many things.

7. WEDNESDAY. Positive. You can wake up feeling refreshed and ready for life this morning. Stop thinking about applying for a promotion or pay increase and just do it. The sooner you do, the sooner it will come through, and you will need some extra cash over the next few weeks. Get your holiday card list compiled. Organize your plans for the silly season so that you won't miss out on anything. Take your car in for service and check any other mechanical or electronic equipment you rely on. It will be cheaper to service them than have to repair a breakdown. Research and revise a diet that isn't working. You might prefer to simply cut out fats than give up the good life at this time of year.

8. THURSDAY. Confusing. Plans can change on you and leave you wondering how you can juggle your personal and professional spheres. Perhaps it would be easier if you considered what is most important to you personally. Then make sure that this area of your life is satisfied first. You will find that everything else will fall into place after that. Your partner could be sending mixed messages. Instead of trying to guess, just ask straight out what is going on. At least this way you might circumvent the buildup of frustration that is bound to happen if the situation continues. Satisfy the traveler inside you by dining at ethnic restaurants in your community.

9. FRIDAY. Tense. Steer clear of arguments and any conflict with your significant other. There is no use trying to work out resolutions at the moment. You are more likely to create new misunderstandings. It might be better to send messages of love and at least nurture the good part of your relationship. Write your resentments down on a piece of paper and bury them in the backyard. Give them to the universe and start your day afresh. Forgive and forget is your best motto. A legal matter can be held up and demand more paperwork. Be thankful for this chance to make sure you have done everything properly. If this problem hadn't occurred, a successful conclusion might have eluded you.

10. SATURDAY. Distracting. You could spend hours on the phone chatting, catching up with people you haven't seen for ages, while the housework stays undone. Instead of getting your planned activities under way, you may go out for a game of golf, or participate in some other sport or social interest in your life. Regardless of what you end up doing, you may possess a sense of inner restlessness that tells you you should be doing something else. Consider what it is you are avoiding and how long you wish to keep doing so. At least then you will be conscious of what is really going on. You may be afraid to visit a parent because of unfulfilled expectations. Face up to it and clear your conscience.

11. SUNDAY. Fair. Trust your instincts and don't believe all you are told. Be discerning; don't buy something just because you can afford it. Use the installment plan if you can't afford the total cost up front. Shopping for presents can be challenging as you try to find that special something for the main people in your life. A spiritual or philosophical gathering can be very powerful, touching you with a sense of the magical and mystical. A workshop in chanting or another equally wild art will add a new perspective on the ordinary, and allow you to express the artist within. Wondrous coincidences might occur to remind you that the universe works in mysterious ways.

12. MONDAY. Innovative. The changing face of your social group can give you insight into your own personal growth. You might be acting as a mentor for your partner at the moment and find that your abilities surpass your expectations . You both might decide to join your talents and start a business partnership that allows you both more freedom and initiative. Do be careful of extravagance. Your exuberance for the aspects of life that you love is not based on the practicalities of daily life. Business matters look promising. You have new contacts who can help you restructure your approach toward a wider market. If you are planning to employ others, check out the insurance coverage and costs.

13. TUESDAY. Slow. Whichever way you look today, there is likely to be some sort of problem or blockage. Throw out your timetable and accept that you will need to work through each one by one. Your partner or colleagues could question what you are doing now, and bring your attention to something important you have overlooked. So don't jump to conclusions or get annoyed too fast. You may have been avoiding an issue in the workplace, but today you can't do that anymore. Whether you like it or not, you will be held accountable for past mistakes. A property or investment matter could dominate business discussions. Be prepared to let go of the old to make way for the new.

14. WEDNESDAY. Smooth. Colleagues as well as outside vendors should follow your lead now. Your business manner is persuasive. You can achieve the things you set out to achieve and then some. Plan your day well so that you can cover all aspects of your business. Mercury, the planet of communication, has moved direct. Now misunderstandings and delays can be cleared away. Contracts and agreements, as well as business negotiations, are also likely to move toward finalization. Travel plans can be made, and you are likely to stumble upon a great bargain-basement price for the destination of your choice. A nagging suspicion about a deceitful colleague could prove to be right.

15. THURSDAY. Dreamy. Plans for the future can interfere with your work in the here and now. Keep your mind on the job, and you won't have any slipups or accidents. Furthering your career can open up new avenues of learning that will broaden your mind. You may find that you get a taste for new realms of thought and don't want to stop. Philosophical or religious discussions could get out of hand, as the topic strikes a nerve in the participants. You could be very gullible at the moment, so take everything that is said with a grain of salt. Curb a desire to drink if you are going out tonight. Your energy level would benefit much more from good food and an early night.

16. FRIDAY. Bumpy. Be mindful of personality differences, and you can avoid stepping on the toes of others. Problems during your workday may bring up the desire to find a career that gives you independence and initiative. Sagittarius desires freedom and adventure, and you might find this desire somewhat stymied throughout the day. You and everybody else are likely to take more risks than usual. Keep your eyes open when working close to others or traveling in your car. Do not broach subjects with your family or fellows that demand cooperation and compromise. These attributes might be sadly missing in most discussions. If you can, wait another day to achieve a positive and unified outcome.

17. SATURDAY. Fulfilling. Focus on your appearance and your presentation in public, and you will achieve the results you desire. Working with others in a community event will be starred. You are making new contacts and establishing your reputation among your neighbors. The camaraderie and good vibes will make for a fun-filled family day. Social events and commitments might be so thick that you feel like you only go home to sleep. Family Archers should include loved ones in a day activity, or build the evening around them. In the long run, no matter what you do in your life, these are the people with whom you travel the important years.

18. SUNDAY. Spontaneous. Be prepared for the unexpected, and you won't be surprised. You may have planned a day at home to organize the coming week. Instead, you are bombarded with visitors from far and near. Some might descend and expect a bed for the night. Be very straightforward about what you will and won't do. Don't get sucked into lending money, as you might not see it for a long time. A new relationship could be high-maintenance, and you're starting to wonder how you can escape. Be up front, be kind but honest, and you will avoid more painful times. You could be celebrating a birthday and decide to go to a catered venue. There you can relax, and the house will stay tidy.

19. MONDAY. Demanding. Don't soldier on over a problem. Call on your extensive network for the skill and assistance you need. Developing a team effort in the workplace will also bring rewards. Many hands make light work. You could be working on a large-scale project that demands a lot from you by way of responsibility and commitment. Rather than let this weigh heavily on your shoulders, just take one thing at a time. Breaking it down into smaller components will make it easier to focus on. If this is beyond your scope, consider delegating and play the role of overseer while you get more than one thing done at a time. Service in a humanitarian organization may stretch you to the limits.

20. TUESDAY. Low-key. Avoid overloading your workday. This is a hectic time of year, and you might find that there is no need to do as much as it might seem. Take care of the most pressing matters, and find time for yourself as well. Do what you can to recharge your spiritual batteries, whether you attend a worship service, go for a long walk, or spend hours reading a good book. Time for yoga and meditation will also be a treat. As the sensitive Scorpio Moon passes through your twelfth house of secrets and solitudes, any quiet time you can get will be golden. Meet that special someone for lunch and enjoy a romantic moment in between appointments.

21. WEDNESDAY. Favorable. Luscious Venus has moved into Aquarius, your solar sector of communication, and brings affection and good company into your daily life over the next few weeks. Contact with your siblings, neighbors, and friends is likely to pick up. What might start out as a quick call or short lunch can turn into long conversations full of fun and laughter. You might want to bring art or artistic creativity into your daily life now. If you haven't already begun decorating, there is no time like the present. Involve the whole family in making your own decorations. With paint and glue and sparkles, you can have lots of fun together. Your boss might pass out a festive bonus.

22. THURSDAY. Bright. As the loving Sun moves into Capricorn, your second house of money and values, the Moon moves into your sign of Sagittarius and bolsters your popularity. Put yourself first. Make sure you have your plans truly in place before you get side-tracked into helping others. You may have several invitations for the holidays, but you decide you are not going to do the usual thing this year. Some of you might be taking off on a vacation as soon as your work closes down. If you are well organized, you can relax and enjoy early celebrations. Then you won't have to worry about overindulging that would hinder your upcoming plans.

23. FRIDAY. Productive. Pay attention to your finances. You might want to pay your outstanding bills now and not have to worry over the coming week. If you have any gifts left to buy, do it now and don't wait until the crush of tomorrow. You might go to a small shopping center and find something different from the run-of-the-mill fare available at the malls. Objects of art and specialty wares can seem more appropriate to you at the moment. You are in danger of spending big, so leave your credit cards at home to remove that temptation. You might be amazed at the work you get done in between helping others to finalize their projects. Love and laughter are infectious.

24. SATURDAY. Revitalizing. A friendly and relaxed atmosphere may prevail. The company of your family or neighbors can be particularly interesting, just what you need. Today's New Moon in Capricorn lights up your financial sector and brings opportunity to improve this aspect of your life. A business proposal might arise out of a casual conversation with a friend you haven't seen in ages. Unusual and unexpected fortune can sparkle amid your daily routine. An overly optimistic attitude can prompt you to make promises you can't keep, so be mindful of what you are saying in order to avoid future problems. Stay close with loved ones this Christmas Eve. Savor the love and inner peace.

25. SUNDAY. Merry Christmas! There is a strong spiritual flavor today, with the emphasis on helping those less fortunate. Your kind and generous Sagittarius nature is evident. You will be loved by your fellows for your good cheer. Some of you might be far from home. Catch up with family and friends over the Internet while you join in with the different style of celebrations of a foreign land. You may find that your values are changing. You are enjoying pleasures that money can't buy, and are starting to appreciate certain things you normally don't notice. Be cautious traveling on the roads. If you are going a long distance, check the weather forecasts to ensure you are prepared for what is ahead.

26. MONDAY. Successful. Your ruling planet, benevolent Jupiter, has moved direct. All the blockages to expansion or travel will clear away. Work and business opportunities will become clear. You will know when it is the right time to act. Your intuition is strong, your hope for prosperity is justified. Some of you might have a house full of guests from afar. Enjoy the conversation and gossip while everyone shares the tasks of cooking and cleaning. A neighborhood celebration may take you away from your hearth and into the larger family of the community. Dancing and singing are joyful expressions of shared values and commitments.

27. TUESDAY. Opportune. You might get the chance to make some extra money today. You are likely to be mixing with people who have different ideas from yours, and gain a new perspective on your usual life. Sometimes it is helpful to talk to others about problems in a relationship and get the benefit of their objectivity. Just offloading fears and resentments onto an impartial listener helps you to clear out these negative emotions. You might have to cut your holiday short to return to help a family member or because of a business matter. Perhaps, despite all the festive cheer, some people just can't get along. The return to your usual routine and the comfort of home will be reassuring.

28. WEDNESDAY. Disconcerting. Stick to your original plans, no matter how good an idea sounds. Once you start changing one thing, you'll be surprised at the problems that arise later on. Romantic dreams and ideals might distort reality. Today's vibes are much more attuned to creative activities than pragmatic black-and-white issues. If you have an important meeting or appointment, make sure you have a map and clear directions. Mix-ups and delays are a high possibility, as are breakdowns. The feeling of déjà vu can bring back a dream from last night and add a touch of magic to your day. Call that special someone. Make a date to share intimate moments of tenderness and desire.

29. THURSDAY. Satisfying. Your usual daily routine will be rewarding. Chores around the home might bring deep satisfaction as you use your creative skills to improve comfort and pleasure for the loved ones in your life. The chance to take over the training of new employees might inspire you, adding extra enjoyment to the working day. Concentrate on developing your natural talents, and give up trying to be someone you are not. You might be amazed at the opportunities available to you now that you are not imagining the grass is greener elsewhere. A romantic interlude can lead you to a new social group that offers valuable business contacts and friends from unusual backgrounds.

30. FRIDAY. Diverse. There is no reason why you can't mix business with pleasure successfully today. An invitation to a party could introduce you to new business connections or to a chance to advance your career. You may be trying to juggle your professional and home life. Make sure you take your family along so that your partner can get enthusiastic over all the possibilities. A great property investment might come to light and encourage you to think about selling and moving out of state. Family concerns might consume most of your day. Just getting loved ones to sit down together may be a mammoth task. If there is argument over possessions, it might warrant drawing straws.

31. SATURDAY. Eventful. There is sure to be plenty of nervous energy in the buildup to this evening. Most Archers will want to do your own thing now, and a personal project could take precedence over everything else. Children might demand your attention. You might spend most of the day trying to find a babysitter to free you up for the evening. Take some time out to reflect on the year past. Review your achievements and your regrets. Writing a gratitude list will help you to become clear on where to go from here and on your most pressing priorities for the coming year. This will identify what resolutions are necessary to keep you on a steady course next year.

SAGITTARIUS
NOVEMBER–DECEMBER 2010

November 2010

1. MONDAY. Positive. As the new month begins, the universe sends a large number of planetary trends, most promising pleasant and productive situations. Vocational and business affairs could occupy a lot of your time, although love and romance are also vital activities. The Sun continues to glide through your Scorpio house of secrets and solitude while nearing the end of your yearly cycle. Although you still covet serenity and peace, it is unlikely that you will have as much time alone as you would want. Archers in a committed union can enjoy spending an intimate evening with that special person. Make plans early, and prepare to have fun. If you are single, get out and be seen.

2. TUESDAY. Steady. There are only a few minor bumps to maneuver through today. Work conducted behind the scenes or in confidence can be very productive. Sagittarius folks involved in producing creative objects should feel inspired. Immerse yourself in areas where your talent can be exhibited. Later in the day you could be uncharacteristically grumpy or in the mood to challenge decisions made by those in charge. The chance of having to deal with a tricky employment problem increases as the hours pass, demanding care to avoid losing a lucrative contract or an overseas offer. A secret romance should continue to blossom.

3. WEDNESDAY. Uplifting. Relationships with friends and colleagues are apt to be on your mind as the Moon wanders through Libra, your house of friendships and goals. As an Archer you enjoy helping those you befriend. Being available to listen to the woes, worries, or wonders of other people can increase your emotional satisfaction. Pay attention to dreams as Mercury, the thinking planet, continues to slide through Scorpio, your house of subconscious thought. Answers could become clear that help further special goals as well as providing inspiration. Strong creative interests should be utilized constructively. If you are so inclined, handmade festive gifts that you produce would most likely be welcomed by family members and friends.

4. THURSDAY. Varied. Mixed planetary vibes prevail. Make sure you are in control of your impulses and that you avoid rash behavior. Over the next few days you will be in your own world of fantasy and flights of imagination. Sagittarius folks with special talent can continue to put those energies into creative areas, which could save money or increase income. A hint of unrealistic expectations may creep into your thinking, and you could develop a gullible attitude in which you believe what you want rather than what is factual. A separation or a break that occurred with a friend or business associate could happily become a thing of the past.

5. FRIDAY. Reflective. Sagittarius are innately generous folks, and this is often shown through a willingness to help those who are less fortunate. However, sometimes this benevolent attitude can be detrimental to your own health or may cause loved ones to suffer because of time constraints. If there has been family tension due to outside influences, this should now begin to disappear. As your birthday draws closer, spend time in quiet reflection, pondering future plans, evaluating strategies, and thinking about where you hope to be twelve months from now. Consider all options, but don't make any definite plans until the Sun enters your own sign of Sagittarius later in the month.

6. SATURDAY. Foggy. A strange day is likely because you may be dreamier, light-headed, and confused, which is odd and out of the ordinary for those typical of your sign. Concentrating on routine chores and duties could create frustration, and you are likely to find your mind continually wandering to more pleasant and interesting thoughts. Thinking big is a wonderful Sagittarius attribute, but not today. Be sure to take minor points into consideration even while viewing the bigger picture. The New Moon in Scorpio stimulates a desire to renew your spirit and to nurture yourself. Retreat for a little while to meditate or commune with nature, restoring spent energy.

7. SUNDAY. Renewing. Jump at the chance to sleep late this morning if you have the luxury to do so. If you felt a little out of sorts yesterday, you should now begin to spark up as the Moon flits into your zodiac sign. Physical energy becomes recharged, along with the feeling that you can accomplish whatever is in your future. Caution should be applied, however, because impulsive or careless action now may be regretted later on. The fearful attitude that some in your circle are displaying could be difficult to comprehend. Patience and compassion are essential until you come to understand the motivations of those people.

8. MONDAY. Beneficial. Delays or confusion experienced with contracts, negotiations, or transportation could begin to settle down now that foggy Neptune is moving forward in Aquarius, your house of mental processes and communication. Aid in this regard also arrives in the form of informative Mercury settling into your sign, accentuating personality and self-expression. The urge to express yourself could find you more talkative, but take care to avoid the famous Sagittarius foot-in-mouth disease. Intuitive feelings should be on target, so pay close attention and listen to that little voice in your head that says stop or go. Spending time with other people will give you pleasure, so begin planning to visit friends and family members over the coming weeks.

9. TUESDAY. Constructive. Although you have practical Capricorn affecting your personal house of finances, your sign is not noted to be conservative where cash is concerned. Spending rather than saving is generally the motto of Archers, and you have a strong streak of generosity. At times like this, however, you need to take stock. Right now money might be disappearing faster than you can make it. With the expensive festive season looming, this is an appropriate time to balance the budget and to figure out where expenses could be trimmed. You may be pleasantly surprised to discover that there are many planned purchases that are not really necessary or required.

10. WEDNESDAY. Vibrant. Your goal may be to simply get what you need to increase contentment and happiness. Acquiring material possessions could be at the top of your list of desires, which is fine if you take a realistic approach. Appreciation of your treasures will increase if you save in advance for special purchases. Your sign is known to be tolerant of the views and philosophies of other people. Occasionally, however, your sense of self-worth can be eroded by those who are arrogant, picky, or overly forceful. Endeavor to remain cool, calm, and collected if such people cross your path today. Buy yourself a small treat as a reward for all the hard work you recently exerted.

11. THURSDAY. Resourceful. If expenditures exceeded the budget yesterday, careful planning now can soon restore financial stability. Take good care of all that is precious to you and brings you pleasure, including your nearest and dearest. If saving up for a large purchase, you can make good headway. If you have something of value to sell, there is every indication of receiving a good price. When the Moon slides into Aquarius later in the day, creative or unusual ideas and projects can be inspiring, providing you with the ability to express yourself eloquently. Neighbors or siblings might drop in for coffee and a chat, so be sure there are a few extra goodies in the fridge or pantry.

12. FRIDAY. Hectic. Archers involved in any field of communication should have added enthusiasm for work as productivity rises. You might become caught up in an endless round of making phone calls, answering e-mails, or attending meetings. If this has the potential to slow you down too much, avoid this by being prepared with an excuse or explanation. Either shut the office door, hold calls, turn your phone off, or don't even check e-mails. However, you may actually prefer to work in this busy environment because it makes the day pass quicker. A soak in the tub and a night on the couch reading an escapist novel might be the best way to unwind at the end of the busy workweek.

13. SATURDAY. Mixed. Morning trends are not as helpful as later in the day. If you are traveling to visit, to shop, or to go for an appointment, expect delays due to traffic snarls or other annoying holdups. Contacting people you need to see might be impossible. Lapses in memory or concentration could prove embarrassing. Keeping your foot out of your mouth might be hard to do as the urge to express and state your views and opinions causes you to talk first and think later. Writing poetry, music, or romantic fiction could be a positive way to share what's on your mind and also keep away from potential trouble. Spending time in the company of people you know well can be a great way to socialize this evening.

14. SUNDAY. Tranquil. On this idyllic day surround yourself with folks you trust and who support your aims and goals. Not everyone has a sharp, quick mind like you do, so be careful that you are not too straightforward or blunt. Domestic or financial problems should begin to be resolved. If you have been stressed recently over financial issues, positive developments are likely. If the weather is chilly, staying in bed could be a good option, especially if you have a lover or a good book for company. If you are entertaining guests, keep discussions light and breezy to avoid an intense debate that might spiral out of control. Mild discord may be experienced in your romantic relationship.

15. MONDAY. Fortunate. Although this is the first day of the new working week, optimism and enthusiasm should be high. Good fortune swings in your favor as the Sun and your life ruler Jupiter shower you with luck and love. Responsibilities are apt to ease, either thanks to assistance from other people or a more organized approach toward tasks at hand. A home-based business could be given a boost from unforeseen sources, and this could be the window of opportunity you have been seeking in order to move fully into self-employment. Students or those not yet fully employed in the work force might come up with a few novel methods of increasing income. Don't discount your ideas without first giving them serious consideration.

16. TUESDAY. Good. Generally fortunate destiny continues for the luckiest sign of the zodiac. Purchase raffle tickets, invest jointly with friends, or check out an online competition and you may end up ahead of the game. Calculated risks shouldn't be a problem because your instincts and judgment are sound right now. The currently unattached Sagittarius could meet a significant love potential this evening. Couples can deepen loving bonds by setting time aside for togetherness. Making money by utilizing your ingenuity and creative talent is again a strong focus. Opportunities are present if you are able and willing to look outside the box.

17. WEDNESDAY. Promising. A discussion with your boss, lover, or child regarding your goals or the aims of other people could generate positive results that can be put into motion immediately. If your thoughts about a particular desire have been confused or uncertain until now, a sense of order should begin to emerge. You probably have plenty to say, and exchanging thoughts and sharing creative ideas with other people can be emotionally satisfying. Keep in mind the idea that a love union is as much about being friends as it is about romance, and be sure to make time in your busy life for your significant other. Also pamper yourself; you deserve it.

18. THURSDAY. Mystifying. A giant fuzzy cloud descends today as the Sun and foggy Neptune clash. The festive season could begin early for the party-loving Archer, making this a time to dress to impress and socialize to your heart's content. Jupiter, your jolly ruler, begins moving forward, ending any delays associated with an arranged celebration to be held at home. Venus also moves out of retreat, indicating a promised pay raise or promotion that was on hold could now be delivered. This will bring a wide smile to those who have been waiting patiently for well-deserved rewards. Dancing, attending the theater, or playing a musical instrument of choice could prove delightful and relaxing this evening.

19. FRIDAY. Fulfilling. Doors can open for you in a variety of ways. Intuitive faculties are strengthened, allowing Sagittarius folks to sift through the many opportunities to move ahead that may be presented. Archers involved with a club or association could be voted to take the lead role. Or you might receive an award for past hard work and effort that helped raise the profile of a group. A fluffy friend with four legs may be due for extra special attention; a romp in the park or an additional fishy or meaty treat might be in order. Assistance from other people could suddenly be granted. Sharing exciting adventures with children can be fulfilling and fun.

20. SATURDAY. Energetic. Today's dynamic energy increases the chance of reaching current goals. Communicating with feeling increases due to planetary vibes. You could be inclined to talk more. There may also be a tendency to speak sharper than intended, so curb your tongue a little to avoid negative fallout. Other people might not be acting very rationally, but it would be wise to ignore their bad behavior unless it impacts negatively on you. Regular health checkups are essential even for the robust Sagittarius. If it has been a while since your last visit to the doctor, make an appointment now so you have peace of mind regarding your general well-being.

21. SUNDAY. Useful. Bearing grudges is not usually your style. So if you are feeling resentment toward someone who you think acted against your best interests, seek closure and then move on. The Taurus Full Moon impacts your house of health, work, and service, affecting conditions relating to these areas. A situation regarding employment could come to a head during the next two weeks. Although this might not initially be to your liking, in the long term it may be beneficial. Dealing with a tricky problem at home could test your patience and resolve. Applying common sense can be the best way to find a quick and practical solution and avert any lasting tension.

22. MONDAY. Happy Birthday! A celebration can now start as your own personal new year begins with the movement of the Sun into your sign of Sagittarius. Even if other people shower you with gifts over the coming few weeks, put aside a small sum of cash so you can purchase a personal treat as a reward for the hard work you have exerted over the last twelve months. Communicate desires clearly and concisely, whether in private or to a public audience. Archers who are politically inclined can make good progress garnering support and raising finances to further your aims. Couples can share happy rapport this evening.

23. TUESDAY. Cooperative. Diverse energies make an impact today. However, not worrying too much about what is outside your sphere of influence or control will create a happy day. The Moon continues to slide through your opposite sign of Gemini, highlighting relationships with the other people in your life. Sharing ideas and redefining mutual or group goals should be a satisfying experience as the ability to cooperate increases. Energy exerted organizing your environment should be time well spent. Restlessness can be utilized constructively by preparing your home for anticipated festive guests, generally tidying up your living space, or filing away office or personal paperwork.

24. WEDNESDAY. Helpful. Memories of the past are likely to spring to mind as the Moon glides into the family-oriented sign of Cancer. The urge to dig deep arrives, making this a good period for those involved in studying the human psyche, doing research work, or looking into matters that need to be investigated. If a financial audit is required, or if it is essential to get accounting in order, begin now and you should make steady progress. Applying for an educational grant or filling out forms for a loan or for a mortgage should be easier and appear less complicated. Archers considering starting your own business should do your homework to find the best interest rates if funds are required for start-up capital.

25. THURSDAY. Sensitive. Expect an emotional and edgy day, although confidence should be high. Direct your energy in a positive manner and you should have no major upsets. However, informative Mercury is challenging excessive Jupiter, so you may be prone to laziness, which could limit productivity. If you do slack off, make sure no one is watching; at least pretend to be busy if a bossy family member intrudes on your space. There is also a danger of promising more than can be delivered, overlooking the fine print, and blurting out comments that upset other people. Listening probably won't be your strong suit either. Plans can be made as long as grandiose ideas are shelved.

26. FRIDAY. Refreshing. Review and evaluate long-term aspirations and aims. Socialize with the boss, an important client, or someone who can assist your progress up the career ladder. Chances are good of receiving a boost. Mixing business with pleasure is a powerful way to move ahead. Travel and adventure arouse interest as the Moon moves through Leo, your solar house linked to these activities. If you have time, take a trip to explore interesting vistas close to home. A little escapism is good for the soul, so get out the map, plan your route, and head off into the great unknown even if you can only afford to be gone a few hours. Look forward to loving vibes throughout the weekend.

27. SATURDAY. Uneasy. Concentration could be difficult to achieve as dreamy influences combine with edginess. Your mind is likely to drift to faraway destinations or be consumed by interesting daydreams, lessening the chance of performing your duties to the satisfaction of other people. Postpone routine chores if these can be left until next week. Good news connected to communications or a writing assignment could be received. However, a sudden development involving property or a family matter might arouse anger or annoyance. Spontaneous or rash behavior should be guarded against because it could lead to unexpected difficulties.

28. SUNDAY. Stimulating. Planning strategies and implementing ideas should be easier once you decide if basic plans have merit or are unrealistic. Nervous energy remains high; a brisk walk, a session in the gym, or an indoor game of volleyball or basketball could be the answer to releasing anxiety and stress. Socializing with colleagues or your boss can be enlightening and informative, possibly paving the way to increased recognition or responsibility on the job. An honor or recognition for charity work might be bestowed, delighting those who have worked long and hard to serve other people. A trip to a thrift shop or antique mall should uncover a few bargains.

29. MONDAY. Tricky. With the focus on career and business interests, you can make great strides climbing the career ladder. However, how far you advance and how quickly may depend on your ability to curb your loose tongue and be more aware of the moods of other people. An overly generous attitude while energetic Mars is in conflict with your ruler, abundant Jupiter, could lead to squandering resources. Put off making definite decisions. If something seems too good to be true, it will be. The self-employed Archer should be wary of overextending business or professional affairs. Be careful with any do-it-yourself activities because you could encounter problems when attempting projects on your own.

30. TUESDAY. Supportive. Errors made now could become obvious at an inappropriate time, so take extra care with paperwork and important communications. The need for stimulation increases, encouraging you to boost social and entertaining activities. This is a good time to arrange a company party or to host a dinner in your own home for friends or colleagues. Obtaining a sense of financial security and stability is a prime focus as Mercury, planet of logic, powers into your Capricorn house of money and values. Mercury here conveys a practical and sensible approach to spending with an emphasis on receiving quality for money spent.

December 2010

1. WEDNESDAY. Spirited. In this new month and last one of the calendar year, the Sun continues to move through your own sign until December 21. This is your time to shine and to take your rightful place in the spotlight. Physical energy remains at a high peak, conveying enthusiasm and an increased zest for life. Right now you are not afraid to speak your mind. Expressing yourself will be relatively easy, helping you to obtain what you want and need. With lover Venus moving through the twelfth zone of solitary action, some Archers might be involved in a clandestine affair that is providing both pleasure and joy. The tempo of your social life should pick up as your power of attraction increases.

2. THURSDAY. Reflective. A bundle of cosmic trends is about to descend. Try to complete labor-intensive tasks early because your energy is likely to flag as the day goes on. If you intend to celebrate the upcoming festive period, try to finish gift shopping by midmonth. This will give you plenty of time left to enjoy social get-togethers and extended family connections. Don't wait to formulate strategies, plans, and goals for the year ahead; start now so you get a strong sense of where you are and where you are going. Spending time with friends is important. However, as the Moon slides into the solitary sector of your solar chart, scheduling periods for self-nurturing time is also essential.

3. FRIDAY. Disconcerting. Restlessness prevails. Today could be filled with difficult hurdles, but excitement and manageable chaos are also likely. Dynamic Mars and rebellious Uranus are in conflict. This can indicate accidents and mishaps around the house unless extra care is taken, especially when handling hot or sharp instruments and any electrical items. Discard and replace old or faulty household products that may be a risk to personal safety. Reach out to folks you haven't seen for some time; send an e-mail or a festive card, or make a phone call. Both motorists and pedestrians should take extra care on the roads and avoid any hasty action or inattention.

4. SATURDAY. Serene. Restful vibes will prevail by the time you rise and shine this morning. Take it easy; putter around finishing essential tasks without beginning any new projects. If you aren't scheduled to be on the job, consider getting a relaxing massage or attending a gentle exercise class. Later in the day your energy level begins to lift, and by this evening you should again be the bright and bubbly personality that is the Sagittarius hallmark. Spending time with other people should then be very pleasurable as your desire to socialize and be seen becomes stronger. This is also a good time to form an alliance that has the potential to turn current visions into reality.

5. SUNDAY. Smooth. The power of attraction and attracting is strong, and you can turn on the charm and bask in the glow of the spotlight. The New Moon culminates in your own sign of Sagittarius, bringing you a new lease on life as your annual astrological cycle begins all over again. You have a competitive edge; use the energy wisely and personal opportunities are bound to open up. The chance to meet other folks who can help you launch a new project or enterprise rises considerably. If you have been too busy to pay much attention to grooming, appearance, or self-nurturing, take a break now and do something for yourself. Make an appointment for a haircut, register at a weight-loss clinic, or hire a personal trainer. In a short space of time a new you should emerge.

6. MONDAY. Charming. Vibrant charm and charisma remain on display, attracting favors and special treatment from other people. Although Archers prone to shyness are in the minority among members of your zodiac sign, no Sagittarius should be afraid to express feelings and discuss current interests. It is now your time to shine. Holiday parties should appeal to those who love to socialize. However, if you have to work, try to concentrate on the job at hand at least until the close of the working day. Business owners could have a number of excellent opportunities to network, so be alert and don't waste any chances that are presented.

7. TUESDAY. Pleasing. The rewards for time and effort you have put into employment duties or special projects should be evident today. The promise of a pay increase or promotion could come to fruition, allowing you to put a few extra dollars in the bank in time for the upcoming holiday. The self-employed might be notified of success with a lucrative contract or offer. Those of you with a sharp eye for business could discover an investment opportunity that is worth further research to gauge its likely potential. A special gift of money or a bonus can be gratifying, putting a smile on your face. If you happen to miss out on a financial reward, purchase a small treat for yourself so you can also participate in the excitement of the day.

8. WEDNESDAY. Intense. This is another great day promising an abundance of love, joy, and sharing. Your ability to generate money and to grasp opportunities as they are presented is excellent. Refrain from putting yourself down and you can realize current potential. Lover Venus and intense Pluto meet in a happy connection, spreading passion and delight. Romance heats up. Sagittarius folks who are attached should be able to find a positive outlet for increased desire and love. If you can afford to treat a lover to an extravagant dinner with all the trimmings, plan a night to remember. Those of you who have exceptional culinary skills might prefer to serve a home-cooked meal, complete with candlelight and soft music.

9. THURSDAY. Meaningful. An extra dose of power and intensity remains for those who are in a committed union. Single Archers should put yourselves in a situation where you have a good chance of finding someone who meets your expectations for love and romance. If you feel tied down or held back because of a certain situation, it may be time to consider making changes that can help you meet your objectives. Enrolling in a class that sparks interest could be a good way to meet new people, especially if you are new to the neighborhood, and can also add to your knowledge. With energetic Mars now gracing Capricorn, your personal money house, there should be plenty of chances to generate more income throughout the coming weeks.

10. FRIDAY. Wary. Finances appear to be fine. But if you are heading out to shop be aware of budgetary limits and write a list to avoid overspending. Listen carefully to what other people convey. Otherwise you are apt to misunderstand their intentions, especially as mischievous Mercury moves into retrograde motion today. Confusing situations are likely during the next three weeks involving your cash flow and personal possessions. Choose festive gifts with care to avoid deciding on one item and then changing your mind before even arriving home. There is also more likelihood of purchasing a gift that is broken or faulty but can't be returned.

11. SATURDAY. Stimulating. Although Venus, the lover of good times, remains in your hidden twelfth house, the urge to socialize may be growing stronger. You will find that the inclination this month is toward self-empowerment and discovering the best way to bring your desires to fruition. Listen to your good Sagittarius intuition. Guidance from within is the wisest advice to take now.

Double-check arrangements and make sure you have the right address if meeting friends at a new social venue. Take along your cell
phone as backup because of the chance of miscommunication. Welcome a newcomer into your social group.

12. SUNDAY. Enjoyable. Make an effort to keep the day going
according to plan and you can expect a pleasant and happy time.
You may need to reconsider a number of plans if they include lots
of physical action and hard work. Becoming motivated for anything other than relaxing and socializing could be difficult. If there
is nothing pressing that must be done, take a backseat and enjoy
some downtime with stimulating company. There might be family upheaval later this evening. Extricate yourself from a situation
where you might be drawn into someone else's drama. Going to
bed early would be a smart way of avoiding possible fallout.

13. MONDAY. Invigorating. Look forward to a very interesting
day ahead as informative Mercury, energetic Mars, and passionate
Pluto all interconnect. A number of problems can be resolved, and
worrying financial concerns could magically disappear. You may be
speaking to a group of people, presenting an important sales report,
or lecturing to an academic body. Captivating and holding the attention of an audience should be extremely easy even if you are not
accustomed to speaking in public. The power of your message is
unlikely to go unnoticed, so take your place center stage and shine
brightly.

14. TUESDAY. Diverse. Communicating on an emotional level
remains enhanced because your ability to deeply connect with
other people is supported by current influences. This is a good
time to bond with a lover. Intimacy can help you find exactly the
right words needed to express love and affection. A number of irritations and annoyances may be confronted, requiring Archers to
keep cool. You also need to remember to bite your tongue when
angered. The demands of children could increase stress. Sagittarius
parents should find a babysitter rather than dragging youngsters
out to stores if shopping is on the agenda. Give social events a miss
tonight because most folks, including you, may be crankier than
usual.

15. WEDNESDAY. Bumpy. This is likely to be an irritating day, although you might only experience angst due to the increased pressure and strain brought on by the demands of the upcoming festive
season. Pay more attention to the concerns of children. Playing with
youngsters may be a good way to release pent-up stress. Postpone

important communications with an older family member or author-ity figure until tomorrow at the earliest. Put aside routine obliga-tions for a short period and participate in family fun. Or spend time on a favorite hobby that draws on your creative self-expression. Allow inspiration free rein and you could come up with a number of trendy or crafty ideas that can become handmade gifts.

16. THURSDAY. Indulgent. The mood is a little lighter now as the Moon continues journeying through your Aries house of pleasure. But your ruler, good-time Jupiter, is being challenged by the Sun and Venus, warning Archers of all ages to be more moderate. This isn't the best day to head to the stores because the potential to over-indulge and overspend is extremely high. Guard against grandiose ideas. Keep flamboyant behavior to a minimum or both your health and wallet may take a battering. An issue with a superior or a father figure could be creating anxiety, but it is unlikely that a satisfactory resolution can be found until a more opportune time.

17. FRIDAY. Watchful. Continue to strive for moderation. You will probably be tempted to go overboard and indulge in a luxury item that can severely deplete your bank balance. If you are worried about the current state of your health or weight, do something con-structive. Join a gym, eat healthier food, or remove bad habits from your lifestyle. To make the most of the holiday period you need to be worry-free so you can be uplifted by special celebrations. If you are stressed, put on your running shoes and get physical. Be aware of the moods of coworkers. It could be all too easy to say the wrong thing and cause upsets in the working arena.

18. SATURDAY. Hopeful. Many and varied universal trends are forming. Although there are apt to be positive occurrences through-out the coming days, also prepare for a number of troubling issues that will need your undivided attention. One of the main rules to follow is to avoid jumping to conclusions even though uncertain instincts are more than likely to plague you. Dealing with a rebel-lious child could spoil part of the day. As a Sagittarius you are one of the signs that desires freedom and independence, so giving a loved one personal space if needed shouldn't be an issue for you. Taking this approach could help move your relationship to another level.

19. SUNDAY. Variable. Keeping secrets is apt to be difficult. A confidence might be disclosed, creating unpleasant vibrations for you or for someone you love. Archers who are holding back on information that should be revealed would be advised to get it out into the open once and for all. If you have a difficult predicament to deal with, there are other people who would be willing to help so ask for assistance. A problem shared is a problem halved, and the advice you receive could get you back on the right track. If festive cards, e-mails, or phone calls have escaped your attention, make amends now. You should be in the mood to celebrate, so plan a spontaneous gathering, or seek outside entertainment.

20. MONDAY. Unsettled. Messenger Mercury clashes with erratic Uranus during the next few days. Be prepared for more disruptions and chaos than would normally occur at this time of the year. Your natural ability to articulate and speak with conviction continues, and you can use self-expression to gain the attention of people you want to impress. However, you may also be more argumentative than perhaps you should be. Aggression may be directed at parents or those who share your residence. Archers juggling friends, family, work, and social events may be trying to keep too many folks happy, and that could be wearing you out. Be good to yourself also.

21. TUESDAY. Demanding. A challenging day ahead appears likely. It will be up to you to handle emotional trends. Issues relating to a personal or business partnership may be under a cloud. A Full Moon in your opposite sign of Gemini conveys an added need for cooperation and compromise. However, an opportunity to discuss lingering differences or repetitive problems can be found if you are willing to apply necessary effort. Try to set time aside to bring order back into the domestic environment. Decluttering your home can help clear your mind. Today the Sun enters Capricorn, joining Mars and Pluto there in your house of income, values, and self-worth.

22. WEDNESDAY. Lively. Expect another busy day, with large doses of discretion and tact required if you are to remain unscathed. Pay attention to the price and quality of goods before deciding to make a purchase on the spur of the moment. Refrain from making any extravagant decisions. Spending more money than you earn is a dangerous habit that should be avoided if financial security is your aim. Although as a Sagittarius you are the original party animal, you don't have to accept every invitation you receive. Practice saying no to reduce the possibility of burnout and to keep more money in your wallet. Romance takes on a rosy glow as passion rises.

23. THURSDAY. Constructive. Canny shoppers heading for large department stores are bound to find many festive bargains. Even though the season to be jolly is extremely close, clearing debts and improving money management procedures can be helpful. Contact an expert, enroll in a course, or read a financial magazine to expand your knowledge and expertise. Taking a proactive approach can steer you to the right monetary path that will produce benefits in the future. Moving in with a friend, partner, or relative could be the focus of discussion as a way to share costs and save money. Singles might find romance with an older or more mature person very attractive.

24. FRIDAY. Mixed. Archers leaving early this morning to travel a long distance may not really be up to the hassle or at least not looking forward to the lengthy day ahead. Brace yourself. The day improves a little as the hours pass, and the rewards at the end of the trip should make any discomfort worthwhile. Constructive decisions can be made. If you have a myriad of chores to complete, your plans should fall easily into place during midafternoon. A group function or making merry with colleagues, friends, or associates should swing into top gear as festive bonding begins. Last-minute bargains can be found by the savvy, but check that you are receiving what you pay for.

25. SATURDAY. Merry Christmas! Expect a few crises to disrupt preparations this morning. One or two dramas usually occur when everyone is busy, and these can add to the exciting ambience of the day. A valuable gift from your partner or father may be a very pleasant surprise, making you realize that you are indeed lucky. Aside from the usual family festivities, Sagittarius folks with a high profile could spend part of this special day attending a public function or in some form of meeting and greeting. Make sure everyone is involved in entertainment activities to ensure family members unite together closely while sharing congenial times.

26. SUNDAY. Busy. Cleaning away the remnants of yesterday's festivities could be the first chore tackled this morning. With the Moon transiting perfectionist Virgo, a clean and tidy environment may be a priority. The self-employed Archer could even decide to put nose to the grindstone and complete outstanding work orders or tasks. Willpower and determination are strong, so steer clear of the after-Christmas sales. Stay home and spend time with family members, enjoy festive gifts, or visit friends who were unable to drop by yesterday. Don't go to any location that harbors a dangerous element. Carry a cell phone if venturing far from home because an accident or breakdown could leave you in the lurch.

27. MONDAY. Satisfying. The new workweek begins on a positive note. If you are not lucky enough to be on vacation, at least take solace that important headway can now be made in career and business matters. Your personal power remains strong and can be used advantageously in the professional arena. Other people could have difficulty meeting your high standards, especially if you are back at work. You have a reputation for excellence to uphold. Delays with personal plans could become frustrating, but patience is needed for a little while longer. Romance is highlighted, so plan entertainment just for two.

28. TUESDAY. Cautious. Romantic relationships are not well starred, but those in a committed union can look forward to mild satisfaction. Beware get-rich-quick schemes, and make sure security measures are in place to protect personal belongings. Returning unwanted or malfunctioning gifts for credit might not be as easy as expected; it would be better to leave this chore until Friday. Practice the art of delegation if your workload is becoming increasingly heavier. Support from colleagues should be easily obtained if there are important duties that need to be completed quickly. Sharing the busy and quiet times with fellow employees can increase the bonds of friendship on the job.

29. WEDNESDAY. Subdued. Patience and quietness are attributes that require constant effort to achieve, especially for those born under the fiery sign of Sagittarius. Both of these characteristics may be needed today as your enthusiasm and energy take a downward plunge. Although you have been born under a lucky star, the universe is sending a reality check to those who have been reckless when it comes to finances. If credit cards were overextended during the festive season, start cutting expenses now so you can pay your way next month. A night at home could relax body and mind, and also help to restore your good humor.

30. THURSDAY. Steady. If you are suffering pangs of guilt over the amount of food and drink consumed during the festive season, don't despair. Take it easy now and resolve to begin a new health kick on the first day of 2011. List your goals for the New Year and place them in a highly visible location where you will be reminded every day. Inspired imagination can be used to plan an end-of-year party that will be memorable. The thought of socializing might not appeal right now as your lunar low makes an impact. But by tomorrow evening the urge to merge and mingle should return to full strength. Mercury now begins moving forward, freeing up stalled personal plans.

31. FRIDAY. Fair. If work isn't a priority, rest up for much of the day so you have plenty of energy for the evening ahead. Spiritual interests could bring contentment. Sagittarius folks who are on vacation should be enjoying the chance to restore and recharge run-down batteries. Singles going out this evening should dress to impress. Your charisma and charm are to the fore, and romantic potentials are bound to be plentiful. Take a responsible approach to socializing. Refrain from drinking and driving; take a cab or hire a chauffeur if you don't want to use public transportation. Split expenses with friends, and welcome in 2011 happy in the knowledge that you will arrive home safely.

TALK TO THE EXPERTS

The Most Respected Psychic Service

PSYCHIC SOURCE™

$10 FOR TEN MINUTES*
satisfaction guarantee

CALL NOW
1.866.408.8511
or visit PsychicSource.com

MC40015   For Ent. Only. 18+.   *New Members Only.

Train at home in your spare time to

Be a Medical Billing Specialist

10 Years	
5 Years	**Increase In Demand!***
Now	

*U.S. Dept. of Labor projects significant growth for specialists doing billing for doctors' offices.

Take the first step to earning up to $40,000 a year and more!

Now you can train in the comfort of your own home to work at home or in a doctor's office, hospital or clinic making great money...up to $40,000 a year and more as your experience and skills increase! It's no secret, healthcare providers need Medical Billing Specialists. In fact, the U.S. Department of Labor projects a significant increase in demand for specialists doing billing for doctors' offices!

Nationally accredited training... be ready to work in as little as four months!

Our experts train you step by step to perform the job of a qualified Medical Billing Specialist. Everything is explained in easy-to-understand language with plenty of examples. You learn exactly what to do and how to do it! You can graduate in as little as four months and be ready to take your first step into this exciting, high-income career.

No Previous Medical Experience Required. Compare the Money You Can Make!

We make it easy to learn how to prepare medical claims for Medicare, Medicaid and private patients. And since every medical procedure must be properly billed, there's plenty of work available. You'll make great money working with doctors as a part of the medical team doing a job that really helps people.

WORK AT HOME!

You Get Toll-Free Support!

You are never alone with USCI training. Just email us or call our toll-free hotline if you ever need help from our expert instructors.

" I would like to thank you from the bottom of my heart for the WONDERFUL course of Medical Billing... I want to encourage others who are thinking about taking the course. Go ahead! IT'S THE BEST DECISION YOU'LL EVER MAKE! "
Sincerely, Scarlet M.

Because of the demand, more and more billing specialists work from home!

SENT FREE!

Get FREE Facts! Call 1-800-388-8765 Dept. SPHB2A70

U.S. Career Institute, Dept. SPHB2A70
2001 Lowe Street, Fort Collins, CO 80525
www.uscareerinstitute.com

Or mail this coupon today!

Yes! Rush me my free information package with complete details about training at home to be a Medical Billing Specialist. I understand there is absolutely no cost and no obligation.

Name:_____ Age:_____

Address:_____ Apt:_____

City:_____ State:_____ Zip:_____

E-mail:_____

CL210

FREE
PARTY LINE

Make new friends, have fun, share idea's never be bored this party never stops! And best of all it's FREE!

Never Any Charges!
Call Now!

712-338-7722

Only Regular Low Long Distance rates apply where applicable

FREE LOVE READING

Powerful Love Psychics. Gifted & caring, waiting to provide you with FREE answers on love, relationships, lost love, passions, romance, fortune, destiny & more!

PSYCHIC D ANNE
Master Psychic Advisor

1-800-710-3511
AskNow.com

18+ ENT. PURPOSES ONLY. CALL FOR DETAILS.

WHAT DOES YOUR FUTURE HOLD?

DISCOVER IT IN *ASTROANALYSIS*—

**COMPLETELY REVISED THROUGH THE YEAR 2015,
THESE GUIDES INCLUDE COLOR-CODED CHARTS FOR
TOTAL ASTROLOGICAL EVALUATION,
PLANET TABLES AND CUSP CHARTS,
AND STREAMLINED INFORMATION.**

ARIES	0-425-17558-8
TAURUS	0-425-17559-6
GEMINI	0-425-17560-X
CANCER	0-425-17561-8
LEO	0-425-17562-6
VIRGO	0-425-17563-4
LIBRA	0-425-17564-2
SCORPIO	0-425-17565-0
SAGITTARIUS	0-425-17566-9
CAPRICORN	0-425-17567-7
AQUARIUS	0-425-17568-5
PISCES	0-425-17569-3

Available wherever books are sold or at penguin.com

B093

Incredible Psychic Solutions!

5 Minutes FREE!

Speak to one of our highly trained professional psychics for answers to YOUR questions!
LOVE, ROMANCE, MONEY, HEALTH, HAPPINESS!
Your answers are only a call away!

1-888-799-2428

18+ Ent. Only